Public Management in Times of Austerity

Since 2008, the world has experienced an enormous decrease of wealth. By many measures the impact of the crisis was severe. The fall in GDP, the collapse of world trade, the rise in unemployment, and the credit slump reached bigger proportions than in any other crisis since World War II. Although the economic figures seem to improve in some countries, the crisis continues being a challenging issue and is said to be one of the most important problems governments face today.

The crisis has put public finances under ever-increasing pressure, and governments have responded through austerity measures such as cutbacks of public spending and new fiscal rules and budgeting procedures.

Public Management in Times of Austerity seeks to explore the austerity policies adopted by European governments and their consequences to public management. It asks how governments have cut back on public expenditure, and how they have implemented new rules leading to more stringency in public budgeting and financial management. These questions are examined comparatively through case studies in different parts of Europe, and variations across countries are discussed and interpreted.

Throughout the volume, the consequences of the crisis and austerity policies for public management are discussed. What is the relationship between crisis and decision-making in the public sector, and how does austerity affect public-sector organisation? As the previous crisis in the 1970s resulted in a major reform movement, which was later referred to as New Public Management, *Public Management in Times of Austerity* seeks to understand whether the current crisis also leads to a wave of public management reform and, if so, what is the content of this?

Eva Moll Ghin is postdoctoral researcher in public administration at the Department of Political Science, University of Copenhagen, Denmark.

Hanne Foss Hansen is professor in public administration and organization at the Department of Political Science, University of Copenhagen, Denmark.

Mads Bøge Kristiansen is associate professor at the Department of Political Science and Public Management, University of Southern Denmark.

Routledge Critical Studies in Public Management
Edited by Stephen Osborne

For a full list of titles in this series, please visit www.routledge.com

The study and practice of public management has undergone profound changes across the world. Over the last quarter century, we have seen

- increasing criticism of public administration as the overarching framework for the provision of public services,
- the rise (and critical appraisal) of the 'New Public Management' as an emergent paradigm for the provision of public services,
- the transformation of the 'public sector' into the cross-sectoral provision of public services, and
- the growth of the governance of inter-organizational relationships as an essential element in the provision of public services.

In reality these trends have not so much replaced each other as elided or coexisted together—the public policy process has not gone away as a legitimate topic of study, intra-organizational management continues to be essential to the efficient provision of public services, while the governance of inter-organizational and inter-sectoral relationships is now essential to the effective provision of these services.

Further, while the study of public management has been enriched by contribution of a range of insights from the 'mainstream' management literature, it has also contributed to this literature in such areas as networks and inter-organizational collaboration, innovation and stakeholder theory.

This series is dedicated to presenting and critiquing this important body of theory and empirical study. It will publish books that both explore and evaluate the emergent and developing nature of public administration, management and governance (in theory and practice) and examine the relationship with and contribution to the overarching disciplines of management and organizational sociology.

Books in the series will be of interest to academics and researchers in this field, students undertaking advanced studies of it as part of their undergraduate or postgraduate degree and reflective policymakers and practitioners.

Public Management in Times of Austerity
Edited by Eva Moll Ghin, Hanne Foss Hansen, and Mads Bøge Kristiansen

Public Management in Times of Austerity

Edited by Eva Moll Ghin,
Hanne Foss Hansen, and
Mads Bøge Kristiansen

Routledge
Taylor & Francis Group

LONDON AND NEW YORK

First published 2018 by Routledge

2 Park Square, Milton Park, Abingdon, Oxfordshire OX14 4RN

52 Vanderbilt Avenue, New York, NY 10017

Routledge is an imprint of the Taylor & Francis Group, an informa business

First issued in paperback 2018

Library of Congress Cataloging-in-Publication Data
Names: Ghin, Eva Moll, editor. | Hansen, Hanne Foss, editor. | Kristiansen, Mads Bøge, editor.
Title: Public management in times of austerity / edited by Eva Moll Ghin, Hanne Foss Hansen, and Mads Bøge Kristiansen.
Description: New York : Routledge, 2017. | Includes index.
Identifiers: LCCN 2017004166 | ISBN 9781138680531 (hardback) | ISBN 9781315563916 (ebook)
Subjects: LCSH: Public administration—Cost control. | Administrative agencies—Management. | Recessions.
Classification: LCC JF1351 .P8284 2017 | DDC 352.4/3—dc23
LC record available at https://lccn.loc.gov/2017004166

ISBN: 978-1-138-68053-1 (hbk)
ISBN: 978-0-367-24305-0 (pbk)

Typeset in Sabon
by Apex CoVantage, LLC

Contents

Tables and Figures

Tables

Figures

Preface

This book discusses the effects on public management of the recent financial, economic and fiscal crisis and the austerity policies that emerged in its wake. It is primarily aimed at a readership with special interest in austerity policies and public-sector changes and reforms.

The book offers an international perspective with special attention to Eastern, Southern, Western, Northern and Central Europe, analysing the country cases of Estonia, Italy, Ireland, Denmark and Germany. The principal themes to be addressed are crisis responses, cutbacks and budgetary reform and the impact they have had on public management changes and reforms.

More specifically, Part I presents the research questions, reviews the literature and introduces the case countries. Part II examines the crisis responses and the cutback initiatives in the case countries, while Part III investigates budgetary reform. Finally, the book provides a comparative cross-country analysis and conclusion.

This book is a result of the *SPARK* project, SPARK being an abbreviation of the Danish words for economize (*spare*) and crisis (*krise*). We are grateful to the SPARK members and network for comments on the ideas presented in the book as well as on the drafts to the introductory and concluding chapters. Special thanks to Søren Kjær Foged, Gunnar Gjelstrup and Caroline Howard Grøn. We are also grateful to colleagues at the Department for Political Science and Public Management at The University of Southern Denmark, who took the time to comment on a draft of the concluding chapter. Furthermore, our two former colleagues who are now professors at Copenhagen Business School, Carsten Greve and Lotte Jensen, took the time to read, comment and discuss an early version of the manuscript at an international seminar assembling the chapter authors held at the Department of Political Science, University of Copenhagen, in June 2016. Our warm thanks also go to them. Finally, we are grateful to the Velux Foundation for the generous financial support they provided to the SPARK project. Without this support, the book project would not have been possible.

Eva Moll Ghin, Hanne Foss Hansen and Mads Bøge Kristiansen
Copenhagen 15 December 2016

Part I

Introduction

1 Introduction

Eva Moll Ghin and Mads Bøge Kristiansen

The amount of wealth in the world fell dramatically from 2008. By many measures, the impact of the crisis was severe. The fall in GDP, the collapse of world trade, rising unemployment and the credit slump were worse than in any other crisis over the last 70 years (Lin and Treichel 2012, 10). Although economic figures have improved in many countries, the crisis seems to have marked the beginning of a new 'age of austerity'[1] characterised by increased levels of (perceived) scarcity and a tougher stance on public spending. Governments have cut spending on public organisations and services and they have reformed their budgetary institutions with a view to restraining expenditure.

It could be argued that tougher attitudes towards public expenditure are likely to be accompanied by higher ambitions to spend money (more) efficiently and effectively and thus to pressure for public management reform. These changes may follow along the path of reforms that have already been pursued in the public sector for decades (Pollitt and Bouckaert 2011), but it is also possible that the sense of crisis will provide the necessary pressure for radical departures from accustomed ways of organising, managing—and reforming—public organisations and services (Peters, Pierre and Randma-Liiv 2011). Indeed, there is some precedent for significant new reforms in conditions of fiscal stringency (Hood 2010, 7), and the previous crises of the 1970s and 80s are often assigned the role as catalyst of the international wave of reforms that later became known as 'New Public Management' (NPM) (Wollman 2003; Pollitt and Bouckaert 2011, 6–7).

The objective of this book is to provide insight into the policies of austerity in European countries and the consequences of such policies for public management. The book reports studies of how five different European countries have managed cutbacks of public expenditure, how they have reformed their budgetary institutions, and what the consequences have been for public management. It addresses three main research questions:

1. What is the character of the changes to public management that are taking place under present-day austerity?

2. Does austerity lead to path-breaking and/or path-dependent change?
3. Why are different and/or similar patterns of change observed in different countries?

The first two questions are aimed at analysing the character and scale of changes in public management, whereas the third aims at *comparing* how austerity policies are implemented and the consequences they have for public management in different countries—and to offer some interpretation of the observed differences and similarities across countries.

Before proceeding further, we want to clarify our understanding of the crisis and the times of austerity, how we expect crisis and austerity to affect public management, and our reasons for focusing the analysis on cutback management and budgetary reform. We will also offer some justification for our choice of intensive case studies as a means of investigating the relationship between austerity and public management, and we will account for the structure of the book.

Times of Austerity

This book is about public management in times of austerity. While 'austerity' can refer to government efforts to reduce budget deficits through expenditure cuts or tax increases, for many the term carries connotations regarding an ideological preference for quick expenditure cutbacks (Hood, Heald and Himaz 2014, 5). Other recent publications have therefore focused on 'the politics of fiscal consolidation', referring to political efforts aimed at the 'reduction of budget deficits and debt accumulation, by expenditure cuts and revenue increase' (Kickert and Randma-Liiv 2015, 52) or 'the politics of fiscal squeeze', similarly referring to 'efforts made by politicians and governments to correct the public finances by raising taxes or cutting spending or a mixture of the two'[2] (Hood, Heald and Himaz 2014, 4). We prefer to use the term austerity because it is widely used in both academic publications (e.g. Diamond and Liddl 2012; Lodge and Hood 2012; Blyth 2013) and in public discourse to denote both a course of government policy and a political and psychological climate that results in a 'tough stance' on public expenditure. We do not mind the term's connotations towards a preference for expenditure cutbacks, and we are more interested in the implementation and management aspects of austerity than the previously mentioned publications that deal with the *politics* of fiscal consolidation or squeeze.

This book views 'times of austerity' as something that has grown out of the global financial crisis and as a set of policies that have been adopted by all of the European countries at more or less the same time (with the possible exception of oil-rich Norway; see Kickert and Randma-Liiv 2015). We understand the global crisis as consisting of several stages (cp. Kickert 2012; Kickert and Randma-Liiv 2015, 26ff). In the first stage, *the banking—or financial—crisis*, banks and other financial institutions faced serious problems and bankruptcy. To avoid the collapse of the financial system, governments stepped in and 'bailed out' their banks with large sums of public money. The second stage, *the economic crisis*, was characterised by falling national product and rising unemployment. It led some governments to take stimulus measures such as relieving taxes or increasing public expenditure (e.g. through forwarding investments). The third phase, *the fiscal crisis*, began as a result of debts incurred through bank takeovers in many countries and deficits resulting from stimulus measures and the effect of automatic stabilisers in times of economic decline. Governments responded by consolidating their fiscal balances by reducing public expenditure and/or increasing taxes. The fiscal crisis remains acute in some countries, whereas in others it has given way to more permanent attitudes of stringency towards public spending; that is, austerity. According to Kickert and Randma-Liiv (2015), we may also speak about a fourth phase of the crisis, *the Eurozone crisis*, when a troika of international economic institutions organised bailouts for Greece, Ireland, Portugal and Cyprus under conditions of severe budget cuts and reforms.

We thus understand austerity to be a course of policy that is adopted by governments more or less voluntarily in response to or justified by the fiscal crisis. Austerity policies are intended to reduce debts and deficits by holding back and reducing public expenditure but may also prepare the public sector for future challenges, such as the socio-demographic changes related to ageing (Lodge and Hood 2012). We focus primarily on cutbacks in the public sector rather than reduced government transfers to the private sector, as we are interested in the role and consequences of austerity for public management. Austerity policies may also concern institutional reforms that are meant to strengthen the position of 'budget guardians' vis-à-vis 'advocates' in budgeting. In other words, we view the crisis and austerity policies such as cutbacks and budgetary reform as drivers for public management change.

Public Management in Times of Austerity

The term 'public management' may be understood as referring to decisions about the activities involved in running public-sector organisations and to the structures and procedures (i.e. institutions) of the public sector and its organisations. 'Public management' overlaps with 'public administration', but compared to the latter term it denotes a modern, reformed approach to running the public sector in which public officials are not just responsible for administering legal rules but are also expected to use professional management techniques from the private sector. Following Pollitt and Bouckaert (2011, 77), we focus on selected components of public management, including financial management, personnel management, organisational restructuring and performance measurement.

The first aim of the book is to understand whether and how austerity leads to centralisation and a stronger focus on coordination, coherence and organisational scale advantages in public management consistent with the alleged transformation of NPM in the direction of 'post-NPM' reform (Christensen and Lægreid 2007; 2011). The second aim is to understand whether austerity constitutes a 'critical juncture' that opens a window for major change in public management, consistent with the interest in crisis in historical institutionalism. The third aim of the book is to understand how the interplay between the economic conditions and political and administrative institutions influence austerity and changes to public management. The book is informed by a broad institutional framework in which historical institutionalism in particular looms large. The three main aims of the book are further outlined in the following section.

The Character of Change: Centralisation, Coordination and Larger-Scale Organisations?

One of the most common expectations regarding the effects of fiscal crisis and austerity is that they lead to *centralisation*. When there is a crisis, people look to their political leaders for a response (Peters 2011), and central government actors are expected to try to exert control (Boin et al. 2008). In the public sector, centralisation is expected because budget units are given stronger powers to impose spending limits and cuts that other subunits are unlikely to undertake voluntarily (Raudla, Savi and Randma-Liiv 2013, 24–5).

Another aspect of how austerity leads to change is whether it leads to *coordination* becoming a higher priority in the public sector. Austerity is likely to increase the demand for the coordination of scarce budgetary resources and might also lead to increased demands for the coordination of policies as a means of increasing cost-effectiveness (Peters, Pierre and Randma-Liiv 2011).

Last but not least, austerity is likely to accelerate the ongoing search for *rationalisation of public organisations* through agency mergers, downsizing of back-office functions via the creation of shared-service centres etc. (Kickert and Randma-Liiv 2015, 2010ff). These organisational reforms may be conceptualised as a cost-saving device making use of (perceived) scale advantages and/or as a means of supporting the goals of centralised steering and coordination in the public sector by reintegrating functions into larger, multipurpose organisations.

Path-Breaking Changes?

Shortly after the crisis, it was discussed whether government responses to the crisis would reinforce existing path-dependencies, or whether the crisis would become the source of potentially fundamental change of the kind that we associate with a critical juncture in historical institutionalism (Peters 2011; Peters, Pierre and Randma-Liiv 2011). As a contribution to this discussion, we analyse whether austerity only leads to minor changes along the existing path; whether it reinforces ongoing reforms; whether it works against the realisation and implementation of ongoing reforms; or whether it is used as a window for fundamental changes to public management. The ambition is to add to the discussions of continuity and change in public management by offering analyses of how austerity and cutbacks affect reform trajectories in different countries, focusing on financial management, organisational restructuring, personnel management and performance measurement (Pollitt and Bouckaert 2011, 77).

Different and/or Similar Patterns of Change in Different Countries?

In addition to exploring how each country implements cutbacks and budgetary reforms we also want to offer some interpretations of why approaches vary between countries. First, economic conditions may be important for the choice of reforms and cutback strategies in the current times of austerity. For example, we expect the countries that have been hit hard by the crisis to carry out radical budgetary reform and large cutback programmes that include comprehensive changes to public management and its institutions. Second, different countries may follow different trajectories of public management reform, and we consider history to be important to understanding present choices. Third, we expect popular management ideas to influence the character of change. Fourth, the institutions of the political system may be significant for the chosen approach to expenditure cutbacks and to the centralisation of budgeting. Fifth, we expect administrative traditions, structures and regulations to influence how public management changes.

Cutback Management and Budgetary Reform

As previously argued, this book approaches its overall ambition of investigating the role of and changes in public management in times of austerity through country-specific analyses of the adoption and implementation of expenditure cutbacks and budgetary reform. Both policies have been adopted throughout Europe as a reaction to the fiscal crisis, and they both represent the overall tough stance on public spending that we associate with austerity. Both policies are implemented by public organisations and they concern the resource management of the public sector itself.

Cutback management is not a reform but a process of implementing budgetary decisions to cut back public expenditure. Cutback management may, however, also involve public management reforms such as chang-ing organisational structures or work procedures or modes of delivering public services (Pollitt 2010). Budgetary reform can be understood as deliberate changes to budgeting institutions such as the rules and regula-tions according to which budgets are drafted, approved and implemented (Alesino and Perroti 1996, 401).

We refer to 'budgetary' institutions and reforms rather than 'fiscal' institutions and reforms because we are less interested in the use of taxa-tion and spending to influence the economy and more in how govern-ments try to steer and manage resources. At the same time, we talk about 'budgetary' rather than 'financial management' reform, as we also want to include those reform aspects in our analysis that have to do with budg-etary decision-making in democratic political systems and how fiscal discipline is attained in such systems, rather than just focus on the prepa-ration and implementation of budgets and management of resources in public organisations. We conceptualise budgetary reform as an independ-ent course of policy—most likely with important consequences for finan-cial management in the public sector.

Cutback management and budgetary reform are likely to interact in ways that increase the demand for both. Cutbacks may generate a demand for new budgetary decision-making procedures (Levine 1985; Pollitt 2010). At the same time, budgetary reforms in the context of austerity likely favour expenditure guardians and decisions to consoli-date public finances (Schick 2010), thus generating a need for cutback management. Moreover, cutback management and budgetary reform are likely to affect other public management institutions such as structures and procedures related to personnel management, organisational restruc-turing and/or performance measurement.

As regards cutback management, we focus on cutbacks at the cen-tral government level, except in the German case where the Länder level (but not local governments) is included in the analysis. We analyse how governments combine across-the-board and targeted strategies to cutting back public operational expenditure, and how cutback strategies interact with public management reform. On the one hand, cutback management that relies on across-the-board strategies resembles budgetary reform that institutionalises aggregate fiscal targets in that the power over aggre-gate cuts is centralised but the power over the implementation of the cuts is decentralised to organisational managers. Targeted cuts, on the other hand, could be seen as the expression of another kind of centralisation in which priorities are set at the central level. Each case study may exhibit different kinds of interactions between the choice of cutback strategies and centralisation.

With regard to budgetary reform, we analyse how the reforms that are aimed at fiscal discipline interact with those that are aimed at effective-ness in allocation and efficiency in the administration of public resources.

Budgetary reform that relies on fiscal targets represents a particular form of centralisation in which the power over aggregate fiscal outcomes is centralised, but it does not necessarily represent centralisation in the sense of central priority-setting or standardised strategies for achieving efficiency gains. If fiscal targets are complemented with performance-oriented reforms, the scope for centralised priorities and strategies may increase, but those reform elements often entail decision-making competencies being delegated with respect to some aspects of resource management. In other words, the interaction between budgetary reforms aimed at fiscal discipline and those aimed at performance may have important implications for the relationship between centralisation and decentralisation in public management.

Summing up, we are interested in how public management and its institutions change in a context of austerity. More specifically, we are looking at how cutbacks are implemented in central government, which cutback strategies and measures are chosen, and how this leads to changes in public management (judged by their character and scale). We also focus on how budgetary institutions are changed in the context of austerity and the consequences of this for public management. Finally, we analyse how the economic and institutional context influences how cutbacks are implemented and how budgetary and public management institutions are changed.

Case Studies as Research Methodology

This book builds on case studies in five countries: Germany, Italy, Denmark, Ireland, and Estonia. It thus consists of five case studies on cutback management and five case studies on budgetary reform in the same countries. Each of the case studies is based on a combination of document studies, quantitative data and/or qualitative interviews.

Austerity and its consequences for public management is a topic in which many hard-to-operationalise variables interact in complex ways. Consequently, we have opted for a strategy in which priority is given to presenting the reader with in-depth analysis of a small number of cases in order to better understand case-specific contexts. Consistent with our ambition to present deep, case-specific knowledge, each chapter has been written by national experts. The studies focus on country-specific concerns but are also guided by a common framework based on a reading of the literatures on institutional change, cutback management and budgetary reform (see Chapter 2).

The comparative analysis in the book is guided by the literature but we do not primarily rely on analysis of correlations between cases to test pre-formulated hypotheses. Instead, we combine several logics of comparative case analysis. First, we use the cases for drawing general inferences regarding the relationship between cutback management, budgetary reform and changes in public management. In this regard, it is advantageous to have cases with widely varying economic and institutional conditions. If there are common findings across these widely different cases, we have a stronger case that they are probably valid for many other European cases based on a 'most different' logic of comparative case studies (Przeworski and Teune 1970). Second, we use the variations between our cases to look for patterns of correspondence between economic and institutional factors and the adoption and implementation of expenditure cutbacks and budgetary reform. This comparative analysis is guided by expectations and a model from the literature regarding the influence of different economic and institutional factors on public management reform. However, the analysis is not of the strict hypothesis-driven kind in which the relative influence of different factors is assessed. Instead, we use the literature to inform and enrich our analysis and for discussion of the cases and variations between them. Third, our investigation of the relationship between economic and institutional factors and the approaches to cutback management and budgetary reform is based on in-depth analysis of the individual cases.

Case Selection and Country Characteristics

We have selected our cases based on the expectation that the management of austerity in each country is likely to depend on a combination of economic factors and political and administrative institutional factors (Christensen and Lægreid 2002; Pollitt and Bouckaert 2011). The economic factors include how hard the country has been hit by the crisis and whether it has been the object of international interventions (Troika conditionality). The degree of crisis is described in terms of the severity of the recession, which occurred in most countries after 2008, budget deficits and public debts. The main national institutional (political and administrative) factors are type of government, administrative structures, administrative and civil service traditions, and reform trajectories (Pollitt and Bouckaert 2004; 2011; Wollmann and Kuhlmann 2014). The main characteristics of each country are outlined in Table 1.1. and are further described in Chapter 3.

The Structure of the Book

The book is structured as follows: First, three chapters introduce the reader to (1) the purposes of the book, (2) the existing literature on public management reform, cutback management and budgetary reforms and (3) the selected case-countries. Second, five chapters focus on expenditure cutbacks in each of the selected countries (Germany, Italy, Denmark, Ireland, Estonia). Third, five chapters look into recent budgetary reforms in the same countries. In the comparative analysis and conclusion (Chapter 14), the main findings are outlined and the character of changes and

Table 1.1 Main Characteristics of the Case Countries

	Germany	Italy	Denmark	Ireland	Estonia
Recession	Moderate, rapid recovery	Moderate, prolonged	Moderate, relatively long	Deep, relatively long	Deep, rapid recovery
Budget Deficits after the Crisis	Modest	Moderate	Moderate	Large	Modest
Level of Public Debt after the Crisis	Moderate	High	Modest	High	Modest
State Structures	Federal	Unitary-decentralised	Unitary-decentralised	Unitary-centralised	Unitary-centralised
Members of the Eurozone	Yes	Yes	No (due to opt-out)	Yes	Yes (from 2011)
Troika Conditionality	No	No	No	Yes	No
Types of Government, (2007–15)	Grand or majority coalitions	Majority coalition, technocratic government, grand coalition	Minority coalition	Majority coalition	Majority coalition, minority coalition
Administrative Traditions	Continental European (Federal) Rule-of-law	Continental European (Napoleonic) Rule-of-law	Scandinavian Rule-of-law	Anglo-Saxon Public interest culture Pragmatism	Central and Eastern European Rule-of-law
Reform Approach Before the Crisis	Maintain-Modernise	Modernising-managerial	Modernising-participatory	Modernising (reform laggard)	Marketisation-minimisation (NPM radical)

the patterns of change of public management in times of austerity are discussed. Finally, the differences and similarities between the selected countries are analysed and discussed.

Notes

1   British Conservative leader David Cameron became famous for promising his party a new 'age of austerity' in a 2009 speech shortly before winning the 2010 general elections (conservative-speeches.sayit.mysociety.org).
2   Hood, Heald and Himaz (2014) deliberately choose fiscal squeeze over fiscal consolidation, as the latter may both be the result of 'belt-tightening' politics or economic growth, and they only want to address the politics of increasing revenues or reducing expenditure, regardless of the outcomes of such policies.

References

Alesina, Alberto and Roberto Perotti. 1996. "Fiscal Discipline and the Budget Process." *The American Economic Review* 86(2):401–7.

Blyth, Mark. 2013. *Austerity: The History of a Dangerous Idea.* Oxford: Oxford University Press.

Boin, Arjen, Paul 't Hart, Eric Stern and Bengt Sundelius. 2008. *The Politics of Crisis Management: Public Leadership Under Pressure.* Cambridge: Cambridge University Press.

Christensen, Tom and Per Lægreid. 2002. *New Public Management: The Transformation of Ideas and Practices.* Aldershot: Ashgate.

Christensen, Tom and Per Lægreid. 2007. *Transcending New Public Management: The Transformation of Public Sector Reforms.* Farnham: Ashgate.

Christensen, Tom and Per Lægreid. 2011. "Beyond NPM? Some Development Features." In *The Ashgate Research Companion to New Public Management*, edited by Tom Christensen and Per Lægreid, 391–404. Aldershot: Ashgate.

Diamond, John and Joyce Liddle. 2012. *Emerging and Potential Trends in Public Management: An Age of Austerity.* Bingley, GB: Emerald Group.

Hood, Christopher. 2010. *Reflections on Public Services Reforms in a Cold Fiscal Climate.* London: 2020 Public Services Trust.

Hood, Christopher, David Heald and Rozanna Himaz. 2014. *When the Party Is Over: The Politics of Fiscal Squeeze.* Oxford: Oxford University Press.

Kickert, Walter. 2012. "State Responses to the Fiscal Crisis in Britain, Germany and the Netherlands." *Public Management Review* 14(3):299–309.

Kickert, Walter and Tiina Randma-Liiv. 2015. *Europe Managing the Crisis: The Politics of Fiscal Consolidation.* London: Routledge.

Levine, Charles H. 1985. "Police Management in the 1980s: From Decrementalism to Strategic Thinking." *Public Administration Review* 45:691–700.

Lin, Justin Yifu and Volker Treichel. 2012. *The Unexpected Global Financial Crisis: Researching Its Root Cause.* Policy Research Working Paper 5937. Washington, DC: World Bank.

Lodge, Martin and Christopher Hood. 2012. "Into an Age of Multiple Austerities? Public Management and Public Service Bargains Across OECD Countries." *Governance* 25(1):79–101.

Peters, B. Guy. 2011. "Governance Responses to the Fiscal Crisis: Comparative Perspectives." *Public Money and Management* 31(1):75–80.

Peters, B. Guy, Jon Pierre and Tiina Randma-Liiv. 2011. "Global Financial Crisis, Public Administration and Governance: Do New Problems Require New Solutions?" *Public Organizational Review* 11:13–27.

Pollitt, Christopher. 2010. "Public Management Reform During Financial Austerity." *Statskontoret.* www.statskontoret.se/globalassets/publikationer/om-offentlig-sektor-1-11/om-offentlig-sektor-2.pdf. Accessed on 19th of December 2016.

Pollitt, Christopher and Geert Bouckaert. 2004. *Public Management Reform: A Comparative Analysis.* Oxford: Oxford University Press.

Pollitt, Christopher and Geert Bouckaert. 2011. *Public Management Reform: A Comparative Analysis: New Public Management, Governance, and the Neo-Weberian State.* Oxford: Oxford University Press.

Przeworski, Adam and Henry J. Teune. 1970. *The Logic of Comparative Social Inquiry: Comparative Studies in Behavioral Sciences.* New York: Wiley-Interscience.

Raudla, Ringa, Riin Savi and Tiin Randma-Liiv. 2013. *Literature Review on Cutback Management.* COCOPS workpackage 7 deliverable 1: COCOPS. www.cocops.eu.

Schick, Allen. 2010. "Post-Crisis Fiscal Rules: Stabilising Public Finance while Responding to Economic Aftershocks." *OECD Journal on Budgeting* 10(2): 1–16.

Wollmann, Hellmut. 2003. "Evaluation in Public Sector Reform: Towards a 'Third Wave' of Evaluation." In *Evaluation in Public Sector Reform*, edited by Hellmut Wollman, 1–11. Cheltenham: Edward Elgar.

Wollmann, Hellmut and Sabine Kuhlmann. 2014. *Introduction to Comparative Public Administration.* Cheltenham: Edward Elgar.

2 Public Management in Times of Austerity—The Literature

Eva Moll Ghin and Mads Bøge Kristiansen

Introduction

As explained in the introduction to this volume, its ambition is to elucidate the role of public management in the formulation and implementation of austerity policies such as cutbacks and budgetary reforms and the consequences of such policies to public management. The book addresses three main research questions: (1) What is the character of the changes to public management that are taking place under present-day austerity? (2) Does austerity entail path-breaking change and/or path-dependent patterns of change? (3) Why are different and/or similar patterns of change found in different countries?

This chapter reviews the literature on institutional continuity and change in public management and the literatures on cutback management and budgetary reform to help us qualify our expectations about the likely character and pattern of changes to public management in times of austerity. The chapter first discusses continuity and changes to public management at a general level. Then it zooms in on the literature on cutback management and budgetary reforms, and finally it discusses the likely consequences of austerity to public management in different countries.

Continuity and Change in Public Management

This section deals with continuity and change in public management (e.g. Aucoin 1990; Pollitt and Bouckaert 2004; 2009; 2011; Christensen and Lægreid 2007). We conceptualise the likely character of change under austerity and different patterns of change, and we present a model for understanding similarities and differences between countries.

The Character of Change

When discussing the character of changes to public management, it is almost unavoidable to refer to the large literature on the New Public Management (NPM) as reform paradigm and likely changes to this paradigm (e.g.

Hood 1991; Christensen and Lægreid 2007; Pollitt and Bouckaert 2011). NPM is based on a somewhat paradoxical combination of managerialism and new institutional economics (Aucoin 1990; Hood 1991) that includes a bundle of specific concepts and practices such as: organisational disaggregation, managerial flexibility, performance measurement (focusing on outputs), incentive-based controls, and treating service users as 'customers' (Hood 1991; Dunleavy et al. 2006; Pollitt and Bouckaert 2011). Although reform ideas related to NPM have been popular across a broad range of countries, and it has been discussed whether it leads towards international convergence (e.g. Kettl 2000; Pollitt 2001; Christensen and Lægreid 2002), it is also a common idea that countries pursue different 'reform trajectories' (Pollitt and Bouckaert 2007; 2011, 75ff; Ongaro 2009) towards different end-goals (Pollitt and Bouckaert 2011, 76).

More recently NPM has been diluted and merged with other streams of reform ideas, which have been referred to as 'Digital Era Governance' (Dunleavy et al. 2006), 'Second Wave Digital Era Governance' (Margretts and Dunleavy 2013), 'New Public Governance' (Osborne 2006; 2010) or 'Post-NPM' (Christensen and Lægreid 2007; 2011). Advocates of New Public Governance argue that modern public management must be based on cooperation and networks, boundary-spanning partnerships, citizen involvement and co-production (Osborne 2006). Other scholars have argued that NPM has been superseded by 'Digital Era Governance' involving organisational reintegration, needs-based holism and digitisation (Dunleavy et al. 2006). Similarly, advocates of 'Post-NPM' argue that we have entered an era of reforms that have the purpose of increasing the central steering capacity of the state through among other things vertical and horizontal reintegration and coordination (Christensen and Lægreid 2007; 2011). On the basis of these different trends, it is interesting to examine the character of the changes that are taking place under present-day austerity.

A common expectation in the literature on crisis and austerity is that it leads to *centralisation* in the sense of a concentration of power and decision-making (Aucoin 1990, 120; Boin et al. 2008). Centralisation is expected because budget units are given stronger powers to impose spending limits and cuts that other subunits are unlikely to undertake voluntarily (Raudla, Savi and Randma-Liiv 2013, 24–25). Centralisation can be achieved through standardisation of procedures, empowering the central budgetary departments, setting limits and ceilings to organisational spending, or by general priority-setting (Pollitt 2010; Peters 2011; Raudla, Savi and Randma-Liiv 2013). However, austerity need not lead to centralisation on all aspects. It can also be argued that austerity requires consensus and involvement of those decentralised units that must take responsibility for implementing it (Peters, Pierre and Randma-Liiv 2011). Furthermore, it is likely that centralisation will happen in cascades, meaning that central government leaders and budgetary units are not directly involved in the implementation of cuts at lower levels of organisation. They are probably more likely to exert their powers through aggregate guidelines and ceilings that must be implemented at lower levels of organisation, leading to a centralisation at those lower levels (Raudla, Savi and Randma-Liiv 2015).

Another common expectation is that austerity will be followed by increased demands for 'whole-of-government' coordination as a means of increasing cost-effectiveness (Peters, Pierre and Randma-Liiv 2011) or keeping the budgets. Coordination means that fragmentation (departmentalism) of policy and budgetary decision-making and the diffusion of power therein is challenged by central corporate authorities (Aucoin 1990, 120) and that central political and administrative capacity is strengthened, more scrutiny instruments and regulatory agencies established etc. (Christensen and Lægreid 2007, 12). It may also entail that horizontal specialisation is countered by networks and collaboration across institutions that increase the overall coordination of the system (Christensen and Lægreid 2007, 12). In the history of public management reform, coordination can be seen to represent one pole in a dichotomy between coordination and deregulation (Aucoin 1990) because the demand for coordination may translate into procedures and directives that each organisational subunit must consider when doing its work. Some decades ago, the dictum of (NPM-inspired) public management reform was that public managers should be set free to pursue their own organisational goals within overall guidelines. However, during the last decade or so, a larger emphasis on coordination has been observed and taken as a sign of transformation towards a post-NPM paradigm (Christensen and Lægreid 2007).

In the recent crisis literature, it has also been found that fiscal consolidation leads to rationalisation of public-sector organisations via agency mergers, downsizing back-office functions via creation of shared-service centres etc. (Kickert and Randma-Liiv 2015, 2010ff). These organisational reforms may both be conceptualised as a cost-saving device making use of (perceived) scale advantages and/or as a means of supporting the goals of centralisation and coordination through the reintegration of functions in larger multipurpose organisations.

In other words, we find it relevant to characterise the changes to public management by determining whether they continue the original NPM-paradigm and its combination of centralisation and decentralised managerial discretion, and/or they reinforce the transformation towards 'post-NPM' reforms where centralisation, coordination and organisational reintegration are central values.

The Pattern of Change: Path-Breaking and/or Path-Dependent?

After the crisis, it was discussed whether the crisis would become an exogenous shock that opened possibilities for sudden radical change of governing and administrative institutions (a critical juncture), or whether government responses to the crisis would reinforce existing governing patterns and institutions (Peters 2011; Peters, Pierre and Randma-Liiv 2011). The question has been addressed in a recent volume on fiscal consolidation in Europe, where it was found that the crisis led to the planning—but not always implementation—of new administrative reforms in most of the countries under study, and that the crisis also boosted reforms that were initiated before the crisis in many countries. It was, however, also found that the crisis led to cancellation, postponements or hindrance of ongoing reforms in some cases (Kickert and Randma-Liiv 2015, 196–210).

We propose that the different effects of crisis and austerity on reforms can be conceptualised in a systematic way by drawing on recent contributions to historical institutionalism (Streeck and Thelen 2005; Pollitt and Bouckaert 2009; Mahoney and Thelen 2010) that distinguish between *processes* of change, which may be gradual or abrupt, and *results* of change, which may amount to either continuity or discontinuity in relation to existing institutions and traditions. The combination gives four different types of institutional change shown in Table 2.1:

Table 2.1 Patterns of Institutional Change Under Austerity

		Result of Change	
		Within-Path, Incremental (Continuity)	*Pathbreaking, Transformation (Discontinuity)*
Process of Change	Gradual	A. Austerity leads to minor changes along the existing path.	B. Austerity reinforces the existing reform trajectory which may possibly lead to transformational change over time.
	Abrupt	C. Austerity leads to cancellation, postponement, hindrance or reversal of existing reforms.	D. Sudden radical change (punctuation): Austerity as a 'critical juncture'.

Source: Our adaptation of Pollitt and Bouckaert (2009, 18) and Streeck and Thelen (2005, 9) to the times of austerity.

In the first pattern (Box A) the process is characterised by small gradual changes, and they do not add up to fundamental changes of existing administrative institutions and traditions. It is possible that austerity only leads to small changes that fit into this path-dependent pattern.

In the second pattern (Box B), the process of change is gradual but the direction of change is constant leading eventually to fundamental change. Austerity may reinforce and 'boost' ongoing reforms and thus contribute to major long-term transformations. It is, however, not always straight-forward to distinguish between gradual within-path changes and gradual changes that are path-breaking and transformational, as it depends on time (Pollitt 2008, 47). In other words, if austerity reinforces ongoing reforms, it may—or may not—lead to path-breaking changes of existing institutions over time.

In Box C, the crisis has an immediate effect on reforms, but it is negative. Within this pattern of change austerity leads to more path-dependence in public administration because it works against the realisation of ongoing reforms through cancellation, postponement or hindrance.

In Box D, the process of change is abrupt, and the results are transformational. Within this pattern, the economic crisis has the role of exogenous shock that makes quick and radical changes possible, leading to comprehensive redesign of institutions (Thelen and Steinmo 1992, 15).

On the basis of this typology, we hope to be able to provide a more nuanced picture of the patterns of change to public management that occur as a result of crisis and austerity in different countries. In the following section, we will discuss why countries pursue different reform trajectories, and how this may matter to their patterns of change in times of austerity.

Understanding Differences and Similarities Between Countries

As argued earlier, it has been discussed whether economic globalisation and the circulation of ideas would lead towards convergence, or whether national administrative institutions are likely to remain divergent. Pollitt and Bouckaert (2004; 2011) have added to the discussion by arguing that different countries pursue different 'reform trajectories'. They have presented a model which may help us conceptualise the forces that drive and restrain changes and lead to similarities and differences across countries, and in the following we will adapt the model to the comparative analysis of changes to public management in times of austerity.

In Bouckaert and Pollitt's model, institutional change is understood as 'reform', i.e. as the result of key reform decisions that are taken by national governments (Pollitt and Bouckaert 2011, 32). At the centre of the model are politicians' and senior civil servants' decision-making. Decision-making is influenced by decision makers' perceptions of what is desirable and feasible, reflecting for example that there are different cultural preferences and conservative forces which resist change (Pollitt and Bouckaert 2011, 33). Surrounding decision-making are three large groups of factors: economic factors, political factors and administrative factors. It is from the interplay between these elements that public management reforms emerge.

As this book focuses on changes in the wake of the financial crisis, *economic forces* are of special interest. Economic crises may be a vital background for changes of administrative institutions, and may serve as an exogenous shock that opens things up (e.g. Pierson 2000), allowing for change. Although the international crisis has been a common driver for change, it does not necessarily elicit similar responses. Each country may, to some extent, be argued to have had its own distinct crisis driven by different mixes of factors (Lindquist, de Vries and Wanna 2015). Furthermore, the impact of the crisis acts through other intervening factors such as management ideas concerning how the public sector could be better organised (Pollitt and Bouckaert 2011, 36). The circulation of popular reform ideas are often promoted by international bodies such as the OECD, the World Bank, EU or IMF (see e.g. Sahlin-Andersson 2001), but when they meet the national context they tend to flow into a larger pool of ideas drawn from a variety of sources (Pollitt and Bouckaert 2011, 38–40), and their realisation often depends on a 'window of opportunity', which allows reform entrepreneurs to couple reform ideas to problems and political circumstances in a way that draws the attention of elite decision makers (Kingdon 2003).

However, even when reforms are on the national agenda, the different political and administrative systems shape reforms in different ways.

The *political system* may enable or constrain reforms in several ways. First, we must take account of the structural and institutional features of different political systems, such as the role of law, the type of government (minority, majority or grand coalition), the political culture, and the constitutional protection of local government. Pollitt and Bouckaert also place dynamic elements in the 'political system' box, such as party-political ideas or pressure from citizens. However, in the comparative

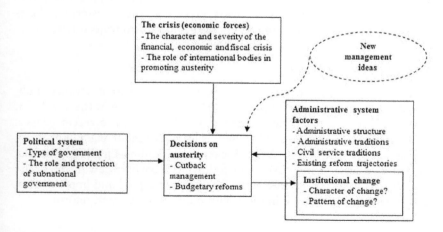

Figure 2.1 A Model of Institutional Change

Source: Inspired by Pollitt and Bouckaert (2011, 33).

analysis of public management under austerity, we mainly pay attention to the institutional features of the political system.

The *administrative system* is also an important source of enabling and constraining factors. For example, it may be important whether the civil service consists of a core of generalists or a staff trained in law. The structure of the administration may also influence the shape and timing of institutional change; it makes a difference whether the state is a unitary state or a federation, and whether the unitary state is decentralised or centralised. Personnel regulations may also serve as notable constraints on reform, and public service unions are likely trying to prevent any changes that may result in staff reductions or deterioration of their members' conditions (Pollitt and Bouckaert 2011, 42–43). Finally, previous reform trajectories may influence the extent and character of institutional change, for example through learning from previous processes of implementation (Pollitt and Bouckaert 2011, 46).

Summing up, Pollitt and Bouckaert's reform model can help us to understand how austerity affects the trajectories of public management reform in different countries. Under austerity, the studied countries are affected by some similar pressures, including the fiscal policies of the European Union and the circulation of ideas. However, as they enter the times of austerity from different starting points, and they have different political and administrative systems, and they were affected differently by the crisis (see Chapter 3), austerity is likely to have different consequences to public management.

In the next section, we will dig more into the literature on cutbacks and budgetary reforms, i.e. two responses to the crisis that represent austerity in the sense of a stern attitude on public spending. We will discuss how cutbacks and budgetary reforms are likely to be adopted and implemented, before we return to the questions of how these austerity policies affect public management and its changes and reform trajectories.

Cutback Management

Cutback management was the object of a relatively coherent stream of public administration research in the late 1970s and early 80s (Levine 1978; 1985; Jørgensen 1981; Dunsire and Hood 1989), and in recent years a number of researchers have taken up this literature again (e.g. Pollitt 2010; Overmans and Nordegraaf 2014; Kickert and Randma-Liiv 2015; Raudla, Savi and Randma-Liiv 2015). In the following, we will review the literature and discuss how expenditure cutbacks may be adopted and implemented, and how they are likely to interact with public management reform.

Cutback Strategies and Measures

The most basic distinction that emerges from the literature on cutback management is that between across-the-board and targeted cuts.

Across-the-board cuts refer to cuts in equal amounts or percentages for all organisations, whereas targeted cuts imply that some organisations or sectors face larger cuts than others (Raudla, Savi and Randma-Liiv 2015). The across-the-board tactic has also been called decrementalism (Levine 1985) or cheese-slicing (Pollitt 2010). Decrementalism has the advantages of reducing decision-making costs, minimizing conflict and being perceived as equitable, but it is also criticised for not reflecting the public's needs and preferences, for penalising efficient organisations, ignoring the varying needs of different units and for leading to decline in service levels or quality (Pollitt 2010; Raudla, Savi and Randma-Liiv 2015). Targeted cuts have the opposite pros and cons; they have high decision-making costs and risk stirring up conflict but they may also preserve the level and quality of core services. In most of the literature, the 'targeted cuts' strategy is thought to involve a higher level of rational analysis and prioritisation, and it is also argued to be based on more centralised decision-making (e.g. Pollitt 2010; Kickert and Randma-Liiv 2015). It can, however, not be ruled out that targeted cutbacks emerge from decision-making with elements of randomness or 'garbage can' traits (Raudla, Savi and Randma-Liiv 2015).

In addition to the decremental and targeted approaches, some researchers have proposed an intermediary level of analysis and prioritisation. Jørgensen (1981) proposed distinguishing between decremental, managerial and strategic approaches. More recently, Pollitt has presented a similar distinction between cheese-slicing, efficiency gains and centralised priority-setting (2010). Whereas cheese-slicing entails an equal distribution of cuts on the involved units, efficiency gains are based on analysis of the opportunities for rationalisation and innovation in different areas. Centralised priority-setting entails that some programs are prioritised at the expense of others. This may be based on assessment of their relative cost-effectiveness, and/or on strategic analysis that helps the organisation distinguish between high- and low-priority programs.

In the literature, it is expected that adopted strategies and measures reflect the context. Levine (1985) argued that as the situation of fiscal stress grew more long-term and severe in organisations, more radical approaches became workable, and the demand for strategic capacity increased. Similarly, Jørgensen (1981) argued that as the crisis grows longer and deeper, and the psychological climate gets more pessimistic, organisations will move through different stages of cutbacks; from decremental to managerialist and strategic approaches. The empirical evidence on the stages model is mixed (Dunsire and Hood 1989; Pollitt 2010), but it is still influential. Recently, Kickert and Randma-Liiv (2015) found that the size and speed of cutbacks increased in subsequent phases of consolidation between 2007 and 2012, and that decision-making changed from across-the-board to targeted and priority-setting strategies.

The concept of cutback approaches or strategies refers to how decisions are reached and rationalised. It does not tell us the concrete measure through which costs are reduced, whether through staff layoffs, hiring freezes or wage reductions or through savings on building maintenance or acquisitions. In our conceptualisation, each cutback strategy may lead to cost reductions through different measures. For example, efficiency cuts may be based on a reorganisation of work processes that reduce the needed number of staff, which may then be decreased through layoffs or hiring freezes.

Raudla, Savi and Randma-Liiv (2015) argue that cutback strategies can be applied at the macro or *national policy* level (when cutback decisions are taken by government cabinets) or at the *organisational level* (within individual ministries or agencies). Among the early studies of cutback management, many took the perspective of individual agencies or departments (e.g. Levine 1978; Jørgensen 1981) or of local governments (Levine, Rubin and Wolohojian 1981), while a few took the perspective of national government (Dunsire and Hood 1989). There were, however, not many who paid attention to the question of how cutback decisions are delegated from one level of organisation to another.

Across-the-board cuts at one level may entail that decisions on the implementation of cutbacks are delegated to the next level of organisation (e.g. from cabinet to the ministerial level), and in that sense, it may represent a decentralisation of decision-making. At the next level of organisation, leaders again face the choice between different cutback strategies and measures—and so forth. Raudla, Savi and Randma-Liiv (2015) explored some of the implications of this logic of delegation when they found that ministries of finance make their increased power more felt at the top hierarchical levels of agencies, whereas managers at lower hierarchical levels perceived that decision-making powers were being centralised to the top managers and budgetary units of their respective organisations rather than directly to the Ministry of Finance itself. Cutback management thus leads to a cascading dynamic of centralisation at the various levels of organisation in the public sector (Raudla, Savi and Randma-Liiv 2015).

Cutbacks and Public Management Reform

In this context, we are not only interested in how cutback decisions are made but also in the relationship between cutbacks and public management reform. Related to this, Pollitt (2010) argues that both cheese-slicing, efficiency gains and centralised priority-setting may lead to public management reform, albeit in different ways. With *cheese-slicing*, it is up to operational managers to find ways of reducing their budgets. This may involve the adoption of public management reforms at the decentralised levels. We could thus expect that cheese-slicing will lead to minimal reforms or a variety of decentralised reforms which are tailored to the circumstances of each organisation. It is also possible that the pressure for cutbacks will induce decentralised entities to look to each other for ideas, leading to the adoption of homogenous reform elements (DiMaggio and Powell 1983). *Efficiency gains* by definition entails that savings come from more efficient ways of organising and providing services at levels above line managers (Pollitt 2010). These reforms may reflect recent advances in organisational technologies or a process of learning from recent generations of reform, but it is also possible that the adoption of efficiency-oriented reforms will reflect prevalent cultural beliefs about which organisational forms are most effective (Meyer and Rowan 1977; Røvik 2007). *Centralised priority-setting* may result in reforms, which entail that some services are not offered anymore or are drastically reduced. Centralising priority-setting also increases the demand for reforms that increase strategic capacity in public organisations such as new decision-making procedures and calculative techniques (Pollitt 2010).

Christopher Hood (2010) has also discussed the relationship between crisis and reforms of public services, distinguishing between three types of reform strategies: (1) resetting of recent reforms, (2) system redesign, (3) East of Suez moments.[1] The resetting strategy signifies a reorientation of recently introduced instruments from the objective of expanding public services and improving their quality to the objectives of cost reductions and productivity improvements. The redesign strategy involves more radical reorganisations or redesigns of services, and the East of Suez moments concern decisions to terminate programs to focus scarce resources on other programs.

On the basis of the typologies offered by Pollitt (2010) and Hood (2010), Hansen and Kristiansen (2014) argue that we need to reflect on cutback strategies both on a dimension related to how decisions are made and another related to the logic and content of the strategies. Thus, their typology combines whether the process of change is incremental, managerial or strategic, and whether strategies are anchored in a cost-saving logic, reorganisation logic or programme logic. Incremental processes of change include minor adjustments, managerial processes refer to re-engineering in order to obtain efficiency gains, and the strategic processes cover more radical decisions. On the other dimension, using a cost-saving logic means making decisions on levels of cost savings and afterwards discussing how to implement these. Using a reorganisation logic means making decisions on organisational reform under the belief that organising differently can redeem savings. Finally, using a programme logic means responding to cutbacks through changing programmes, services, regulations and inspection procedures. As shown in Table 2.2., thinking along these lines reveals nine different strategies:

In practice, the nine strategies are not independent. Politicians may for instance decide to cut back the budgets of ministries by 5% using strategy 1: cheese-slicing. If politicians do not decide how the cuts are to be

Table 2.2 Cutback Strategies

Logic/Process	Cost-Saving Logic	Reorganisation Logic	Programme Logic
Incremental	1. Incremental cost savings	4. Resetting reform elements from the past to an age of fiscal consolidation	7. Marginally changing programmes, services and inspection routines
Managerial	2. Assessing potential for savings or efficiency gains through business cases	5. Intra- and interorganisational reorganisation through rationalising work procedures	8. Innovating programmes, services and inspection routines
Strategic	3. Substantial savings	6. Systems redesign	9. Strategic prioritising and cutting away programmes, services and regulation regimes

Source: Hansen and Kristiansen (2014: 232)

implemented, ministries may choose to implement the political decision in distinct ways. In this context, strategies may transform from decision to implementation and/or through delegation.

A similar typology has been presented by Overmans and Nordegraaf (2014) and Overmans and Timm-Arnold (2015). In the latter publication, a distinction is made between four types of austerity measures: fiscal cuts, fiscal change, organisational cuts and organisational change. In particular, the category of 'organisational change' involves changes to public management.

Budgetary Reform

Budgeting and budgetary reform is the topic of a large and diverse literature. Budgeting is both regarded as a rational exercise of allocating public money to the uses where it can achieve most of society's agreed-upon goals (Lewis 1952) and as an outcome of the 'who gets what' of government politics (Wildavsky 1974). It is a long-standing discussion whether budgetary reforms make a difference, or whether public budgets are fundamentally the expression of the political balance of power (Wildavsky 1961) and/or of economic cycles (Blöndal 2003). Nonetheless, budgeting has been reformed for generations, and it has been argued that each generation of reforms addresses the dominant problems of their time in public budgeting and management (Schick 1966).

It may also be argued that different parts of the literature address different problems in budgeting. For example, the literature on 'fiscal institutionalism' is primarily concerned with institutional solutions to the problem of maintaining fiscal discipline at the societal level (e.g. Hallerberg, Strauch and Hagen 2009), whereas the performance-budgeting literature is focused on ways of using budgeting for the stimulation of efficiency and effectiveness in the public sector (e.g. Curristine 2007). Furthermore, the focus of analysis varies from the effects of political institutions and budgetary rules on fiscal outcomes (Hagen 2007) to the role of public managers in the implementation of budgets and of different financial management principles (Pollit and Bouckaert 2011, 77ff). Budgetary reforms may also be analysed from the perspective of general institutionalist theory (e.g. Raudla 2010; Wanna, Jensen and de Vries 2010; Cohen and Karatzimas 2014).

In the following section, we will provide a definition of budgetary reform, and we will look at justifications and explanations of budgetary reform from the perspectives of fiscal discipline and performance. Last but not least, we will consider how an economic crisis is likely to affect budgetary reforms.

What Is Budgetary Reform?

Budgetary reforms may be defined as changes to budgetary institutions, i.e. the rules and regulations according to which budgets are drafted, approved, and implemented (Alesina and Perroti 1996).

Budgetary reform can have a 'macro-budgetary', 'distributive' or 'micro-budgetary' character. Macro-budgetary reforms are meant to strengthen fiscal discipline, distributive budgetary reforms are meant to rationalise the allocation of expenditure between programs and organisations, and micro-budgetary reform is meant to rationalise operational resource management (Schick 2001). According to Wanna (2010, 285), budgetary reforms from the 1980s to the 2000s have primarily been motivated by macro-budgetary and micro-budgetary objectives whereas less emphasis has been put on the distributive objective of reallocation. This possibly reflects the preoccupation with operational productivity that has been central to the understanding of performance in NPM (van Dooren 2008). Contemporary budgetary reforms are strongly motivated by fiscal discipline, particularly those reforms that reflect the implementation of the common fiscal policies of the European Union. It is, however, also conceivable that these reforms will be complemented by reforms that are meant to improve the allocation and management of scarce resources.

Budgetary Reform From the Perspective of Fiscal Discipline

The literature on fiscal institutionalism focuses on 'collective action' problems in budgeting and on solutions to these problems from a rational institutionalist perspective (Hagen 2007; Hallerberg, Strauch and Hagen 2007). The main problem concerns the *common pool problem* of public finance, referring to the argument that the total of spending-wishes from different groups typically exceeds the 'pool' of expenditure that society is willing to fund. The common pool problem is considered particularly large if there are many groups in the political system (Hagen 2007, 28).

The main solution offered is to *centralise* budgeting. Centralisation of the budget process may occur at different phases. The *planning phase* is centralised when it promotes the setting of budgetary targets at the outset (Raudla 2014, 6). The *approval phase* is centralised when the executive has an important role in setting the agenda of budget proceedings in the legislature, when it can (1) limit legislative amendments to the budget, (2) require amendments to be offsetting, (3) postulate the legislature to vote on the total budget size before the approbation of single provisions and (4) raise the political stakes of rejecting the executive's budget (Raudla 2014, 6). The *implementation phase* is centralised when it is difficult to change the existing budget document during the fiscal year, when transfers of funds between chapters are forbidden or limited, when unused funds cannot be carried over to the next year's budget, and when the minister of finance has extensive powers to monitor and control spending flows during the fiscal year (Raudla 2014, 6).

In the literature on fiscal institutionalism, distinctions are made between three types of budgetary institutions, which may all be adapted to the purpose of centralising budgeting: (1) rules concerning the transparency and comprehensiveness of budgeting (2) fiscal targets or rules and (3) budgetary procedures (Alesina and Perotti 1996; Hagen 2007). The first category concerns whether all claims on public expenditure are made in the central budget process. The second category includes rules about budget outputs, such as balanced budget rules or rules about maximum allowable deficits or debts. Traditionally, fiscal rules have addressed the actual, 'nominal' balance, but recently some countries—and the EU—adopted so-called 'second-generation fiscal rules' (Schick 2010) that regulate the so-called 'structural balance' which is calculated in ways that take account of cyclical fluctuations in the economy. These rules are more flexible than traditional fiscal rules. The third type of budgeting institutions are rules and norms that define the budgetary process. These procedural rules may focus on decision makers (e.g. the authority of the Ministry of Finance) or on procedural content, e.g. top-down budgeting or the use of medium-term expenditure frameworks. The literature on fiscal institutionalism distinguishes between two modes of centralisation. In the *delegation* approach, centralisation is achieved by delegating power to a strong 'fiscal entrepreneur', usually the Ministry of Finance. In the *contracts* approach, centralisation is achieved by letting the budgeting process start with an agreement among the main actors on a set of binding fiscal targets. The theory on fiscal institutionalism predicts that the delegation approach is more functional in single-party majoritarian political systems where the same party controls the Ministry of Finance and spending ministries whereas the contracts approach is more functional in coalition governments (Hallerberg, Strauch and Hagen 2007; 2009).

Economic crises play a major role in the literature as 'windows' for institutional change that centralise budgeting. For example, in the literature on fiscal institutionalism, crises make the disadvantages of weak expenditure control apparent to the population, which is then likely to support reforms that institutionalise fiscal discipline (Hallerberg, Strauch and Hagen 2009; Suenson, Nedergaard and Christiansen 2015). If we use Kingdon's imagery, crises open windows of opportunity that make it possible for policy entrepreneurs, for example in the shape of ministries of finance, to create couplings between the problem of fiscal discipline, the politics of crisis and reform policies (Kingdon 1993).

Budgetary Reform From the Perspective of Performance

In addition to fiscal discipline, budgetary reforms may be aimed at allocative effectiveness and operational efficiency. These aspects of resource management are addressed by the literature on performance budgeting (e.g. Curristine 2007; Kelly and Rivenbark 2011). The idea behind performance budgeting is that budgetary allocations should be shaped less by detailed rules and past allocation patterns and more by information on performance. Curristine and the OECD distinguish between three categories: *presentational performance budgeting* (where performance information is included as background information in budget documents), *performance-informed budgeting* (performance information is used to inform budget decisions indirectly) and *direct/formula performance budgeting* where allocations are tied directly to units of performance, generally outputs (Curristine 2007).

Performance considerations may also be integrated in budgeting through accrual budgeting and accounting. Accrual accounting may be understood as macro-budgetary reform because it decreases the scope for misrepresenting the costs of budgetary decisions (Schick 2001), but it is also a kind of 'micro-budgetary' reform because it makes the productivity of public organisations comparable to other organisations. However, the introduction of accruals also bears the risk of making the financial implications of budgetary decisions less readily understandable (Pollitt and Bouckaert 2011).

Budgetary reforms may also be intended to improve allocative effectiveness, corresponding to the distributive dimension of budgetary reform. Providing budgets with a program structure can represent a step in this direction (Cohen and Karatzimas 2014). Other tools for allocative effectiveness include evaluations, outcomes measurements, and strategic planning (Schick 2001). *Spending reviews* can also be used to identify potentials for budgetary reallocations.

According to Pollitt and Bouckaert, the *savings* objective of budgetary and financial management reform (i.e. fiscal discipline) does not always fit well with reforms to encourage performance improvements because the top-down imposition of cutbacks may generate an unpredictable and negative environment for operational managers (Pollitt and Bouckaert 2011, 78). However, one way of making top-down cutback targets more compatible with performance incentives is through frame- or block-budgeting, which has been used for example in the Scandinavian countries (Pollitt and Bouckaert 2011, 78). This means that the central ministry sets overall ceilings but delegates the responsibility for detailed allocations to the levels of ministries, agencies or local governments. In other words, centralisation of decision-making on overall targets is combined with decentralisation of detailed allocations and cutbacks to budget units at lower levels of organisation. Indeed, top-down budgeting is sometimes defined as a combination of centralised setting of expenditure ceilings and delegation of detailed resource allocation decisions to line ministries (Kim and Park 2006).

It is not clear from the literature how crises and austerity will affect those budgetary reforms that are meant to improve performance (Kelly and Rivenbark 2011, 9). One viewpoint is that the scarcity of resources increases the need for rational allocation and management, and this should speak for increased use of performance information in a broad sense (Dunsire and Hood 1989; Raudla 2013). On the other hand, scarcity may make it harder to implement performance-oriented reforms since they can no longer be lubricated with new money (Dunsire and Hood 1989; Raudla 2013). It is also possible that austerity will focus policymakers' attention on short-term fiscal control and discipline and crowd out their attention to performance-oriented reforms (Cepiku and Savignon 2012; Cohen and Karatzimas 2014), or that they will not want to pursue reforms that make the consequences of cutbacks on public services more transparent (Pollitt 2013).

Changes to Public Management in Times of Austerity: Expectations

Thus far, we have reviewed literature on continuity and change in public management, cutback management and budgetary reform. In the following sections, we use the literature to develop some more detailed expectations with regard to the three main research questions of the book.

The Character of Changes

As argued earlier, we find it relevant to characterise the recent changes by considering whether they continue the original NPM-paradigm and its combination of centralisation and decentralisation, and/or whether they reinforce the transformation towards 'post-NPM' reforms where centralisation, coordination and organisational reintegration are central values. In order to help us address this rather abstract question, we find it appropriate to focus on different components of public management reform. For the sake of simplicity, we have chosen to focus on four so-called 'substance' components derived from Pollitt and Bouckaert's framework (2011, 77): financial management, personnel management, organisational restructuring and performance measurement.

Financial Management

The trajectory of financial management has been driven by two pressures: to restrain the growth of public expenditure (fiscal discipline) and to increase efficiency and effectiveness (performance) (Pollitt and Bouckaert 2011). As argued earlier, fiscal discipline often speaks for centralisation, but sometimes the central setting of overall expenditure ceilings may be combined with decentralisation of detailed allocations and increases in managerial freedoms at the implementation phase of the budget. We can thus expect that financial management reform will move in the direction of centralisation, which may or may not be combined with decentralisation.

Personnel Management

Traditionally a typical civil servant was assumed to be a tenured career appointment, promoted in relation to qualifications and seniority, and part of a unified civil service within a distinct national framework of terms and conditions (Pollitt and Bouckaert 2011, 90). NPM-inspired reforms related to these features adopted in many countries during the 1980s and 1990s, however, changed personnel management toward less secure careers, linking promotion more clearly to performance, and decentralising personnel authority i.e. through a widening range of terms and conditions (Pollitt and Bouckaert 2011, 91–95). We want to explore whether personnel management in times of austerity is characterised by further movements towards decentralisation of personnel authority increasing managerial discretion, or whether it is characterised by more centralisation, coherence and traditional features of civil servants.

Organisational Restructuring

Organisational restructurings may be classified according to three features: (1) specialisation; (2) centralisation/decentralisation and (3) scale (Pollitt and Bouckaert 2011). In NPM 'flat', flexible, specialised, decentralised and therefore relatively small organisations were preferred, whereas the recent 'post-NPM' trend of reasserting coordination has led to mergers and reabsorptions of arm's-length bodies into central departments (Christensen and Lægreid 2011; Pollitt and Bouckaert 2011, 104). Thus, whereas disaggregation and small-scale organisations were preferred in the 1980s and 1990s, recentralisation, mergers and larger scale organisations seem to have been preferred in the 2000s, either as a means of realising scale advantages and/or as a means of facilitating coordination and centralised steering. We will explore whether the recent times of austerity have been characterised by recentralisation, mergers, less specialised and larger scale organisations, or by specialised, decentralised and small organisations.

Performance Measurement

Performance measurement is a central feature of NPM-inspired reform in most countries, and it may be an institutionalised part of the three other components mentioned earlier. Performance measurement for example may be adopted through performance-informed budgeting, as a means of coordination between organisations through performance contracts, and as performance-related pay. Further, performance information may serve as a basis for decisions on cutbacks. Over time, performance measurement seems to have become more extensive, intensive and external in public management (Pollitt and Bouckaert 2011, 106). Overall, we can expect performance measurement to continue becoming more extensive, intensive and external, possibly with the purpose of increasing coordination, and/or we can expect setbacks to the use of performance information in public management.

Path-Breaking or Path-Dependent Changes?

As previously argued, economic crises are often associated with radical changes in the literature on budgetary reform and institutional change more generally. It is, for example, conceivable that the crisis helps ministries of finance and similar reform actors achieve political support for sudden radical changes to financial management or personnel management. It is also conceivable that large-scale strategic cutbacks may entail path-breaking changes of existing institutions and reform trajectories (pattern D).

It is, however, also conceivable that austerity leads to more path-dependent patterns of change. If we use the stages model of cutback management, we may expect that the short-term implementation of cutbacks will be based on decrementalism, and that such cutbacks will take away the resources that are needed for public management reform (Pollitt 2010) and/or favour reforms that are similar to previous reforms. In other words, we may expect within-path changes that either do not change the existing reform trajectory or that may work against existing reform ambitions (patterns A and C discussed earlier). In the medium term, we may expect cutbacks that are based more on managerialist approaches. These approaches are more likely to affect the existing path, for example by intensifying the pressure for reforms and helping administrative elites overcome resistance from public-sector unions and others, thus reinforcing and speeding up ongoing reforms. Hence, managerialist cutbacks are likely to be associated with the previously discussed pattern of gradual changes (pattern B).

The Influence of Economic and Institutional Factors

If we use the model of public management reform, which was presented earlier, it is to be expected that the degree and character of changes will depend both on the character of the economic crisis and on the institutions that define the political and administrative systems of each country.

The decisions on cutbacks and budgetary reforms and their effects on public management are likely to depend on the *character of the economic and fiscal crisis* in each country. First, the volume of cutbacks is likely to depend on the financial-economic situation; severe crises lead to large budget deficits that are likely to be handled through large consolidation plans and cutbacks which also entail radical changes to public management. Second, the pressures of the crisis have been mediated by the policies and actions of international actors such as the IMF or the EU, and different countries have been exposed to different degrees of intervention from such bodies.

With regard to the political system, it is a common assumption that one-party majoritarian types of governments are more likely to carry out swift, large and targeted cuts that involve radical reforms than coalition and minority governments (Kickert and Randma-Liiv 2015, 173). Grand majorities are, on the surface, able to force through radical changes, but given the need to find agreement within a heterogeneous government coalition they are probably unlikely to embark on radical reforms. The political system may also matter in the sense that it is easier to decide on large reforms in unitary states where there are fewer constitutional rules regulating the relationship between national and subnational governments, and subnational governments do not have a formal role in policymaking.

With regard to the *administrative structures*, it can be argued that governments of states with high degrees of vertical decentralisation are likely to delegate cutback decisions to local governments and agencies, whereas governments in centralised states are more likely to impose targeted cuts that involve public management reform. *Administrative cultures* and *civil service traditions* are also likely to influence the choice of cutback measures and their consequences to personnel management, as they determine whether it is possible or not to layoff personnel, lower wages etc.

Finally, the choice of cutbacks and reforms and their consequences on public management is likely to depend on existing reform trajectories. According to Pollitt and Bouckart (2004), the reform trajectories of different European countries have either been characterised by 'marketising', 'modernising', 'minimising', or 'maintaining' reform strategies in the past. It is likely that the choice of reforms under austerity will be influenced by the countries' different starting points as well as it may also reflect processes of learning from those past reform experiences.

Note

1   East of Suez moments refers to the historic decision by Harold Wilson's Labour government in 1968 to abandon most of the chain of overseas military bases Britain had formerly maintained from the Mediterranean to the South China Sea (Hood 2010, 8).

References

Alesina, Alberto and Roberto Perotti. 1996. "Fiscal Discipline and the Budget Process." *The American Economic Review* 86(2):401–7.

Aucoin, Peter. 1990. "Administrative Reforms in Public Management: Paradigms, Principles, Paradoxes and Pendulums." *Governance* 32(2):115–37.

Blöndal, Jón. 2003. "Budget Reform in OECD Member Countries: Common Trends." *OECD Journal of Budgeting* 2(4):7–26.

Boin, Arjen, Paul 't Hart, Eric Stern and Bengt Sundelius. 2008. *The Politics of Crisis Management: Public Leadership Under Pressure.* Cambridge, UK: Cambridge University Press.

Cepiku, Denita and Andrea B. Savignon. 2012. "Governing Cutback Management: Is There a Global Strategy for Public Administrations?" *International Journal of Public Sector Management* 25(6/7):428–36.

Christensen, Tom and Per Lægreid. 2002. *New Public Management: The Transformation of Ideas and Practice.* Aldershot: Ashgate.

Christensen, Tom and Per Lægreid. 2007. *Transcending New Public Management: The Transformation of Public Sector Reforms.* Aldershot: Ashgate.

Christensen, Tom and Per Lægreid. 2011. "Beyond NPM? Some Development Features." In *The Ashgate Research Companion to New Public Management*, edited by Tom Christensen and Per Lægreid, 391–404. Aldershot: Ashgate.

Cohen, Sandra and Sotirios Karatizimas. 2014. "Reporting Performance Information in the Public Sector: The Moral Behind the (non)Application of Program Budgeting in Greece." *International Review of Administrative Sciences* 80(3):619–36.

Curristine, Teresa. 2007. *Performance Budgeting in OECD Countries.* Paris: OECD.

DiMaggio, Paul J. and Walter W. Powell. 1983. "The Iron Cage Revisited: Institutional Isomorphism and Collective Rationality in Organizational Fields." *American Sociological Review* 48(2):147–60.

Dunleavy, Patrick, Helen Margetts, Simon Bastow and Jane Tinkler. 2006. "New Public Management Is Dead: Long Live Digital-Era Governance." *Journal of Public Administration Research and Theory* 16(3):467–94.

Dunsire, Andrew and Christopher Hood. 1989. *Cutback Management in Public Bureaucracies, Popular Theories and Observed Outcomes in Whitehall.* Cambridge: Cambridge University Press.

Hagen von, Jürgen. 2007. "Budgeting Institutions for Better Fiscal Performance." In *Budgeting and Budgetary Institutions*, edited by Anwar Shah, 27–52. Washington, DC: World Bank.

Hallerberg, Mark, Rolf Strauch and Jürgen von Hagen. 2007. "The Design of Fiscal Rules and Forms of Governance in European Union Countries." *European Journal of Political Economy* 23:338–59.

Hallerberg, Mark, Rolf Strauch and Jürgen von Hagen. 2009. *Fiscal Governance in Europe.* Cambridge: Cambridge University Press.

Hansen, Hanne Foss and Mads Kristiansen. 2014. "Styring af besparelser." In *Offentlig Styring: Forandring i krisetider*, edited by Caroline Howard Grøn, Hanne Foss Hansen and Mads Kristiansen, 227–56. Copenhagen: Hans Reitzels.

Hood, Christopher. 1991. "A Public Management for All Seasons?" *Public Administration* 69(1):3–19.

Hood, Christopher. 2010. *Reflections on Public Services Reforms in a Cold Fiscal Climate.* London: 2020 Public Services Trust.

Jørgensen, Torben Beck. 1981. *Når staten skal spare.* Copenhagen: Nyt fra Samfundsvidenskaberne.

Kelly, Janet and William Rivenbark. 2011. *Performance Budgeting for State and Local Government.* Armonk: Sharpe.

Kettl, Donald. 2000. *The Global Public Management Revolution: A Report on the Transformation of Governance.* Washington, DC: Brookings Institution.

Kickert, Walter and Tiina Randma-Liiv. 2015. *Europe Managing the Crisis: The Politics of Fiscal Consolidation.* London: Routledge.

Kim, John and Chung-Keun Park. 2006. "Top-Down Budgeting as a Tool for Central Resource Management." *OECD Journal on Budgeting* 6(1):87–235.

Kingdon, John Wells. 2003. *Agendas, Alternatives, and Public Policies.* New York: Longman.

Levine, Charles H. 1978. "Organizational Decline and Cutback Management." *Public Administration Review* 38(4):316–25.

Levine, Charles H. 1985. "Police Management in the 1980s: From Decrementalism to Strategic Thinking." *Public Administration Review* 45:691–700.

Levine, Charles H., Irene Rubin and George G. Wolohojian. 1981. "Resource Scarcity and the Reform Model: The Management of Retrenchment in Cincinnati and Oakland." *Public Administration Review* 41(6):619–28.

Lewis, Verne B. 1952. "Toward a Theory of Budgeting." *Public Administration Review* 12(1):42–54.

Lindquist, Evert, Jouke de Vries and John Wanna. 2015. "Readiness, Resilience, Reform and Persistence of Budget Systems After the GFC: Conclusions and Implications." In *The Global Financial Crisis and Its Budget Impact in OECD Nations*, edited by Evert Lindquist, Jouke de Vries and John Wanna: 309–42. Cheltenham: Edward Elgar.

Mahoney, James and Kathleen Ann Thelen. 2010. *Explaining Institutional Change, Ambiguity, Agency, and Power.* Cambridge: Cambridge University Press.

Margetts, Helen and Patrick Dunleavy. 2013. "The Second Wave of Digital-Era Governance: A Quasi-Paradigm for Government on the Web." *Philosophical*

Transactions: Series A, Mathematical, Physical, and Engineering Sciences 371(1987): 1–17.

Meyer, John Wilfred and Brian Rowan. 1977. "Institutionalized Organizations: Formal Structure as Myth and Ceremony." *American Journal of Sociology* 83(2):340–63.

Ongaro, Edoardo. 2009. *Public Management Reform and Modernization: Trajectories of Administrative Change in Italy, Greece, Portugal and Spain.* Cheltenham: Edward Elgar.

Osborne, Stephen P. 2006. "The New Public Governance?" *Public Management Review* 8(3):377–88.

Osborne, Stephen P. 2010. *The New Public Governance: Emerging Perspectives on the Theory and Practice of Public Governance.* London and New York: Routledge.

Overmans, Tom and Mirko Nordegraaf. 2014. "Managing Austerity: Rhetorical and Real Responses to Fiscal Stress in Local Government." *Public Money and Management* 34(2):99–106.

Overmans, Tom and Klaus-Peter Timm-Arnold. 2015. "Managing Austerity: Comparing Municipal Austerity Plans in the Netherlands and North Rhine-Westphalia." *Public Management Review* 18(7):1–20.

Peters, B. Guy. 2011. "Governance Responses to the Fiscal Crisis: Comparative Perspectives." *Public Money and Management* 31(1):75–80.

Peters, B. Guy, Jon Pierre and Tiina Randma-Liiv. 2011. "Global Financial Crisis, Public Administration and Governance: Do New Problems Require New Solutions?" *Public Organization Review* 11:13–27.

Pierson, Paul. 2000. "Increasing Returns, Path Dependence, and the Study of Politics." *The American Political Science Review* 94(2):251–67.

Pollitt, Christopher. 2001. "Clarifying Convergence: Striking Similarities and Durable Differences in Public Management Reform." *Public Management Review* 3(4):471–92.

Pollitt, Christopher. 2008. *Time, Policy, Management. Governing With the Past.* Oxford: Oxford University Press.

Pollitt, Christopher. 2010. "Public Management Reform During Financial Austerity." *Statskontoret.* www.statskontoret.se/globalassets/publikationer/om-offentlig-sektor-1-11/om-offentlig-sektor-2.pdf.

Pollitt, Christopher. 2013. "The Logics of Performance Management." *Evaluation* 19(4):346–63.

Pollitt, Christopher and Geert Bouckaert. 2004. *Public Management Reform: A Comparative Analysis.* Oxford: Oxford University Press.

Pollitt, Christopher and Geert Bouckaert. 2009. *Continuity and Change in Public Policy and Management.* Cheltenham: Edward Elgar.

Pollitt, Christopher and Geert Bouckaert. 2011. *Public Management Reform: A Comparative Analysis: New Public Management, Governance, and the Neo-Weberian State.* Oxford: Oxford University Press.

Raudla, Ringa. 2010. "The Evolution of Budgetary Institutions in Estonia: A Path Full of Puzzles?" *Governance* 23(3):463–84.

Raudla, Ringa. 2013. "Budgeting during Austerity: Approaches, Instruments and Practices." *Budgetary Research Review* 5(1) 30-39

Raudla, Ringa. 2014. "Budgetary Institutions." In *Encyclopedia of Law and Economics*, edited by Jürgen Backhaus, 1–9, Springer eBook, New York: Springer.

Raudla, Ringa, James W. Douglas, Tina Randma-Liiv and Riin Saavi. 2015. "The Impact of Fiscal Crisis on Decision-Making Processes in European Governments: Dynamics of a Centralization Cascade." *Public Administration Review* 75(6):842–52.

Raudla, Ringa, Riin Savi and Tiina Randma-Liiv. 2013. *Literature Review on Cutback Management.* COCOPS workpackage 7 deliverable 1: COCOPS. www.cocops.eu.

Raudla, Ringa, Riin Savi and Tiina Randma-Liiv. 2015. "Cutback Management Literature in the 1970s and 1980s: Taking Stock." *International Review of Administrative Sciences* 81(3):433–56.

Røvik, Kjell Arne. 2007. *Trender og translasjoner, ideer som former det 21: århundrets organisasjon.* Oslo: Universitetsforlaget.

Sahlin-Andersson, Kerstin. 2001. "National, International and Transnational Constructions of New Public Management." In *New Public Management: The Transformation of Ideas and Practice,* edited by Tom Christensen and Per Lægreid, 43–72 Aldershot: Ashgate.

Schick, Allen. 1966. "The Road to PPB: The Stages of Budget Reform." *Public Administration Review* 26(4):243–58.

Schick, Allen. 2001. *Does Budgeting Have a Future?* OECD, 22nd annual meeting of Senior Budget Officials, Paris, May 21–22, 2001.

Schick, Allen. 2010. "Post-Crisis Fiscal Rules: Stabilising Public Finance while Responding to Economic Aftershocks." *OECD Journal on Budgeting* 2:1–18.

Streeck, Wolfgang and Kathleen Ann Thelen. 2005. *Beyond Continuity, Institutional Change in Advanced Political Economies.* Oxford: Oxford University Press.

Suenson, Emil Lobe, Peter Nedergaard and Peter Munk Christiansen. 2015. "Why Do You Want to Lash Yourself to the Mast? The Case of the Danish 'Budget Law.'" *Public Budgeting and Finance* 36(1):3–21.

Thelen, Kathleen Ann and Sven Steinmo. 1992. "Historical Institutionalism in Comparative Politics." In *Structuring Politics: Historical Institutionalism in Comparative Analysis,* edited by Sven Steinmo, Kathleen Thelen and Frank Longstreth, 1–32. Cambridge: Cambridge University Press.

van Dooren, Wouter. 2008. "Nothing New Under the Sun? Change and Continuity in the Twentieth-Century Performance Movements." In *Performance Information in the Public Sector: How Is It Used?* edited by Wouter van Dooren and Steven van de Walle, 11–23. Houndmills: Palgrave Macmillan.

Wanna, John. 2010. "The Work in Progress of Budgetary Reform." In *The Reality of Budgetary Reform in OECD Nations: Trajectories and Consequences,* edited by John Wanna, Lotte Jensen and Jouke de Vries, 281–98. Cheltenham: Edward Elgar.

Wanna, John, Lotte Jensen and Jouke de Vries (eds). 2010. *The Reality of Budgetary Reform in OECD Nations: Trajectories and Consequences.* Cheltenham: Edward Elgar.

Wildavsky, Aaron. 1961. "Political Implications of Budgetary Reform." *Public Administration Review* 21(4):183–90.

Wildavsky, Aaron. 1974. *The Politics of the Budgetary Process.* Boston: Little, Brown & Company.

3 The Five Case Countries

Eva Moll Ghin and Mads Bøge Kristiansen

Introduction

This book includes case studies of cutback management and budgetary reform from five European countries: Germany, Italy, Denmark, Ireland and Estonia. The cases have been selected according to a 'most different' strategy in which it is important to have case countries representing different crisis experiences and political and administrative systems. This chapter presents the reader with comparative information concerning the economic crisis and the political and administrative systems in the case countries.

The selected cases are all EU countries. They include the largest and fourth-largest EU countries in terms of population (Germany and Italy, with 81.5 million and 61 million inhabitants, respectively) as well as three smaller countries: Denmark (5.7 million), Ireland (4.6 million) and Estonia (1.3 million). Since the analysis focuses on public-sector austerity and cutbacks, it is also relevant to mention that the public sector varies greatly in size in these five countries. In Denmark, public employment constitutes around 33% of the labour force, in Estonia it constitutes approximately 23%, in Ireland 17%, in Italy 16%, and in Germany 15% (OECD 2015).[1]

In the following section, we describe and compare the influence of the global financial and economic crisis in the case countries before providing comparative information on the other, intermediating, factors in our model on public management reform (see Chapter 2); that is, the political and administrative systems and public management reform trajectories.

The Crisis (Economic Factors)

As argued in Chapter 1, the crisis can be understood as a banking and financial crisis that led to an economic crisis with declining production levels and rising unemployment and a fiscal crisis with mounting deficit and debt levels. Different governments responded with different measures, including bank bailouts, economic stimulus measures and fiscal consolidation. In the European context, the fiscal crisis and politics of fiscal consolidation were also a matter of common EU policy and of sovereign 'bailouts' and conditionality by the so-called 'Troika' consisting of the European Commission, International Monetary Fund (IMF) and European Central Bank (ECB). In the following, we will describe how the case countries were affected by each stage of the crisis.

The Financial and Economic Crisis

At the global level, the crisis began as a banking crisis and broader financial crisis in late 2007, when leading American financial institutions began experiencing liquidity problems due to their overextension in the 'bubble economy' that had emerged in the real estate market. European banks started experiencing similar problems in 2008, and governments had to step in with rescue packages to prevent the collapse of financial institutions that were deemed 'too big to fail' (Lindquist, de Vries and Wanna 2015, 2–5). Among our case countries, Ireland, Denmark and Germany spent substantial means on saving domestic banks. Estonia had no domestic banks and, hence, no domestic banking crisis, and Italy had no banking crisis at this stage of the crisis.

The financial crisis led to an economic crisis when the turbulent financial markets infected the broader economy, leading to huge falls in production and GDP in 2008 and particularly in 2009 (see Table 3.1). Ireland, Estonia, Denmark and Germany all had high growth rates before the crisis, and the pre-crisis growth in Ireland, Denmark and Estonia was accelerated by overheated property markets. The crisis substantially reduced economic production levels in all five case countries, the Estonian GDP falling by no less than 14.7% in 2009. Germany already bounced back out of the crisis in 2010, however, and Estonia also returned to high growth rates rather quickly. Denmark and Ireland took a little longer to pull out the crisis, but Denmark has had growth rates around the EU average, and Ireland has had very high growth in recent years—although the 26% surge in 2015 was largely driven by foreign companies switching

Table 3.1 Real GDP Growth Rate—Volume (Percentage Change on Previous Year)

GEO\TIME	2005	2006	2007	2008	2009	2010	2011	2012	2013	2014	2015
EU (28 countries)	2.1	3.3	3.0	0.4	−4.4	2.1	1.7	−0.5	0.2	1.6	2.2
Germany	0.7	3.7	3.3	1.1	−5.6	4.1	3.7	0.5	0.5	1.6	1.7
Italy	0.9	2.0	1.5	−1.1	−5.5	1.7	0.6	−2.8	−1.7	0.1	0.7
Denmark	2.3	3.9	0.9	−0.5	−4.9	1.9	1.3	0.2	0.9	1.7	1.6
Ireland	5.8	5.9	3.8	−4.4	−4.6	2.0	0.0	−1.1	1.1	8.5	26.3
Estonia	9.4	10.3	7.7	−5.4	−14.7	2.3	7.6	4.3	1.4	2.8	1.4

Source: Eurostat (2016a)

tax domiciles to Ireland to take advantage of low corporate tax rates. Italy has found it hardest to pull out of the crisis, with low growth from 2010 to 2015 and negative growth rates in 2012–13.

The Fiscal Crisis

The financial and economic crisis also became a fiscal crisis in 2010; public deficits and debts had increased sharply due to falling economic production and because of government outlays for bank bailouts and economic stimulus, and governments had to cut back budgets in order to adapt public expenditure to their falling income and rising debt levels (Kickert 2012). Whether the crisis led to high pressures for austerity is also likely to depend on the shape of public finances before the crisis. Countries with high deficits and debts were particularly vulnerable to pressures from volatile financial markets, leading to massive pressure for change.

If we consider the period until 2007, Denmark, Ireland and Estonia all had relatively sound public finances with government deficits and debts far below the EU average. Germany had deficits and debts near the EU average, and among our case countries only Italy had a record of high public deficits and debts. All of the cases experienced a sharp deterioration in 2008–09 (see Table 3.2), after the rescue measures during the banking crisis, the subsequent economic recovery measures and the effects of the financial crisis on the national economies. The deterioration was clearly worst in Ireland, where the deficit reached 32.3% in 2010. This record-high deficit was in large part due to the country's large bailout costs for its banks, but deficit levels remained above the EU average and the 3% deficit limit of the European Growth and Stability Act (see upcoming discussion) until 2014. The deficit levels were moderate in Italy compared to the EU average but violated the European 3% deficit limit until 2015. Estonia, Denmark and Germany had relatively low deficit levels, although Germany breached the 3% limit in 2009 and 2010 and Denmark did so in 2012.

Table 3.2 General Government Deficit and Surplus (Percentage of GDP)

GEO/TIME	2005	2006	2007	2008	2009	2010	2011	2012	2013	2014	2015
EU (28 countries)	2.5	−1.6	−0.9	−2.4	−6.6	−6.4	−4.6	−4.3	−3.3	−3.0	−2.4
Germany	3.4	−1.7	0.2	−0.2	−3.2	−4.2	−1.0	0.0	−0.2	0.3	0.7
Italy	−4.2	−3.6	−1.5	−2.7	−5.3	−4.2	−3.7	−2.9	−2.7	−3.0	−2.6
Denmark	5.0	5.0	5.0	3.2	−2.8	−2.7	−2.1	−3.5	−1.1	1.5	−1.7
Ireland	1.6	2.8	0.3	−7.0	−13.8	−32.1	−12.6	−8.0	−5.7	−3.7	−1.9
Estonia	1.1	2.9	2.7	−2.7	−2.2	0.2	1.2	−0.3	−0.2	0.7	0.1

Source: Eurostat (2016b)

Table 3.3 General Government Gross Debt—Annual Data (Percentage of GDP)

GEO/TIME	2005	2006	2007	2008	2009	2010	2011	2012	2013	2014	2015
EU (28 countries)	61.5	60.1	57.5	60.7	72.8	78.4	81.1	83.8	85.7	86.7	85.0
Germany	67.0	66.5	63.7	65.1	72.6	81.0	78.7	79.9	77.5	74.9	71.2
Italy	101.9	102.6	99.8	102.4	112.5	115.4	116.5	123.3	129.0	131.9	132.3
Denmark	37.4	31.5	27.3	33.4	40.4	42.9	46.4	45.2	44.7	44.8	40.4
Ireland	26.1	23.6	23.9	42.4	61.7	86.3	109.6	119.5	119.5	105.2	78.6
Estonia	4.5	4.4	3.7	4.5	7.0	6.6	6.1	9.7	10.2	10.7	10.1

Source: Eurostat (2016c)

The developments during the crisis were reflected in the public debt levels. All of the countries have had rising debt levels (see Table 3.3), but the development has been particularly marked in Ireland, which went from a low-debt to a high-debt country over the course of the crisis. The Irish debt/GDP ratio fell below the EU average in 2015, but this figure should be considered on the background of its highly volatile level of recorded economic production (as discussed earlier). In Italy, the crisis led to a dramatic increase to its already high debt levels, whereas Estonia remained among the EU countries with the lowest debt levels and Denmark remained at the low end of the scale. The German public debt level was above the EU average until 2008 and increased in connection with the crisis, but its debt level has been falling since 2010, reflecting both the country's positive economic development and low annual deficits.

The Role of EU Fiscal Policy

In the European context in which our cases are placed, the effects of the fiscal crisis were mediated by EU policies that are meant to support the credibility of its common currency: the euro. In the following, we will account for the main developments in EU fiscal policy since the early 1990s and for how the case countries were affected by EU policies.

In 1992, the 'Treaty on the European Union' (the Maastricht Treaty) set out to establish an economic and monetary union and a common currency. The treaty specifies a set of economic convergence criteria for potential member states, including two criteria for fiscal outcomes; (1) general government *budget deficit must not exceed 3% of GDP*, and (2) gross *government debts must not exceed 60% of GDP*. In 1997, as a further step in the preparations for the euro, the member states agreed to the 'Stability and Growth Pact' (SGP), which is meant to ensure that countries in the EU pursue 'sound public finances' and coordinate their fiscal policies. It contains a preventive and a corrective arm. The former sets out the same short-term fiscal targets as the Maastricht Treaty plus a medium-term target that countries should aim for a fiscal balance 'close to balance or in surplus'. The latter obliges the European Commission to monitor individual countries and to initiate an Excessive Deficit Procedure (EDP) against countries with a budget deficit exceeding 3% of GDP. This procedure requires that the country in question presents a plan for restoring compliance with the short-term targets; otherwise a fine can be imposed on the country. Among the case countries in this volume, only Estonia has never been under an EDP. Germany has been under EDPs in 2002–07 and 2009–12, Italy in 2005–08 and 2009–13, Denmark in 2010–14 and Ireland in 2009–16 (European Commission 2016a).

The SGP was revised in 2005 to make the implementation of fiscal rules more flexible. With the revision, the medium-term objective was formulated in terms of the *structural* fiscal balance, which is adjusted for the influence of economic cycles and extraordinary events, thus rendering it easier to avoid an EDP by referring to extraordinary developments (Kukk and Staehr 2015). The revised SGP also stipulated that the structural deficit could be at most 1% of GDP, and countries with an excessive deficit were to correct their deficit by at least 0.5 percentage points of GDP annually.

After the crisis, the Eurozone countries reached agreement on several reforms. The 'Six Pack' from 2011 contained six components to strengthen fiscal performance and surveillance. EU budgetary surveillance was synchronised in a new process called the 'European Semester', and the structural balance requirement was complemented by expenditure benchmarking and explicit debt reduction targets for debt exceeding 60% of GDP. It also became easier to adopt sanctions.

In 2012, most member states adopted a new 'Treaty on Stability, Coordination and Governance in the Economic and Monetary Union' including the so-called 'Fiscal Compact', which stipulates that the budgetary position of general government must be balanced or in surplus. This provision is specified to mean that the annual structural balance must be at its country-specific, medium-term objective *with a lower limit of a structural deficit of 0.5* (or 1% if the debt level is below 60% and there is no doubt about the sustainability of public finances); that is, the medium-term structural deficit may not exceed 0.5% of GDP. Deviations from the target trigger an automatic correction mechanism. According to the Compact, these provisions must be passed into national law, preferably constitutional law, and the administration of these provisions must be overseen by a national fiscal council. The provisions are very restrictive at first glance, but the Compact does allow deviations under exceptional circumstances and stipulates that the deviations from the medium-term target must be substantive to trigger the correction mechanism (Kukk and Staehr 2015).

In 2013, the 'Two Pack' added a new assessment procedure of draft budgetary plans to the European Semester and strengthened the monitoring of countries under the EDP. Each country also became obliged to set up an *independent fiscal council* that was responsible for monitoring fiscal performance and the observation of national fiscal rules (Kukk and Staehr 2015).

The Eurozone Crisis

Beginning in 2010, the financial crisis led to unsustainable debt levels and the threat of sovereign defaults in several Eurozone countries, including Greece, Ireland, Portugal, Cyprus and Spain. This was perceived by euro-area decision makers as a threat to the financial stability of the whole Eurozone; to prevent defaults, they agreed on a number of financial support mechanisms.

Furthermore, a tripartite decision-making group was formed consisting of the European Commission (EC), the European Central Bank (ECB) and International Monetary Fund (IMF) to handle the deepening Eurozone debt crisis. The so-called 'Troika' has provided bailouts for Greece, Ireland, Portugal and Cyprus, which have been conditional on 'economic adjustment programmes' in the affected countries, including the reorganisation of the banking sector, labour market structural reform and fiscal consolidation (e.g. European Commission 2011; 2016b). Greece and Ireland entered the programme in 2010 followed by Portugal and Cyprus. Ireland was the first country to exit the programme in 2013. Only Greece remains in the programme at the time of writing in 2016.

In other words, conditionality has been an important external driver of austerity in one of our case countries, Ireland, and Italy has been under great pressure from the EU and IMF to reduce its deficit and debt and carry out reforms, although it has not received bailouts or been under conditionality. The remaining three case countries have not been under Troika conditionality.

The Political Systems

The political system is an important intermediating factor in the shaping of decisions on cutbacks and reforms. For example, it is important whether reforms are constrained by constitutional law, whether the political system is consensual or majoritarian, and how subnational governments are protected by the constitution. We will focus on two features that can be described comparatively with relative ease: the type of government and the constitutional protection of subnational government.

As argued in Chapter 2, it is probably more likely that normal majority governments (whether single-party or coalition) will carry out large and swift cutbacks and reforms than minority governments or grand coalitions that include the main opposing parties in the political system. Among our case countries (see Table 3.4), Germany has been governed by coalitions under Christian Democrat leader Angela Merkel since 2005. The

Table 3.4 Types of Government During the Crisis

Germany	Italy	Denmark	Ireland	Estonia
2005–09 Merkel (grand coalition)	2008–11 Berlusconi (majority coalition)	2001–09 Fogh Rasmussen (minority coalition)	2002–08 Ahern (majority coalition)	2007–09 Ansip (majority coalition)
2009–13 Merkel (majority coalition)	2011–13 Monti (technocratic government)	2009–11 Løkke Rasmussen (minority coalition)	2008–11 Cowen (majority coalition)	2009–11 Ansip (minority coalition)
2013–present Merkel (grand coalition)	2013–14 Letta (grand coalition)	2011–15 (Thorning-Schmidt (minority coalition)	2011–16 Kenny (majority coalition)	2011–14 Ansip (majority coalition)
	2014–present Renzi (majority coalition)	2015–present (Løkke Rasmussen (minority coalition)		20115 Rõivas (majority coalition)
				2015–16 Rõivas (majority coalition)

Source: Information from the contributors to this volume.

first Merkel cabinet (2005–09) was a grand coalition of the CDU, CSU and Social Democrats. Her second cabinet was a majority coalition of the CDU, CSU and the liberal FDP, and her third cabinet, formed in 2013, was another grand coalition. Italy has had a succession of different governments during the crisis. From 2008 to 2011, it was governed by a majority coalition under Silvio Berlusconi consisting of three (later four) centre-right and right-wing parties. From 2011 to 2013, it was governed by a technocratic government under Mario Monti. The 2013 elections did not make it possible to form a government to one side of parliament, and Enrico Letta from the centre-left Democratic Party formed a grand coalition after weeks of negotiations. Later in 2013, the centre-right People of Freedom dropped out, and Letta was challenged by Matteo Renzi in 2014, also from the Democratic Party, as the leader of a new majority government.

In Denmark, centre-right minority coalitions governed from 2001 to 2011 under Anders Fogh Rasmussen and Lars Løkke Rasmussen. In 2011, the general elections resulted in a minority centre-left government under Helle Thorning-Schmidt. This government remained in power until 2015 when it lost the national election to a new minority centre-right government under Lars Løkke Rasmussen. In Ireland, majority coalitions with the participation of Fianna Fáil (a centre-right populist party) and the conservative Progressive Democrats had been in power since 1997 (since 2007 with participation of the Green Party). At the 2011 elections, a broad majority coalition of the center-right Fine Gael and the Labour Party was formed and remained in power until 2016. In Estonia, a majority coalition with the participation of liberal, conservative and a social democratic party was formed in 2007 with Andrus Ansip as prime minister. In 2009, the Social Democrats dropped out of the coalition, and the government continued as a minority coalition. In 2011, the liberals and conservatives won the elections and governed as a majority coalition, still under Andrus Ansip, until 2014. From spring 2014 until the elections in March 2015, the coalition government, led by Taavi Rõivas, included the liberals and the Social Democrats. After the 2015 elections, Taavi Rõivas became the head of a new majority coalition government with participation of the same liberal, conservative and social democratic parties from the 2007–09 government.

In Chapter 2 it was also argued that it is probably easier to extend the subnational reach of budget and administrative reform in unitary states than in federal states with many constitutional rules regulating the central–local government relationship. Among our case countries, Germany is a federal state with sixteen local state (*Länder*) governments. The Länder have extensive powers entrenched in the constitution, and their interests are further protected by their control of the upper house of legislature *Bundesrat* (Gallagher, Laver and Mair 2011, 188). In Italy, the level of autonomy given to regional and local government is a politically contested issue. It is not a federal country, but in 2001 a new constitutional law was passed that introduced a quasi-federal framework. Denmark, Estonia and Ireland are all small unitary states with fewer constitutional obstacles to the extension of reforms.

The Administrative Systems

The implementation of cutbacks and reforms and their effects on public management are also likely to depend on administrative structures, administrative traditions and civil service systems, and reform trajectories in each of the case countries.

Administrative structures may be described as the level of vertical decentralisation of tasks and competences to local governments and the relationship between central and local government (Kuhlmann and Wollmann 2014, 11). Administrative structures also concern the relationship between ministries and agencies and the level of horizontal fragmentation—or coordination—of authority in central government; that is, to what extent one or two central ministries are able to impose a common direction (or cuts) on other ministries (Pollitt and Bouckaert 2011, 42, 53). In this context, we will focus on the vertical decentralisation or centralisation of the cases described through their basic state structure (see earlier discussion) and the proportion of employees working at the central level of government. Germany, a federal state, is highly decentralised, and only 13% of all public employees work at the central level. Italy has a quasi-federal constitution but public employment is relatively centralised, with 55% of all public employees working in central government. Denmark, however, is a unitary-decentralised country (cp. Kuhlmann and Wollmann 2014), with only 24% of public employees at the central level. Estonia is unitary-centralised with 48% of public employees in central government, and Ireland is a unitary-centralised state with weak local government (Verhoest et al. 2010, 65–66) and 90% of all public employees working in central government (OECD 2013).[2]

Administrative traditions are often categorised in two clusters in Western Europe: the classic Continental European rule-of-law (*Rechtsstat*) and the Anglo-Saxon public interest culture. Civil service systems are closely connected to administrative traditions (Kuhlmann and Wollmann 2014, 28). The administrative rule-of-law tradition, on the one hand, is characterised by the separation of state and society, the idea of the state as an integrating force in society, the comprehensive codification of legal rules, administrative action as implementation of law, and high value attributed to the principles of legality, equal treatment and neutrality of interests. The public interest culture, on the other hand, has no strict separation of the public and private spheres or comprehensive codification of legal rules (common law). The state is regarded as an instrument of government, and legislative acts have the function of political programmes. The dominant values are pragmatism, flexibility and reconciliation of interests (Kuhlmann and Wollmann 2014). According to Pollitt and Bouckaert (2011, 63), the polar classification of Rechtstaat versus public interest is too crude, as most contemporary systems are mixtures. There has been a considerable shift in several countries away from a highly legalistic state but towards something different from a straightforward public interest model. This book bases the selection of case countries on a categorisation of five politico-administrative clusters (Kuhlmann and Wollmann 2014, 14–20); the Continental European Napoleonic model (represented by Italy), the Continental European federal model (Germany), the Anglo-Saxon model (Ireland), Central and Eastern European (CEE) model (Estonia) and the Scandinavian model (Denmark). (See Table 3.5.) The main difference between the first two models is the decentralisation and

Table 3.5 Administrative Traditions and Personnel Systems

	Administrative Tradition	*Personnel System*
Germany	Continental European federal	Career-based
Italy	Continental European Napoleonic	Position-based
Denmark	Scandinavian	Position-based
Ireland	Anglo-Saxon	Career-based
Estonia	Central and Eastern European	Position-based

Sources: Data for Germany, Italy, Denmark and Estonia from Kuhlmann and Wollmann (2014, 14–21, 28–31). Ireland has been categorised by Muiris McCarthaigh for the present volume.

principle of subsidiarity in the Continental European federal model. The Scandinavian model overlaps with the Continental European model, as it is also based on a Roman law tradition, but it has a more open recruiting and career system and is more accessible to citizens. The Central and Eastern European countries are shaped by the imposed Stalinist organisation model, but each country has its own legacy. In Estonia, the reaction to the Soviet past has led to a predisposition towards individualism and distrust in the state (Drechsler 2000; cited in Sarapuu 2011, 69).

Traditionally, the Continental European model of public administration is connected to a closed, career-based civil service system, where public service law and general labour law are separated from one another. The career system is typically seniority-based with a closed recruitment policy. Once a person has obtained civil servant status, he or she is difficult or impossible to fire. The public interest culture, however, typically has civil service systems with no explicit difference between the public and private spheres. The employment relationship is contract-based, and recruitment is position-based. In such systems, public employees are subject to free collective bargaining, and they can be fired. Many European countries use a combination of civil servants and contract staff.

European public administrations have already been subject to reform for several decades. The reform trajectories that different countries follow are largely affected by their political system and administrative structures and traditions. Pollitt and Bouckaert (2004) have categorised countries and the reform trajectories in four clusters: maintain, modernise, marketise and minimise.

The first group of countries, termed *maintainers*, seem to have the relatively modest ambition of 'lightening' the bureaucracy and saving money by tightening up on budgets. The aim is to *maintain* as much as possible by making current structures and practices work better (Pollitt and Bouckaert 2004, 97). The *modernisers* are more adventurous. This group still believes in a major role for the state but acknowledges the need for fairly fundamental changes in the organisation of the administrative system, such as performance-oriented budgetary reform, the loosening of personnel rigidities, decentralisation and the devolution of authority. Within this group, there are different emphases between *managerial* modernisation and *participatory* modernisation (Pollitt and Bouckaert 2004, 97). The *marketisers* favour e.g. large-scale contracting-out and market-testing, contractual-appointments and performance pay for civil servants and a general reduction of the distinctiveness of the public vis-à-vis the private sector (Pollitt and Bouckaert 2004, 97–98). Finally, the *minimisers* opt for massive privatisation and the downsizing of the public sector (Pollitt and Bouckaert 2004, 98).

In *Germany*, the pace of public management reform has been incremental. Its federal structure usually speaks for incremental change, and the etatism and legalist culture has not presented a fertile climate for management concepts and instruments (Kickert 2011, 103). Pollitt and Bouckaert (2004, 97; 2011, 117) place Germany somewhere between a maintaining and modernising approach. In *Italy*, public management reform is pursued actively but is often hindered by the need for a legal basis for decisions. The average pace of reform is therefore low, and Italy is widely perceived as being weak on implementation. According to Pollitt and Bouckaert (2004, 97), Italy's reform trajectory can be characterised as managerial modernisation. *Denmark's* approach to public management reform is a mixture of strategies for modernisation and marketisation with most emphasis on the former (Ejersbo and Greve 2008; cp. Hansen 2011). Pollitt and Bouckaert (2004; 2011) have characterised this reform trajectory as *participatory modernisation*. The *Irish* administrative system shares many traits with the UK, but the Irish approach to public management reform in the 1990s was based on more pragmatic steps. Its reform style seems closer to that of Netherlands and Denmark than the UK, and it is generally characterised by prudence, pragmatism and incremental change (OECD 2001; Hardiman and MacCarthaigh 2010). *Estonia* has been affected by the accession process to the EU. Thus, since regaining independence in 1991, Estonia has pursued a radical reform strategy with a strong market-oriented focus. The underlying theme for the neo-liberal governments in power has been to reduce the role of the state, and the early transition coincided with the NPM fashion in the West, which also contributed to the popularity of NPM-style tools (Tönnisson and Randma-Liiv 2008; Savi and Metsma 2013, 8).

Summing Up

Our case countries represent most of the variation existing in the European Union when it comes to the influence of the crisis and the role of political and administrative systems in mediating that influence.

Crisis-related economic factors would lead us to expect that radical cutbacks and reforms are most likely in Ireland, which experienced a large turnaround in its economic fortune and became the object of an external economic adjustment programme. We can also expect a high level of pressure for austerity in Italy. In Germany and Denmark, the level of economic pressure was lower, and in Estonia the crisis was deep but over relatively quickly. Based on economic factors alone, we would not expect radical changes in these three countries, but it cannot be ruled out that budget guardians there have been particularly ready and able to use the crisis as a window of opportunity.

Political system factors should probably also lead us to expect a relatively slow pace of change in Germany with its federal structure and many veto points and its recent reliance on grand coalitions. Nor should we expect radical reform in Italy, with its quasi-federal structure and propensity for technocratic government and grand coalitions, or in Denmark with its many minority governments. Estonia and Ireland are probably the best candidates for swift, radical change with their (mainly) majority governments and unitary-centralised states.

Based on administrative structures and traditions, the regulation of local finances will likely be an important element in the federal or unitary-decentralised countries (Germany, Italy, Denmark), and the laying off of civil servants is a relatively unlikely tool for cutback management in the German system, with its legalistic administrative traditions. Last but not least, cutbacks and budgetary reform are probably likely to be decoupled from broader managerial reform in maintaining Germany, whereas they are probably more likely to speed up the ongoing reform in modernising and marketising Denmark and Estonia. In Italy, we may expect a combination of modernising ambitions and implementation difficulties, and in Ireland we might expect the crisis and austerity to challenge its existing hesitant approach to public management reform.

All in all, our cases represent most of the variation on economic, political and administrative factors that exists in the EU. We do not have a case country that, like Greece, has been very hard hit by the crisis and has not been able to exit it, or a country with a majoritarian system, public interest culture and a propensity for radical public management reform, like the UK. However, our cases will be able to teach us a great deal about the common characteristics of public management in times of austerity across very different systems, and they can also be used to explore how different economic, political and administrative characteristics possibly influence how a country manages austerity.

Notes

1   OECD 2015. Indicator 3.2: Public sector employment as a percentage of the labour force, 2009 and 2013. The figures in the text are averages of the figures for 2009 and 2013 in Estonia and Italy. In Denmark it is an average for 2011 and 2013, in Germany the figure is only from 2009 and in Ireland from 2013 (due to missing data).
2   OECD 2011. Indicator 5.3: Distribution of general government employment across levels of government.

References

Drechsler, Wolfgang. 2000. "Public Administration in Central and Eastern Europe: Considerations From the 'State Science' Approach." In *Institutions and the Role of the State*, edited by Leonardo Burlamaqui, Ana Célia Castro and Ha-Joon Chang, 267–79. Cheltenham: Edward Elgar.

Ejersbo, Niels and Carsten Greve. 2008. *Moderniseringen af den offentlige sektor*. København: Børsen.

European Commission. 2011. *The Economic Adjustment Programme for Ireland, European Economy, Occasional Papers 76*. Brussels: European Commission, Directorate-General for Economic and Financial Affairs.

European Commission. 2016a. "Corrective Arm/Excessive Deficit Procedure, Country-Specific Procedures." http://ec.europa.eu/economy_finance/economic_governance/sgp/deficit/countries/index_en.html. Accessed on 20th of December 2016.

European Commission. 2016b. *Post-Programme Surveillance Report, Ireland Spring 2016, European Economy, Institutional Papers 035.* Luxembourg: Publications Office of the European Union.

Eurostat. 2016a. "Real GDP Growth Rate—Volume: Percentage Change on Previous Year." http://ec.europa.eu/eurostat/web/products-datasets/-/tec00115&lang=en. Accessed on 29th of November 2016.

Eurostat. 2016b. "General Government Deficit and Surplus—Annual Data." http://ec.europa.eu/eurostat/web/products-datasets/-/teina200. Accessed on 29th of November 2016.

Eurostat. 2016c. "General Government Gross Debt—Annual Data." http://ec.europa.eu/eurostat/web/products-datasets/-/teina225. Accessed on 29th of November 2016.

Gallagher, Michael, Michael Laver and Peter Mair. 2011. *Representative Government in Modern Europe.* Maidenhead and Berkshire: McGraw-Hill.

Hansen, Hanne Foss. 2011. "NPM in Scandinavia." In *The Ashgate Research Companion to New Public Management*, edited by Tom Christensen and Per Lægreid, 113–30. Aldershot: Ashgate.

Hardiman, Niahm and Muiris MacCarthaigh. 2010. "Organising for Growth: Irish State Administration 1958–2008." *Economic and Social Review* 42(3):367–93.

Kickert, Walter J. M. 2011. "Public Management Reform in Continental Europe: National Distinctiveness." In *The Ashgate Research Companion to New Public Management*, edited by Tom Christensen and Per Lægreid, 97–112. Farnham: Ashgate.

Kickert, Walter J. M. 2012. "State Responses to the Fiscal Crisis in Britain, Germany and the Netherlands." *Public Management Review* 14(3):299–309.

Kuhlmann, Sabine and Helmut Wollmann. 2014. *Introduction to Comparative Public Administration: Administrative Systems and Reforms in Europe.* Cheltenham: Edward Elgar.

Kukk, Merike and Karsten Staehr. 2015. "Enhanced Fiscal Governance in the European Union: The Fiscal Compact." *Baltic Journal of European Studies* 5(1):73–92.

Lindquist, Evert A., Jouke de Vries and John Wanna. 2015. "Meeting the Challenge of the Global Financial Crisis in OECD Nations: Fiscal Responses and Future Challenges." In *The Global Financial Crisis and Its Budget Impacts in OECD Nations*, edited by John Wanna, Evert Lidquist and Jouke de Vries, 1–30. Cheltenham, UK and Northampton, MA: Edward Elgar.

OECD. 2001. *Regulatory Reform in Ireland: Government Capacity to Ensure High Quality.* Paris: OECD.

OECD. 2010. *OECD Economic Outlook, Volume 2009 Issue 2.* Paris: OECD.

OECD. 2012. *Restoring Public Finances, 2012 Update.* Paris: OECD.

OECD. 2013. *Government at a Glance.* Paris: OECD.

OECD. 2015. *Government at a Glance.* Paris: OECD.

Pollitt, Christopher and Geert Bouckaert. 2004. *Public Management Reform; A Comparative Analysis.* Oxford: Oxford University Press.

Pollitt, Christopher and Geert Bouckaert. 2011. *Public Management Reform—A Comparative Analysis, New Public Management, Governance, and the Neo-Weberian State.* Oxford: Oxford University Press.

Reichard, Christoph. 2008. "The Study of Public Management in Germany." In *The Study of Public Management in Europe and the US*, edited by Walter J. M. Kickert, 42–69. London: Routledge.

Sarapuu, Külli. 2011. "Post-Communist Development of Administrative Structure in Estonia: From Fragmentation to Segmentation." *Transylvanian Review of Administrative Sciences* 7:54–73.

Savi, Riin and Merilin Metsma. 2013. "Public Sector Reform in Estonia: Views and Experiences From Senior Executives." Country Report as part of the COCOPS Research Project.

Tõnnisson, Kristiina and Tiina Randma-Liiv. 2008. "Public Management Reforms: Estonia." In *Public Management Reforms in Central and Eastern Europe*, edited by Geert Bouckaert, Juraj Nemec, Vitalis Nakrosis, Gyorgy Hajnal and Kristiina Tõnnisson, 93–120. Bratislava: NISPA.

Verhoest, Koen, Paul Roness, Bram Verschuere, Kristin Rubecksen and Muiris MacCarthaigh. 2010. *Autonomy and Control of State Agencies.* Basingstoke: Palgrave Macmillan.

Part II
Cutback Management in Times of Austerity

4 Germany

An Outlier in Terms of Fiscal Adjustment

Jobst Fiedler, Gerhard Hammerschmid and Lorenz Löffler

Introduction

In hindsight, Germany represents an outlier or deviant case, where austerity measures were more extensive in the decade leading up to the crisis than in its aftermath. Major labour market and welfare system reforms carried out in the 2000s together with a period of high fiscal discipline in the pre-crisis years contributed to the rapid German economic recovery after a short, steep fall in GDP in 2009. In 2014, Germany achieved a modest fiscal surplus, which was more the result of record-high employment levels and government revenue combined with low interest rates on public debt than it was the outcome of cutbacks. At the peak of the financial and economic crisis, the new constitutional 'debt brake' introduced by government brought a fundamental change with ambitions for fiscal adjustment. The new fiscal rule requires both the federal and *Länder* governments to balance their budgets, leaving the federal government limited scope for borrowing. Even though full compliance is not required until 2016 and 2020, respectively, the legal—or at least political—commitments to comply with the debt brake rule impact the federal level and the 16 Länder very differently.

This chapter provides insight into the German response to the crisis, applied austerity measures focusing especially on the cutback management at both levels and how Germany achieved its path to fiscal consolidation. We also analyse how far cutbacks and the consequences of the crisis have led to broader changes in public management reforms and structural changes. Due to the specific German federal structure, we also examine important variations between the government levels and across the Länder.

Taking an explanatory approach, we rely on official financial and employment statistics, grey literature from German government bodies, the European Commission and the OECD. Further empirical evidence is provided by survey data from top public officials as part of the COCOPS[1] project. In order to provide a fair comparison of both government levels in Germany,[2] we only use answers from senior executives in federal ministries (n = 58) and Länder ministries (n = 196). Further insights are drawn from interviews with five high-level officials in the Federal Ministry of Finance and 30 senior officials in the ministries of finance and other line ministries of ten representatively sampled Länder.[3] While the timeframe for our case study spans all of the phases of the crisis and the immediate years of recovery, more recent developments are exempted, such as the mass influx of refugees in 2015, which put a strain on the administrative capacity and still has budgetary repercussions.

The chapter is structured as follows: section two traces the economic conditions prior to the crisis (2000–07), the stages of the crisis (2008–10) and the recovery phase (2010–14). The third section turns to a more in-depth analysis of austerity measures and cutback management on both government levels also shedding light on cutback delegation dynamics. Section four discusses the consequences of cutbacks on public management in the context of broader reform trajectories. Finally, the conclusion comments on Germany's ongoing role as 'maintainer' in terms of public management reform.

The Resilient German Economy: Hit Hard by the Crisis But Quick to Recover

The pre-crisis period 2000–07: Throughout the 1990s and early 2000s, economic growth in Germany was substantially lower than in most other European countries. Rising unemployment and stagnating tax revenue led to fiscal deterioration on all government levels (see Figure 4.1.), leading Germany to be labelled 'the sick man of Europe' (e.g. Dustmann et al.

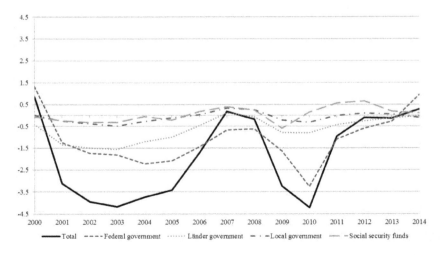

Figure 4.1 Government Deficit/Surplus at the Various Government Levels (% of GDP)

2014). In that sense, the retrenchment had already started in Germany before the crisis hit. Between 2000 and 2007, more than 480,000 public positions (full-time equivalents, or FTE) were cut in the German public sector (10.9% of total public employment).[4] Because civil servants (*Beamte*) and public employees (*Tarifbeschäftigte*) enjoy rigorous protection against dismissal, the decline was mostly based on proportional hiring freezes and retirement-related attrition. The economic and fiscal slump in those years also led to the fundamental overhaul of the German labour market and social policies known as 'Agenda 2010'. In addition, the value-added tax (VAT) was increased by 3 percentage points in 2007 to 19%, substantially contributing to fiscal consolidation. Finally, after more economically prosperous years in 2006 and 2007 (real GDP growth rates of 3.7% and 3.3%, respectively), Germany managed to almost balance its overall budget in the year prior to the crisis.

The crisis years of 2008–10: Already at the beginning of the subprime mortgage and banking crisis in 2007, German banks, including two regional public-sector banks (*Landesbanken*), were affected. Although the government initially expected German banks to be more stable, other banks—including large banks such as Commerzbank and Hypo Real Estate—faced financial troubles over the course of the crisis. Finally, the federal government was forced to set up a €480 billion rescue fund in October 2008 (*Sonderfonds Finanzmarktstabilisierung* 'SoFFin') to issue guarantees on loans and bail out banks directly (e.g. Zohlenhöfer 2011; for an overview, see Kickert 2013). By 2009, the financial crisis had spilled into the real economy and GDP growth dropped by 5.6% over the course of the year, making it one of the highest decreases in all EU countries. Under Chancellor Merkel, the federal government issued a series of Keynesian-style measures intended to offset the effects of the economic crisis. In October 2008, the first recovery stimulus of about €31 billion was immediately adopted to boost investment and prevent unemployment from rising. In January 2009, however, the Merkel administration was forced to launch a second stimulus package, increasing public spending to €80 billion. The forces driving these decisive actions can be seen in the gloomy economic forecast, international pressure for more spending and the upcoming election in September 2009. The main focal points of the second stimulus package were on education (preschool education, schools, universities), infrastructure (roads, housing, broadband) and job training (education and training of the unemployed). One key measure was a job preservation programme allowing companies to reduce employee working hours in order to offset their costs. The employees' loss of income was compensated by state-funded 'short-time working allowances' (*Kurzarbeitergeld*). Individual income tax and health insurance premiums were reduced and child allowances were raised. Finally, a vehicle scrappage scheme was introduced to boost domestic demand for automobiles and curb sales in the import automobile industry.

The recovery period 2010–14: With a surge in GDP growth of 4.1% over the course of 2010, the German economic situation rapidly changed and continued to grow by 3.7% in 2011. Alongside the swift and pragmatic crisis management of the grand coalition of Christian Democrats (CDU/CSU) and Social Democrats (SPD), several factors contributed to this turnaround, which distinguishes Germany from other countries. First, unlike the situation in Denmark, there was no housing bubble that burst in Germany. Second, the turmoil surrounding the euro and the subsequent flight of capital into the 'safe harbour' of German bonds led to historically low interest on government loans, in stark contrast to Italy. Third, unemployment remained rather stable throughout the crisis (with a slight exception in 2009). In fact, the unemployment rate fell continuously to just 5.0% in 2014. Fourth, as a result of a job preservation programme, companies did not lay off workers. This helped the German economy rebound quickly when the main export markets (e.g. China) recovered. As a result of the improvements to the economy, the austerity package (*Sparpaket*) announced by the new coalition government in July 2010 was never fully implemented. After slow economic growth in 2012 and 2013, GDP grew by 1.6% in 2014. Between 2010 and 2014, tax revenues outpaced expenditures, leading to significant deficit reduction, especially at the Länder level. While gross government debt accelerated to 81% of GDP in 2010, debt levels decreased continuously to 74.7% in 2014, although still significantly above the pre-crisis levels. Simultaneously, the general deficit of –4.2% in 2010 turned into a small surplus of 0.3% in 2014.

Rather than a consequence of austerity measures, these improving fiscal conditions can be seen as a consequence of high employment, record-high tax revenues and historically low interest on public debt. In addition, major reforms of the German labor market enacted in the previous decade (the so-called Hartz reforms) had an increasing impact (e.g. Rinne and Zimmermann 2012). In the context of the substantial easing of budgetary pressure, particularly at the federal level, there was less need for major cutbacks, which makes Germany an interesting outlier case compared with most of the other European countries.

Austerity Measures and Cutback Management in Federal and Länder Governments

In the German political system responsibilities are functionally distributed between the federal and Länder level. The relatively small federal government is mostly concerned with policy development and legislation, while major government functions, especially personnel-heavy tasks (e.g. police and education),[5] are delegated to the Länder and local levels. In return government revenues are shared between the federal and Länder level. At the height of the crisis, economic forecasts were alarming and gross government debt reached an all-time high. In this context, the austerity measures, in particular at the federal level, have to be viewed in light of fiscal uncertainty. The fiscal stress was further increased by introduction of the debt brake in 2009, banning the federal government to exceed its structural deficit by more than 0.35% of GDP with effect from 2016 and the Länder to run any structural deficit as from 2020.

Austerity Measures and Cutback Management in Federal Government

In July 2010, the new coalition government announced an austerity package (Sparpaket) proposing expenditure-based cuts (two-thirds) and revenue raises that were to be implemented over a four-year period starting in 2011 (see OECD 2011, 117). On the expenditure side, social security and unemployment benefits were special targets. Formerly mandatory support services for the unemployed became discretionary, and social benefits were either reduced (parental allowance) or cut entirely (heating cost allowance and parental allowance for the unemployed). Employment in federal administration was to be reduced by more than 10,000 FTE through hiring freezes by 2014, along with efficiency savings and a delay of an increase in the annual Christmas allowance for public servants. Further federal-level programme expenditures (exempting education and research) were to be cut. In the context of a larger military service reform (see Katsioulis and Müller-Hennig 2011), compulsory military service was suspended and the number of soldiers was to be cut by 40,000 from around 235,000. On the revenue side, taxes on air travel, nuclear fuel and financial transactions were to be introduced, and an annual dividend was to be paid by the national railway (Deutsche Bahn). All in all, these austerity measures were planned to cut expenditures and raise revenues equalling about 0.5% of GDP in 2011, which were to be followed by amounts corresponding to, on average, 0.25% of GDP in the years 2012–14 (European Commission 2011, 9).

During the 2010–14 recovery period, federal-level government revenues increased sharply (20.9%), while expenditures for debt service and infrastructure declined. This helped reduce the overall fiscal deficit. As a result of easing budgetary pressure, the 2010 cutback package mainly concerning the revenue side was never fully implemented (see Fichtner et al. 2013). For instance, plans for the introduction of a financial transaction tax were shelved after consensus could not be reached at the European level. The nuclear fuel tax revenues also turned out to be significantly less than expected after the immediate shutdown of eight nuclear power plants in the wake of the Fukushima disaster. These revenue shortfalls were partially offset by profits from the state-owned bank for reconstruction (KfW) and—despite the government's intention to the contrary—not eliminating fiscal drag in the income tax system. On the contrary, the federal government passed a series of measures after 2010 that actually increased expenditures (Fichtner et al. 2013, 45). In order to assist the implementation of the legally enshrined right to day care for children three years and younger, the federal government agreed to transfer extra funds to the Länder and local governments. Simultaneously, the CSU pushed through a subsidy for parents wishing to care for their children at home instead of sending them to day care. Moreover, the government slightly reduced the overall pension contribution rate. Additional expenditures were incurred by the abolition of a quarterly fee for medical treatment as well as an increase in the basic tax allowance. Finally, the target for annual personnel cuts in the federal bureaucracy was lowered from 1.5% to 0.4% (European Commission 2013).

The decision-making behind the cutback package of July 2010 evolved during and after the coalition negotiations for the new government in late 2009. In their coalition contract, the CDU/CSU and Liberal coalition government committed to a new constitutional debt brake and an overall policy approach of 'smart cuts' without specifying the details of these measures. Besides some 'golden rules', the only specific measures agreed to were increased nuclear fuel tax revenues (linked to an extension of the operating time of nuclear power plants), efficiency improvements in the federal bureaucracy and revenues from the sale of CO^2 certificates (not included in the cutback package). After the coalition agreement was finalised, the designated Finance Minister Wolfgang Schäuble (CDU) managed to push through 'a substantial cutback package' (Kickert 2013, 295) to balance the books sooner than the FDP and CSU had wanted. Public opinion also played an important role, since Germans generally wanted their government to balance its budget. The Ministry of Finance officials interviewed for this chapter pointed out that cutback proposals already existed in the ministry prior to negotiations. Nevertheless, they reported conflicts at the bureaucratic level during the decision-making process. Generally speaking, the consolidation package reflects a clear, 'proactive' approach even though the nature and size of the cuts were relatively modest from an international perspective. This decision-making fits within a 'rational-comprehensive' approach, even though some elements are more typical for incremental and pragmatic compromises.

Following the logic of the debt brake, the federal government made fundamental changes in budgeting practices. The traditional bottom-up budgeting process consisted of a sequence of negotiation rounds between the Ministry of Finance and line ministries on expenditure items. Beginning in 2011, however, each department was given expenditure ceilings set up front by cabinet decisions and accompanying binding, multiyear financial frameworks. Here it is worth noting that the cutback measures mentioned earlier were implemented in the form of expenditure ceilings. Hence, the government primarily used an across-the-board cutback approach, distributing cutback targets equally between the line ministries, except the Ministry of Defence and the Ministry of Labour and Social Affairs, where targeted cuts imposed a greater budgetary burden. On the other hand, each ministry was free to distribute cuts internally, either proportionally or by setting their own priorities. Regarding the application of the new top-down budgeting procedure, the government made considerable effort to avoid conflict between the coalition partners. According to one Ministry of Finance official, battles between line ministries over the differently derived spending ceilings were to be minimised by negotiations at the state-secretary level prior to a cabinet decision on the budget framework. These instructions came directly from the chancellery. As a consequence of this consensus-oriented, top-down budgeting procedure, budget negotiations have taken place in a rather 'calm atmosphere'. This also reflects the persistence of the bureaucracy's traditional 'coordinating function' in government. Our interviewee also stressed that even though the specifics of the implementation of top-down budgeting were slightly different in every fiscal year since 2010, overall compliance with the new system has been strong. However, the crisis did not provoke a shift towards 'evidence-based' budgetary decision-making; in other words, decision-making still does not systematically incorporate information on the effects of spending items.

Austerity Measures and Cutback Management in Länder Governments

In the aftermath of the crisis, all Länder at least planned some austerity measures but the need for austerity measures was (and still remains) prevalent within the Länder with the most strained fiscal positions. Starting in 2011, five Länder—Berlin, Bremen, Saarland, Saxony-Anhalt and Schleswig-Holstein—committed to reducing their structural deficits by 10% yearly in order to receive annual payments until 2019 to comply with the debt break when it takes full effect in 2020. The so called consolidation assistance is contingent on compliance with the deficit ceilings. While other Länder also established tighter fiscal rules for the transition period, the 'new' Länder in the east faced particular challenges, because federal funding established in the aftermath of German reunification (e.g. funds of the Solidarity Pact II amounted to €9 billion in 2010) will be phased out in 2019. A comparison of debt levels shows that budget pressure varies greatly among the Länder—before and after the crisis. In the city-states of Berlin and Bremen, debt levels are, respectively, two and three times higher than average. They are followed, albeit at lower levels, by Saarland, Schleswig-Holstein and Saxony-Anhalt. Although the debt burden of the Länder in the east is moderate despite a declining and ageing population and structural economic differences. Public debt is also high in the western Länder but significantly smaller in the Länder in the south, even though they were hit particularly hard by the economic crisis due to their highly export-oriented industries.

However, with the quick recovery of the economy, Länder-level government revenues increased by 28.5% in the period 2010–14 and the fiscal balance across all Länder improved substantially despite high annual deficits in some (see Figure 4.2.). As a result, in some federal states fiscal stress was eased substantially. For instance, Bavaria, Baden-Württemberg and the city-state Hamburg, all of which were struck hard by the crisis, achieved surpluses in 2014 due to their rapid economic recovery and thriving government revenues. The eastern Länder (Brandenburg, Mecklenburg-Western Pomerania, Saxony, Saxony-Anhalt and Thuringia) were only mildly hit by the crisis and achieved surpluses in 2014, which also reflects strong fiscal discipline. Finally, the Länder receiving consolidation assistance either cut their deficits by more than two-thirds (Bremen, Saarland, Schleswig-Holstein) or turned a surplus (Berlin, Saxony-Anhalt). In addition to austerity measures, highly indebted Länder profited in particular from sharply decreasing debt expenses due to declining interest rates.

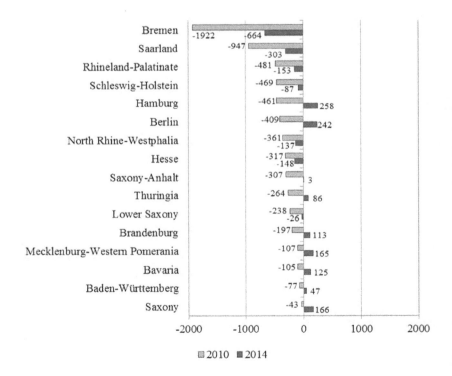

Figure 4.2 Fiscal Balance in 2010 and 2014 (€ per Capita)

Similar to the federal level, the cutback strategies resulting from the crisis involved a shift towards top-down budgeting. City-state Hamburg exemplifies this development, where city departments were instructed to limit their spending increases to 0.88% annually for the legislative period beginning in 2011. A city-state mayor interviewed for this chapter claimed that 'while compliance with the debt brake takes priority at the political level, the cutback measures are the responsibility of senior executives'. This has been a clear deviation from past approaches, when finance ministries would prepare long lists of specific savings to the line departments, often failing because of the information asymmetry. Accordingly, top-down budgeting in Hamburg appears to have led to across-the-board cuts and the delegation of cutbacks to the administrative level. However, the newly formed coalition government had allocated additional financial resources to some policy fields high on their political agenda before top-down budgeting was imposed. In contrast, the setting of departmental ceilings in Baden-Württemberg was clearly a political process involving the prime minister, selected ministers and the heads of the parliamentary groups of both coalition parties. According to one of the interviewees from a state ministry, their main issue was 'how to distribute cuts between personnel and programmes affecting the ministries in different ways'. Targeted cuts to programmes were ultimately in the minority, and the strategy for personnel cuts remained across-the-board. Analysing the public employment records in ten Länder, it is worth noting how cuts and freezes were concentrated on back-office functions. Therefore, the cuts were not directly visible to the general public. One director from a state ministry called this 'a silent saving process' (*lautloses Sparen*). In general, areas with strong public demand (universities, schools, police patrol) were initially exempt from cuts and witnessed an increase in employment in most Länder after the fiscal situation improved (see Figure 4.3.).

If the Länder are viewed as a whole, employment in the core government sector increased by less than 12,000 FTE (0.9%) in the recovery period 2010–14. However, employment in the general government sector increased by more than 100,000 FTE (5.2%), albeit greatly varying across the Länder (see Figure 4.3.). In particular, the Länder in the east and the consolidation Länder Saarland, Schleswig-Holstein and Berlin cut employment, especially in the core government sector. And between 2008 and 2009, Saxony, Saarland, Brandenburg and Mecklenburg-Western Pomerania had already cut their core government sector employment extensively. To be fair, part of the significant changes in personnel can be traced back to 'municipalisation' (*Kommunalisierung*) and privatisation processes. With regard to the general government sector, only Brandenburg, Mecklenburg-Western Pomerania and Saxony-Anhalt cut employment in the recovery period, while all other Länder increased their personnel. In particular, areas with strong public demand were initially exempt from cuts and increased spending on personnel. There

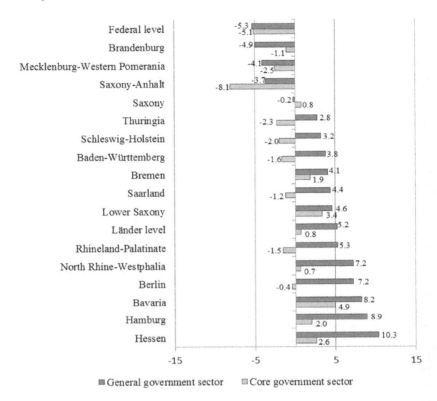

Figure 4.3 Percentage Change in FTE in the Period 2010–14

are several reasons why personnel cuts almost entirely occurred in East Germany: First, the 'new' Länder are still in the process of reforming their administrative structure, which was rapidly rolled out after reunification. Second, all of the reunification subsidies expire in 2019, leaving a tremendous hole in the budget that must be compensated for in order to comply with the debt brake in 2020. And third, the 'new' Länder are particularly affected by an ageing population and the ongoing exodus from rural areas, which is reducing the demand for public-sector personnel, such as teachers.

To comply with the parameters set by the debt brake, austerity measures in the Länder[6] receiving consolidation assistance were more severe. For instance, Berlin agreed to an extensive adjustment programme (2012–16) to avoid a state of budgetary emergency. The city-state administration already underwent restructuring, cutbacks and personnel cuts in the wake of reunification in the 1990s. Cutbacks continued in the 2000s, including cuts to social housing, subsidies, infrastructure maintenance, public employment remuneration and personnel reduction. In the recent adjustment programme, core administration expenses were limited to 0.3% and annual cuts to personnel and public employment remuneration continued. However, the city-state's finances turned around at the end of 2014 due to a growing population and improved revenues. Much of the fiscal surpluses are to be invested in the hiring of additional personnel in key areas where service capacity had been reduced excessively. In addition, special emphasis has been placed on an investment programme addressing the huge backlog in infrastructure repair. Bremen has also participated in an adjustment programme, even though the city-state has been in a state of budgetary emergency since long before 2011. Because the first austerity programme started in 1994, most potential savings had already been exhausted. Nonetheless, personnel are to be reduced by about 7.5% by 2016, with yearly personnel cuts to the core administration of about 1.5% (around 200 FTE). Social spending should be controlled by only allowing an expenditure growth of 1.7% annually. Further gains are to be achieved by strengthening cooperation and restructuring (e.g. merging outsourced segments, reintegration of outsourced units, and dissolution of facilities). In addition, top-down financial planning should be introduced in which departments have to implement global financial frameworks and departmental ceilings. Similarly, Saarland has been dealing with financial pressure since its mining and steel industry underwent a massive structural change. In the 1980s, production volumes were reduced drastically and mines had to be closed, contributing to high unemployment. To deal with the economic consequences and consolidate its budget, Saarland received special supplementary federal grants (*Sonder-Bundeszuweisungen*). In 2004, the grants were phased out and tightening fiscal pressure forced Saarland to adopt restrictive budgetary measures. Even though the budget situation improved until 2008, the positive trend was interrupted by the financial and economic crisis. Finally, the small federal state agreed to an adjustment programme and already applied a series of cuts in 2011 targeting the period 2012–16 and beyond. The programme includes cuts to positions that become vacant due to retirement (education is exempted) and temporary hiring freezes. Other measures included in the programme are pay freezes for public servants, lower starting salaries for civil servants and judges, and cutting the budget for promotions in half. In order to assist in the consistent and effective implementation of the adjustment programme, the state contracted a management consulting firm. Although Schleswig-Holstein is expecting a constant increase of revenues until 2020, the fiscal obligations of the past are severe. A large proportion of public revenues are used to reduce the structural fiscal deficit, interest payments, pensions and benefit payments. The federal state's commitment to an adjustment programme stipulates across-the-board personnel cutbacks, even in education, where fewer teachers are needed due to demographic changes and an increase in the retirement age for police officers. Further measures include reform elements, such as e-government (e.g. digital benefits system), privatisation, the implementation of accrual accounting and controlling, and benchmarking. Schleswig-Holstein also contracted management consultants to assist the different departments in effectively implementing their restructuring tasks.

The adjustment programmes (2012–16) intended to prevent a budget emergency specifically target:

- Personnel cutbacks focusing more on areas of core administration than those close to service delivery
- Cuts to benefits (e.g. pensions by extending retirement age for civil servants)
- Increases to or introduction of state taxes and fees (e.g. real estate transfer tax, tourism levy, day care)
- Reducing investment in infrastructure (e.g. postponing construction)
- Efficiency gains by optimising cross-sectional tasks (e.g. facility management)
- Savings on core administrative expenditures (e.g. necessities and consumables, training, business travel, reports, IT infrastructure)

All four Länder have thus far complied with the agreed ceilings on net borrowing in the period 2012–15. Only Berlin and Schleswig-Holstein are expected to successfully complete the adjustment programme in 2016, however, while Bremen and Saarland still require substantial adjustment efforts. For the year 2016, Bremen is expected to exceed the ceiling of net borrowing by more than double due to increased expenditures related to refugee care and social integration. The stability council therefore launched a formal complaint and requested additional measures. Already in 2013, Bremen was formally requested to intensify its consolidation efforts and Saarland was reprimanded and obliged to strictly follow its course. In contrast, in Berlin and Schleswig-Holstein, favourable fiscal conditions made significant contributions to achieving the set targets so that the consolidation efforts could actually be relaxed.

Finally, on the basis of sixteen Länder with about six to eight departments each, it is hardly surprising that we observe a large variety of austerity measures and cutback strategies, especially according to the extent of fiscal stress in each federal state. Moreover, in six of our ten representatively sampled Länder (especially the financially weaker ones), ministries are subject to departmental ceilings that are set from above. This increases the flexibility to employ whatever works best to perform well (or at least adequately) and cost less. Our interviews have also shown that, all told, there was no uniform reform practice across the Länder during the first years of fiscal consolidation from 2010 onwards.

Consequences of Cutbacks to Public Management

At both levels of government, the rapid economic recovery and increased government revenues averted harsh, large-scale cutbacks. At the federal level, the Länder in eastern Germany and the consolidation Länder, however, personnel cuts and hiring freezes were clearly concentrated on the core government sector, while areas visible to the general public, such as education and policing, were exempted. Because public employees in Germany are protected against dismissal, only hiring freezes could be applied. The cutback approach is clearly path-dependent and fits the recurring reform theme regarding public-sector downsizing and retrenchment since reunification (Schröter 2007). In fact, government sector employment was decreasing substantially on the federal (–10.2%) and state levels (–8.8%) in the pre-crisis period 2000–07, leading to a substantially ageing public workforce. In the case of the federal government, the personnel cuts policy had been relaxed in the late 2000s, signaling a rapid return to previous ways. In terms of cutback measures, the survey findings mainly document the perception of hiring freezes (26% perceived to a great extent) in the federal ministries. Indeed, analysis of public-sector employment records shows that general employment in the federal government sector declined steadily by 5.3% in the period of 2010–14 (around 26,500 FTE), with substantial cuts of 2.0% in 2012 and 2013. The survey data results show that further cutback measures in federal ministries consisted mainly of cuts to existing programmes (26%) and postponing or cancelling new programmes (20%), coinciding with the cutback package. Additional cuts can be traced back to new priorities within the given expenditure ceilings. When asked how to describe the broader approach to cutbacks in their policy area in response to the fiscal crisis, about one-fifth of the respondents identified proportional cuts across-the-board over all areas. By contrast, half of the respondents perceived the cuts as targeted based on priorities and only 17% described them as productivity and efficiency savings. Further insights from qualitative interviews also revealed a shift to the flexible replacement of employees within and between divisions based on capacity and priority. All of this is in line with top-down budgeting intentions, forcing departments to set priorities and realise productivity and efficiency savings instead of tabling new financial demands. However, the degree of priority-setting allowed by this new budgeting did not amount to a fundamental reallocation of spending at the federal level compared to other Eurozone states. Many policy areas, such as social expenditure and subsidies to business, remained nearly unchanged at pre-crisis levels. Similarly, in Länder ministries, senior executives identified hiring freezes (42%), postponing or cancelling new programmes (36%) and cuts to existing programmes (29%) as particular results of the crisis. Because attrition due to age and health determine recruitment levels when personnel cuts are to be made, Länder governments had to resort to hiring freezes in particular to achieve reduction goals. Further cuts involving personnel concerned pay freezes (25%), pay cuts (19%) and the downsizing of back offices (20%). Although monthly wages were not cut or frozen, Christmas bonuses amounting to a thirteenth month of salary were either abolished or strongly reduced in some Länder. In terms of how to describe the broader approach to cutbacks, survey data show that both targeted cuts in specific policy areas (52%) and proportional, across-the board cuts (29%) were applied in Länder ministries in response to the crisis. Regarding public management reform, both government levels lack a strategic approach. Especially in Länder ministries, 48.6% of surveyed top officials view public administration reforms in their policy field as rather partial compared to 30.2% in federal ministries. Instead, a mixture of approaches (e.g. introduction of management tools, streamlining structures and processes, merging smaller organisational units) were applied. For instance, internal services (e.g. ICT, HR, procurement, education and training) were bundled into shared-service centres, demography-sensitive HRM concepts were developed and measures regarding the digitalisation of public services and ICT consolidation were initiated. This also follows a previous path of reforms, which reflected the rather lukewarm reception of NPM reforms in Germany (Hammerschmid and Oprisor 2016) and the impact of developments at the EU level; for example, the EU services directive prescribing the electronic reachability of a single point of contact and the use of electronic procedures for setting up a business. At the Länder level, traditional structural reform approaches prevailed. Since the early 1990s all non-city-states have reduced their bureaucracies substantially by cutting public authorities and personnel (Grotz et al. 2017). In particular, Baden-Württemberg and Lower-Saxony implemented comprehensive administrative reforms in the 2000s (e.g. dismantling duplicated structures of special authorities and district governments, privatising or municipalising tasks and fighting red tape). However, recent reforms at Länder level are more incremental and inclusive (e.g. Ebinger and Bogumil 2016). Finally, compared to other European countries, performance management plays a limited role as a reform trend in German federal and Länder governments. Management tools and performance information are not used extensively and an overall logic of performance management is far from being institutionalised (Hammerschmid and Löffler 2015). As such, it is hardly surprising that a mere 6% of survey respondents in federal ministries and 13% in Länder ministries confirm that the crisis has increased the relevance of performance information. Although insights from our qualitative interviews showed that performance information is developing in areas like policing and schools, this information is not used in budget-related decision-making processes. Given these points, administrative reforms in Germany emerge rather incrementally and management ideas are vulnerable, even in the aftermath of the financial crisis (see Hammerschmid and Oprisor 2016). It is worth noting that in ministries on both government levels, twice as many respondents (41.0%) feel that the reforms are not enough compared to those who perceive them as too much (20.3%).

In terms of fiscal governance, a substantial change towards centralisation on both levels of government can be observed as a result of the fiscal crisis, indicating a kind of deviation from path-dependency. In particular, the power of the Ministry of Finance as the 'guardian of the budget' has increased. Note that the share of surveyed senior executives who perceive a stronger role of the Ministry of Finance is significantly higher in Länder ministries (57%) than in federal ministries (39%). One possible explanation for this is that financial pressure eased faster at the federal level than at the Länder level. A similar pattern of centralisation regarding the budgetary process was found at the organisational level, albeit to a lesser degree. Accordingly, 35% of the respondents in Länder ministries reported that the budget units were given stronger powers due to the crisis compared to 24% of those from the federal ministries. Furthermore, 22% of the senior executives at both levels perceived the decision-making process in their organisation as having become more centralised. These results must also be seen in the context of the new top-down budgeting approach. Following a 'cascading' logic of centralisation (Raudla et al. 2015), target-setting was centralised but the power over implementation was decentralised. In practice, departments were given expenditure ceilings set up front by cabinet decisions, which were then delegated down the line to employ cutbacks. In terms of federal–Länder relations, more coordination regarding budgeting and cutback strategies emerged through the installation of the stability council. At the moment, this only applies to the four Länder that receive consolidation assistance and also agreed upon an adjustment programme. With respect to the other Länder, the implemented procedures have only led to increased transparency, if at all.

Conclusion

The immediate fiscal repercussions of the crisis led to the introduction of the new constitutional debt brake and the stability council in 2009, which can be interpreted as a critical juncture. In doing so, Germany defined its fiscal ambition not only to consolidate its finances up to pre-crisis levels but to a fiscal target far beyond. Another path-breaking change was the introduction of top-down budgeting within the ministries at both levels, leading to a 'cascading' centralisation. On the basis of the debt brake rule, budget caps involving across-the-board cuts were imposed on line ministries by the Ministry of Finance. Within the ministries, budget caps or savings targets were given along departmental lines, leaving the department heads to employ whatever worked to achieve the targets. As regards the overall budgetary process, a slight change towards centralisation within the government levels can be observed, as the ministries of finances increased their power as a result of top-down budgeting. In addition, battles over budget allocations among line ministries were minimised.

From 2011 onwards, fiscal stress eased substantially due to a dramatic increase in government revenues on both levels. At the federal level, across-the-board hiring freezes remained the primary cutback strategy. At the Länder level, the majority even increased their personnel and expenditures in the economic upturn; however, the debt brake rule significantly increased the pressure for structurally weak and highly indebted Länder to balance their budgets. The Länder implementing cutback measures in the period following the crisis had already done so before the crisis. In the consolidation Länder, cutback efforts were mainly targeted at personnel reductions. While areas close to service delivery were often spared, personnel were cut in the core administration in keeping with an across-the-board approach. The same cutback strategy was applied to employment benefits and the general expenses of core administration. In terms of programme cuts, specific policy areas, such as welfare or infrastructure investment, were targeted. It is worth noting that, similar to the federal level, cutback measures were not connected to broader public administration reforms, confirming Germany's role as a maintainer in terms of modernisation (Pollitt and Bouckaert 2011).

Notes

1   The research leading to these results has received funding from the European Union's Seventh Framework Programme under grant agreement No. 266887 (Project COCOPS), Socio-economic Sciences and Humanities.

2   For Germany, the survey targeted senior executives from the first three hierarchical levels in all of the federal and state (Länder) ministries and the first two in all large federal agencies. The data were collected in 2012 in light of the fiscal and economic crisis, with a response rate of 22.8% (n = 445), which is well in line with other public sector surveys. The distribution of respondents with regard to policy field, hierarchical level and organisation type is in line with the targeted population (for further information on the research methodology, see Hammerschmid et al. 2013).

3   Based on a multiyear research project on changes in the fiscal governance and its effects on the fiscal strategies of German Länder between 2010 and 2016 funded by the Bertelsmann Foundation (see chapter 9, this volume).

4   This includes federal, Länder, and local levels as well as social security funds. Our own calculation based on Statistisches Bundesamt 2016a.

5   Personnel costs account for roughly half of the Länder budget, compared to only around 10% of the federal budget.

6   In 2010, the stability council determined all Länder receiving consolidation assistance, except Saxony-Anhalt, to be in a state of an imminent budget emergency. The following analysis is based on an extensive review of documents provided online by the stability council (www.stabilitaetsrat.de).

References

Bundesbank. 2016. "Öffentliche Finanzen in Deutschland." *Finanzierungssaldo (Maastricht-Abgrenzung)*. www.bundesbank.de/Navigation/DE/Statistiken/Zei treihen_Datenbanken/Oeffentliche_Finanzen_in_Deutschland/oeffentliche_finanzen_in_deutschland_list_node.html?listId=www_v27_web011_11a. Accessed on 6 June 2016.

Bundesministerium der Finanzen. 2013. "Entwicklungen der Länderhaushalte im Jahr 2009." *Endgültiges Ergebnis*. www.bundesfinanzministerium.de/Content/DE/Standardartikel/Themen/Oeffentliche_Finanzen/Foederale_Finanzbeziehungen/Laenderhaushalte/2009-2012/Einnahmen_Ausgaben_L%C3%A4nder_2009_endg.Erg.html.

Dustmann, Christian, Bernd Fitzenberger, Uta Schönberg and Alexandra Spitz-Oener. 2014. "From Sick Man of Europe to Economic Superstar: Germany's Resurgent Economy." *Journal of Economic Perspectives* 28(1):167–88.

Ebinger, Falk and Jörg Bogumil. 2016. "Von den Blitzreformen zur neuen Behutsamkeit." In *Die Politik der Bundesländer*, edited by Achim Hildebrandt and Frieder Wolf, 139–60. Wiesbaden: Springer Fachmedien Wiesbaden.

European Commission. 2011. "Assessment of the 2011 National Reform Programme and Stability Programme for Germany." ec.europa.eu/europe2020/pdf/recommendations_2011/swp_germany_en.pdf.

European Commission. 2013. "Assessment of the 2013 National Reform Programme and Stability Programme for Germany." ec.europa.eu/europe2020/pdf/nd/swd2013_germany_en.pdf.

Fichtner, Ferdinand, Simon Junker, Guido Baldi, Jacek Bednarz, Kerstin Bernoth, Franziska Bremus, Klaus Brenke, Christian Dreger, Hella Engerer, Christoph Große Steffen, Hendrik Hagedorn, Katharina Pijnenburg, Kristina von Deuverden and Aleksandar Zaklan. 2013. "Wirtschaftspolitik im Zeichen der Krise." *DIW-Wochenbericht* 80(1/2):39–48.

Grotz, Florian, Alexander Götz, Marcel Lewandowsky and Henrike Wehrkamp. 2017. *Verwaltungsstrukturreformen in den deutschen Ländern: Die Entwicklung der staatlichen Kernverwaltung im Ländervergleich*. Wiesbaden: Springer.

Hammerschmid, Gerhard and Lorenz Löffler. 2015. "The Implementation of Performance Management in European Central Governments: More a North–South Than an East–West Divide." *NISPAcee Journal of Public Administration and Policy* 8(2):49–68.

Hammerschmid, Gerhard and Anca Oprisor. 2016. "German Public Administration: Incremental Reform and a Difficult Terrain for Management Ideas and Instruments." In *Public Administration Reforms in Europe*, edited by Gerhard Hammerschmid, Steven van de Walle, Rhys Andrews and Philippe Bezes, 63–72. Cheltenham: Edward Elgar.

Katsioulis, Christos and Marius Müller-Hennig. 2011. "German Defense Policy at Another Crossroads: Structural Transformation With a European Dimension?" *International Issues & Slovak Foreign Policy Affairs* XX(3):18–28.

Kickert, Walter. 2013. "How the German Government Responded to the Financial, Economic and Fiscal Crises." *Public Money & Management* 33(4):291–6.

OECD. 2011. "Germany." *Special Issue of the OECD Journal on Budgeting* 2:114–18. www.oecd.org/gov/budgeting/47840777.pdf.

Pollitt, Christopher and Geert Bouckaert. 2011. *Public Management Reform: A Comparative Analysis: New Public Management, Governance, and the Neo-Weberian State.* Oxford: Oxford University Press.

Raudla, Ringa, James W. Douglas, Tiina Randma-Liiv and Riin Savi. 2015. "The Impact of Fiscal Crisis on Decision-Making Processes in European Governments: Dynamics of a Centralization Cascade." *Public Administration Review* 75(6):842–52.

Rinne, Ulf, and Klaus F. Zimmermann. 2012. "Another Economic Miracle? The German Labor Market and the Great Recession." *IZA Journal of Labor Policy* 1/3, 1–21.

Schröter, Eckhard. 2007. "Reforming the Machinery of Government: The Case of the German Federal Bureaucracy." In *Public Governance and Leadership*, edited by Rainer Koch and John Dixon, 251–71. Wiesbaden: DUV.

Statistisches Bundesamt. 2011a. "Finanzen und Steuern: Personal des öffentlichen Dienstes 2010." www.destatis.de/GPStatistik/servlets/MCRFileNodeServlet/DEHeft_derivate_00003311/2140600107005.xls. Accessed on 20 December 2016.

Statistisches Bundesamt. 2011b. "Finanzen und Steuern: Vierteljährliche Kassenergebnisse des öffentlichen Gesamthaushalts." 1.-4. Vierteljahr 2010. Fachserie 14 Reihe 2. www.destatis.de/GPStatistik/servlets/MCRFileNodeServlet/DEHeft_derivate_00008993/2140200103245.xls. Accessed on 20 December 2016.

Statistisches Bundesamt. 2015a. "Finanzen und Steuern: Vierteljährliche Kassenergebnisse des öffentlichen Gesamthaushalts." 1.-4. Vierteljahr 2014. Fachserie 14 Reihe 2. www.destatis.de/DE/Publikationen/Thematisch/FinanzenSteuern/OeffentlicheHaushalte/AusgabenEinnahmen/KassenergebnisOeffentlicherHaushalt2140200143245.xlsx?__blob=publicationFile. Accessed on 20 December 2016.

Statistisches Bundesamt. 2015b. "Finanzen und Steuern: Personal des Öffentlichen Dienstes 2014." www.destatis.de/DE/Publikationen/Thematisch/FinanzenSteuern/OeffentlicherDienst/PersonaloeffentlicherDienst2140600147005.xls?__blob=publicationFile. Accessed on 20 December 2016.

Statistisches Bundesamt. 2016a. "Finanzen und Steuern: Personal des Öffentlichen Dienstes 2015." Fachserie 14 Reihe 6. www.destatis.de/DE/Publikationen/Thematisch/FinanzenSteuern/OeffentlicherDienst/PersonaloeffentlicherDienst2140600157005.xls?__blob=publicationFile. Accessed on 20th of December 2016.

Statistisches Bundesamt. 2016b. "Bevölkerung und Erwerbstätigkeit: Bevölkerungsfortschreibung auf Grundlage des Zensus 2011, 2014." Fachserie 1 Reihe 1.3. www.destatis.de/DE/Publikationen/Thematisch/Bevoelkerung/Bevoelkerungsstand/Bevoelkerungsfortschreibung2010130147005.xls?__blob=publicationFile. Accessed on 20 December 2016.

Zohlnhöfer, Reimut. 2011. "Between a Rock and a Hard Place: The Grand Coalition's Response to the Economic Crisis." *German Politics* 20(2):227–42.

5 Italy

A Tale of Path-Dependent Public-sector Shrinkage

Fabrizio Di Mascio, Davide Galli,
Alessandro Natalini and Edoardo Ongaro

Introduction

A number of theoretically relevant contextual features make Italy noteworthy for the study of cutback management in comparative perspective. First, Italy has been exposed to a severe and prolonged pressure for fiscal retrenchment in the context of the wider sovereign debt crisis of the Eurozone southern periphery. Thus, it is a case suitable for the analysis of whether cutbacks have shifted from across-the-board cuts to more selective strategies in the long run (Dunsire and Hood 1989). Second, it is the only case in Southern Europe where the threat of severe fiscal crisis was not unprecedented: the country faced a previous crisis in the early 1990s leading to the consolidation of a repertoire of cutback and modernisation efforts (Di Mascio and Natalini 2015). Therefore, it is a case that could be analysed through the theoretical lenses of those historical institutional accounts of path dependence, namely how earlier responses to crisis constitute repertoires of solutions that affect later responses by proving policymakers with feedback effects (Pierson 2004; Pollitt 2008). Third, it is a case which has been marked by endless political instability throughout the sequence of responses to both the early 1990s and the post-2008 crises. Political instability can be expected to have hindered the phasing of cutback management from sheer dwindling of the public sector to selective measures, as the latter require cohesive governing coalitions (Pollitt 2010). However, Italy is a case where a technical government has been formed to face the crisis in the period 2011–13. This is the fourth feature of the Italian case which, conversely, could have facilitated the implementation of selective cutbacks, since a technical government could be expected to be in the condition to face the crisis without concern for short-term electoral gains so often detectable in risk-adverse party governments (Zahariadis 2013).

By developing an analytical case study of the Italian trajectory of fiscal consolidation, we address the following research question:

RQ: How have contextual features (severe sovereign debt crisis, previous episode of fiscal crisis, political instability, formation of technical governments) affected cutback management in Italy?

In doing so, we adopt a configurational approach to the study of cutback management (Raudla 2013), that is, we look at how the complex patterns of interaction between contextual factors influenced fiscal retrenchment. To preview the main findings of our study, we found that the response to the crisis has been path-dependent: in a context marked by severe and prolonged fiscal pressure, the persistent political instability sustained the adoption of across-the-board cuts inherited from the response to the previous early-1990s fiscal crisis. The shift from across-the-board cuts to selective approaches has occurred only at the level of line ministries in the latest stage of the crisis under the impulse provided by the interaction between cutback management and spending reviews undertaken in the domain of budgetary reforms (see Chapter 10 on budget processes).

Methodologically, the analysis rests on documentary material as well as elite face-to-face interviews with experts knowledgeable about spending reductions. More specifically, in the period October 2012 to November 2015 twelve interviews have been administered to tenured officials from all the institutions tasked with the planning, implementing, and monitoring of fiscal consolidation measures (Ministry of Finance, Ministry of Public Administration, Ministry of Government Program Implementation, Cabinet Office, Parliament, ARAN–National Agency for Negotiation with the Public Sector Unions, Court of Accounts) as well as trade union officials. Moreover, in May 2016 three interviews have been administered to senior public managers from three line ministries.

The involvement of the authors in the FP7 research project 'Coordinating for Cohesion in the Public Sector of the Future–COCOPS' (2010–14) and more recently in a research project based at Erasmus University Rotterdam on the impact of the EU on administrative reform policies under conditions of fiscal consolidation (co-investigators Walter Kickert and Edoardo Ongaro) has also provided opportunities to gather data and acquire knowledge about the dynamics of public management reform in Italy.

This chapter is structured as follows. The next section describes the Italian contextual background focusing on the political, fiscal and economic dimensions of the post-2008 crisis. The following section deals with the response to the crisis in terms of austerity packages in the period 2010–15. The third section outlines cutback management in central government, with a focus on a selection of three line ministries. The fourth section identifies the major effects of cutbacks on public management. Concluding remarks discuss the main findings of our research.

The Italian Context

Italy is a republic based on a parliamentary system of government. The president of the republic has a representative role towards the outer world, as well as a mediatory, moral suasion role internally, mainly acting as a "notary" that guarantees the constitution, but at times incisively steering political processes. The cabinet (Council of Ministers) is a collegial body, implying that the prime minister is only a *primus inter pares* (Cotta and Verzichelli 2007). As for the administrative system, it displays the legalistic conception of public service typical of the Napoleonic tradition (Ongaro 2010).

Until the early 1990s Italy displayed a consensual pattern of executive government with no wholesale alternation between coalitions. The combination of fiscal crisis, prompted by the expulsion of the Italian lira from the European Monetary System, and political crisis, triggered by major corruption scandals, led to the exceptional collapse of the party system. After the 1992–96 transition period when crisis management was entrusted to technical governments, a new majoritarian pattern emerged featuring wholesale alternation in government between pre-electoral coalitions. Yet, the persistent instability of fragmented government coalitions has hindered the implementation of reforms in the post-1996 period (Mele and Ongaro 2014).

The implementation gap of administrative reforms contributed to place Italy in a vulnerable fiscal position when the sovereign debt crisis erupted in Southern Europe. As it already happened in the early 1990s, the fiscal crisis has intertwined with the political crisis since 2011 when a grand coalition was formed to support a technical government led by Mr. Monti. However, the advent of the Monti government has not meant any major reversal in the path of faltering legitimacy of the Italian political class. The success of the new anti-establishment Five Star Movement at the 2013 general elections showcased widespread public discontent with all the major Italian political parties and led to a hung parliament. After two months of political stalemate, an unusual left-right coalition was formed to support the executive led by Mr. Letta. However, the Letta government was short-lived as it was followed by the center–left government led by Mr. Renzi since February 2014.

From the fiscal perspective, Italy entered the crisis in 2008 with a public debt over 100% of GDP and this level has steadily increased over time peaking in 2015 (see Table 5.1.). However, the main problem was not so much the high level of debt, especially when accounting for the relatively low level of private debt and considering that public debt was mostly held domestically. It was the low growth rate of the economy that raised concerns about public debt sustainability.

In the run up to the crisis, the low growth rate basically offset the surplus in the primary balance. The latter resulted from the progressive consolidation of a set of across-the-board cuts which had been implemented by the Italian governments in order to respond to the previous 1992 fiscal crisis as well as meeting the requirements of the European Stability and Growth Pact (Di Mascio, Natalini and Stolfi 2013).

Table 5.1 Italy: Key Economic, Social and Financial Indicators

	2003–07	2008	2009	2010	2011	2012	2013	2014	2015	2016	2017
Real GDP Growth	1.2	–1	–5.5	1.7	0.6	–2.8	–1.7	–0.4	0.8	1.4	1.3
Contribution to potential GDP growth: Total factor productivity	–0.1	–0.2	–0.2	–0.1	–0.2	–0.2	–0.3	–0.3	–0.3	–0.2	–0.1
Private sector debt (% of GDP)	96.7	113.8	120.7	121.5	121	123.4	120.8	119.3	–	–	–
Gross non performing debt (% of total debts and loans)	–	5	7.5	8.4	9.5	11	12.9	15.8	–	–	–
General government gross debt (% of GDP)	100.9	102.3	112.5	115.3	116.4	123.2	128.8	132.3	132.8	132.4	130.6
General government balance (% of GDP)	–3.3	–2.7	–5.3	–4.2	–3.5	–3	–2.9	–3	–2.6	–2.5	–1.5
General government primary balance (% of GDP)	1.4	2.2	–0.9	0	1.2	2.2	2	1.6	1.7	1.8	2.3
Interest payments (% of GDP)	4.7	4.9	4.4	4.3	4.7	5.2	4.8	4.6	4.3	4.1	3.9

Source: European Commission (2016).

Over the crisis period 2008–14, the primary balance remained in surplus but the debt ratio increased on average by 4.7 percentage points. The driver of this substantial increase was the large gap between nearly zero average annual nominal GDP growth (–1.3% real GDP growth) and rather high implicit interest rates paid on debt (4.2% on average).

Austerity Packages

We identify three stages of crisis management drawing on the combined consideration of the varied pressures wielded by financial markets and the changing composition of coalition governments undertaking fiscal consolidation efforts. To track pressures from financial markets, we take into account the dynamics of the spread (interest rate paid on gilts) since rating agencies and financial institutions have relied on the Italian government bond yield spreads to German bunds as a sovereign credit risk indicator.

Germany being considered as the safest sovereign credit in the Eurozone, a country's bond yield increase against German bunds was considered as signal of credit risk rising and political inability to manage the crisis. After remaining below 200 basis points (bps) until June 2011, 10-year bond spreads started to climb, peaking at 552 bps in November 2011. Sovereign spreads tightened for a short period in spring 2012 after the three-year Long Term Refinancing Operations (LTRO) by the European Central Bank, but then widened again reaching more than 500 bps in July 2012. Spreads have come down steadily since the announcement of the details of the European Central Bank's Outright Monetary Transactions (OMT) program in September 2012.

The combined consideration of the dynamics of the spread and the changing composition of government coalitions leads us to identify the following three stages of crisis management: the first stage of rising spread under the center–right Berlusconi government (2008–11); the second stage of peaking spread under the technical Monti government (2011–13); the third stage of declining spread under the governments led by the leaders of the centre-left Democratic Party Letta and Renzi (2013–15).

Table 5.2. reports the fiscal consolidation packages that have been enacted in the post-2008 crisis period highlighting their impacts in terms of variation on both sides of public finance (tax revenue and expenditure) as well as their effects on the net debt. The table shows that the pace of fiscal consolidation accelerated in the period 2010–12 under growing pressure from financial markets as revealed by the adoption of early emergency packages moving up the effect of subsequent budget laws in terms of debt reduction. Conversely, since 2013 the declining pressure from financial markets has led governments to gradually relax their fiscal consolidation efforts.

Table 5.2 Italy: Fiscal Consolidation Efforts in the 2010–15 Period (Millions of Euro)

BERLUSCONI GOVERNMENT (08–11)	2010	2011	2012	2013	2014	2015	2016	2017
Law Decree n.78/2010								
Effects on Net Debt	–31	–12.053	–24.982	–24.979	–47.962			
Tax Revenue Variation	+693	+4.095	+10.091	+8.004	+28.295			
Expenditure Variation	662	–7.958	–14.891	–16.975	–19.677			
Budget Law 2011								
Effects on Net Debt	0	–1	–2	0				
Tax Revenues Variation	76	–18	–308	–335				
Expenditure Variation	–76	–19	–310	–335				
Law Decree 98/2011								
Effects on Net Debt		–2.108	–5.578	–24.406				
Tax Revenues Variation		+1.871	+6.609	+13.285				
Expenditure Variation		–237	+1.031	–11.121				
Law Decree 138/2011								
Effects on Net Debt		–732	–22.698	–29.859	–11.822			
Tax Revenue Variation		+732	+14.068	+22.121	+10.521			
Expenditure Variation		0	–8.630	–7.738	–1.301			
Budget Law 2012								
Effects on Net Debt			–317	–159	–97			
Tax Revenue Variation			+330	–182	+7			
Expenditure Variation			+13	–341	–90			

MONTI GOVERNMENT (11–13)	2010	2011	2012	2013	2014	2015	2016	2017
Law Decree 201/2011								
Effects on Net Debt			–20.245	–21.320	–21.431			
Tax Revenue Variation			+19.366	+16.962	+14.891			

	2010	2011	2012	2013	2014	2015	2016	2017
Law Decree 95/2012								
Effects on Net Debt			−602	−15	−27	−628		
Tax Revenue Variation			−3.392	−6.766	−10.237	−10.300		
Expenditure Variation			−3.994	−6.781	−10.264	−10.928		
Budget Law 2013								
Effects on Net Debt				−2.319	−138	−379		
Tax Revenue Variation				+1.892	−876	−283		
Expenditure Variation				−427	−1.014	−662		
LETTA (13–14) AND RENZI (14–15) GOVERNMENT								
Budget Law 2014								
Effects on Net Debt					+2.458	−3.515	−7.303	
Tax Revenue Variation					+2.244	+234	+1.367	
Expenditure Variation					+4.702	−3.281	−5.936	
Budget Law 2015								
Effects on Net Debt						+5.818	−147	−6.891
Tax Revenue Variation						−124	+6.985	+13.506
Expenditure Variation						+5.694	+6.838	+6.615
Budget Law 2016								
Effects on Net Debt							+17.625	+19.136
Tax Revenue Variation							−17.985	−22.435
Expenditure Variation							−360	−3.299

Source: Ragioneria Generale dello Stato (2010–2016).

Spring 2010–Fall 2011: The Rise of Markets' Pressure Under the Berlusconi Government

As opposed to the situation in most countries, no banking sector rescue package was needed in Italy to tackle the effects of the financial crisis which erupted in the US in 2008 (Quaglia 2009). Therefore, until 2010 the effort of the Berlusconi government was focused on the relaunch of administrative modernisation inspired by New Public Management. A new administrative reform (Legislative Decree 150/2009) was finalised at strengthening the managerial autonomy of senior executives as well as introducing a forced-ranking performance related-pay system. The latter divided civil servants into three groups according to their performance in order to force public managers to tackle underperformance and reward merit.

However, since early 2010 there were increasing international concerns over the Greek crisis and whether it might impact the fiscal stability of other high public debt countries like Italy. The center-right Berlusconi government addressed these international concerns by adopting in late May an emergency fiscal package (Law Decree 78/2010), primarily targeted at reducing expenditure, well before the mandatory deadline for the 2011 Budget Law (mid-October). The latter basically confirmed the target of invariance in the government balance budget. It is worth highlighting that the emergency fiscal package deprived Legislative Decree 150/2009 of the resources needed for its implementation, thus keeping administrative modernisation frozen.

As a result of mounting market pressures, in July 2011 the Berlusconi government adopted a further early emergency package (Law Decree 98/2011), focused mostly on revenues, that substantially moved up the effects of the 2012 Budget Law. This consolidation effort was not enough to assuage market fears of contagion from Greece to Italy. The Berlusconi government responded to mounting market pressures with a new emergency package adopted in mid-August (Law Decree 138/2011), which brought forward to 2013 the goal of achieving a balanced budget mostly by increasing fiscal revenues.

However, even these measures proved to be ineffective in restoring markets' confidence. Therefore, the prime minister started suffering a severe legitimacy crisis and the head of state Mr. Napolitano repeatedly and publicly asked for a change of government. This eventually led to the collapse of the Berlusconi government in November 2011 after the approval by the parliament of the 2012 Budget Law which had no major effect on the reduction of public debt.

Fall 2011–Spring 2013: The Peak of Markets' Pressure Under the Monti Government

In mid-November Professor Mario Monti, former European Commissioner and president of Bocconi University of Milan, was appointed as prime minister by the head of state to gain the confidence of EU institutions and markets. This appointment won the support of all the major parties, pleased to shift the blame of unpopular policies to the non-partisan leadership of Monti, who chose to hold the post of interim finance minister until July 2012 as means to reassure investors. The Monti government, all composed of non-partisan experts, passed a further emergency package in early December 2011 (Law Decree 201/2011) mostly focused on the revenue side. Conversely, a further austerity package enacted in mid-2012 (Law Decree 95/2012) was focused on reducing fiscal revenues balanced by the cut of public expenditure.

In late July 2012 the ECB Governor Mario Draghi pledged to do "whatever it takes" to save the euro, leading to a sharp decline of spread rates. The decreasing pressure of markets led the Monti government to approve a slightly expansionary 2013 Budget Law before resigning four months ahead of the natural term of the legislature. Under the Monti government administrative modernisation was kept frozen: like its predecessor, the executive adopted a risk-adverse approach focused only on cutbacks to restore fiscal soundness.

Spring 2013–Fall 2015: The Decline of Markets' Pressure Under the Letta and Renzi Governments

In order to ensure the achievement of the fiscal commitments (balanced budget in structural terms for 2013, 2014 and 2015) in a context marked by lower tax receipts due to a worsening economy, the Letta government introduced new spending reduction measures in the 2014 Budget Law. The latter was however slightly expansionary in the first fiscal year.

Following the election of the new Democratic Party leader, Matteo Renzi, the Letta government resigned in February 2014. Given the steady decline of the spread, the new government led by Renzi proceeded to give fiscal policy an expansionary turn in the face of a persisting depressed economy.

Unlike the Monti and Letta governments, the Renzi government relaunched administrative reform by adopting a new comprehensive package (Law 124/2015). Yet, if compared with previous efforts, it was less inspired by New Public Management: the emphasis was put less on performance management and more on coordination to be implemented via the reduction of organisational fragmentation and the centralisation around the prime minister.

Cutbacks in Central Government

In the analysis of cutback management in the Italian central government we focus on the personnel domain, an area that is especially exposed to fiscal retrenchment (Derlien and Peters 2008) as revealed by the austerity packages adopted by the OECD countries in reaction to the 2008 crisis

(Kickert and Randma-Liiv 2015). We first analyse public personnel policies adopted at the level of cabinet decision-making. Findings reveal the adoption of across-the-board cuts throughout the period under investigation. When governments opt for across-the-board cuts, reform adoptions are decentralised: the cabinet set the amount of the decrement without choosing what reform types are to be implemented (Pollitt 2010). Therefore, it is essential to follow how cutbacks are implemented at the level of line ministries to understand what activities are affected by cutbacks. To this end, we track reform measures implemented by three line ministries.

Measures Adopted by the Cabinet

Until the early 1990s the Italian public-sector employment regime has been characterised by a high degree of distinctiveness since any aspect of personnel management was densely regulated by public law providing strong guarantees in favour of job stability (Ongaro 2009, Chapter 3). Further, pay rises were automatic and coupled with particularly favourable retirement and pension arrangements. As for recruitment, ordinary procedures were based on competitive examination. However, they were often circumvented by the so called "titularisation" process: candidates were employed on a temporary basis but after a given time, a law was passed by the parliament that changed the employment status, making it permanent for thousands of temporary employees (Cassese 1993). The expansion of the workforce driven by titularisation was not contained by the ceiling of the notional staff, that is the workforce required for executing the job on paper, which has been well far above the actual staff.

In the Italian system there had been no role for performance management until the early 1990s when the fiscal crisis prompted the launch of successive reform packages inspired by the New Public Management doctrine (Ongaro 2011). Labour contracts, negotiated between the government in its capacity as the employer and the unions, became a major source of regulation of the civil service. A two-tier labour contract system (one national and one regarding the individual public-sector organisation) was set up. Second-tier regulation was expected to constitute the prerequisite for staff reorganisation, rationalising its distribution among offices and levels of career to make it proportionate to the salience of tasks.

However, the two-tier regulation produced a perverse effect because the implementation of performance management has been hollowed out by the progressive consolidation of a form of spoils system. In a context where appointments were distributed according to political loyalty rather than performance measurement, public managers had no interest in either reorganising staff nor managing it by objectives and results. Rather, public managers colluded with trade unions to use supplementary allowances, aimed at the differentiation of performance, to distribute an ever-increasing amount of resources among managers and employees (Di Mascio and Natalini 2014). Thus, the two-tier contract system did not keep expenditure under control as the salary mass estimated during the bargaining process at the national level was significantly increased at the decentralised level, without any returns in terms of increased productivity as integrative contracts were not linked to performance.

In a context marked by enduring statutory protections from dismissal and influence of trade unions vetoing the implementation of any reorganisation plan, in the post-1992 period the expenditure has been kept under control mostly by reducing staff turnover. The block of recruitment was introduced in 1992 but too many derogations were admitted, mostly under pressure from unionised temporary workers striving for "titularisation". The block was introduced again in 2001 and reiterated until 2006, while derogations have been progressively circumscribed to a limited number of administrations. Since 2007 a replacement rate has set a cap on staff turnover in the following years at a prefixed percentage of the 2006 terminations. Further, two rounds of across-the-board cuts of the notional staff via a prefixed percentage were enacted in 2004 and 2006. Yet, notional staff has remained higher than the actual staff and this left room for a sort of compensation: while the tenured workforce decreased to 1.9% in the 2003–07 period, the temporary workers grew to 7.4% (Ragioneria Generale dello Stato 2014).

Public employment has been the privileged target of consolidation efforts since the 2010 emergency fiscal package. The response to the crisis has followed the path established since the early 1990s crisis as cutback management has been implemented via across-the-board cuts. Positive feedback effects reinforced the adoption of across-the-board cuts that had proved to be effective in containing expenditure throughout the path to the sovereign debt crisis. Conversely, negative feedback from the perverse effects of previous administrative reforms precluded the relaunch of ambitious modernisation efforts.

Collective bargaining was suspended and wages were frozen at the 2010 total level of compensation until 2014. A pay cut affected salaries exceeding the 90,000 Euros threshold but it was later considered an illegitimate form of discriminative taxation by the Constitutional Court (Sentence 223/2012). The major part of spending reduction has been pursued by reducing the size of public employment. As for the actual staff, it has been squeezed by extending and reinforcing the replacement rate which was already in place: after setting a cap on staff turnover in 2009 at 10% of employee terminations in 2008, for the period 2010–13 the reduction of recruitment was set at 20% of the previous year's terminations, a cap to be removed only in subsequent legislative periods. Emergency fiscal packages adopted in summer 2011 further reinforced and prolonged the replacement rate.

Actual staff numbers have also been affected by the provisions that slashed the budget for fixed-term contracts to 50% of the amount allocated in the year 2009. Further, the practice of titularisation has become less frequent. In the 2008–11 period only 50,000 out of 310,000 temporary workers switched to a permanent status. With regard to the notional staff, it has been reduced by successive rounds of prefixed percentage cuts at both the managerial and non-managerial level included in each emergency fiscal package adopted by the Berlusconi government.

The advent of the Monti government (2011–13) did not bring about any change to the public personnel policy, as it intervened only on the notional staff by introducing a further 20% cut of first and second level managerial positions and further 10% cut of spending for non-managerial personnel (Decree Law 95/2012). In most public administrations the notional staff was eventually aligned to the actual one: after a couple of decades, the ceiling to recruitment based on notional staff finally started to bite.

The 2014 Budget Law adopted by the Letta government prolonged the replacement rate until 2016 and extended it to public–private companies. The relaxing of fiscal constraints allowed the Renzi government to titularise about 100,000 fixed-term teachers in the national education sector. Wage freeze was prolonged for one year by the 2015 Budget Law but individual wage increases resulting from promotions or passages between contractual levels were allowed. Replacement rate was prolonged until 2018 by the 2016 Budget Law. In 2015 the Constitutional Court declared the illegitimacy of the indefinite arrest of collective bargaining (Sentence 178/2015). Therefore, the government was forced to launch a new round of collective bargaining making available only a limited amount of resources for the renewal of collective contracts in all the public sector.

Traditional corporatist linkages between unions and parties in government have been called into question by disaffected citizens pressurised by austerity policies and hence less forgiving towards forms of pervasive influence of organised interests in the public personnel policy. The impact of citizens' disaffection has been greatly intensified by the urgency imposed by the risks of contagion within the Eurozone. Consequently, the unilateral power of the government to set targets for cutback in the domain of public personnel had been strengthened. In 2012 the outright dismissal of public workers was also threatened, though more as a means to send a symbolic sign of addressing the external critique of public employees than as a really countenanced course of action.

Whereas the total amount of cutbacks was imposed on trade unions, they were able to influence the strategy of cutback management in the direction of across-the-board cuts, seen as a way to prevent dismissals resulting from priority-setting. Given the uniformity of the wage-freeze and the security secured to those already in post ('insiders') by the replacement rate, across-the-board cuts suited well the strategy of trade unions which was aimed at maintaining the cohesion of their membership across sectors by shifting the burden of cuts onto the shoulders of non-unionised temporary workers ('outsiders').

Measures Adopted by Three Line Ministries

In order to show how across-the-board cuts have been implemented, we do not take the Italian central government as a single compact entity; rather, we investigate different patterns of cutback management across ministries displaying different features. We track reform measures adopted in three line ministries marked by different size and territorial articulation as shown in Table 5.3.: the Ministry of Justice, a large-sized administration with distribution throughout the national territory; the Ministry of Foreign Affairs, a medium-sized organisation with headquarters in Italy and offices around the world; the Ministry of Environment, a small body with a single territorial headquarter.

We first analyse the evolution of expenditure across the three ministries. As for the Ministry of Justice, the net effects of cutbacks do not appear significant in the period under examination. However, this outcome is also the consequence of the fact that the Ministry of Justice could compensate for cuts with self-financing secured by the so-called Unified Fund for Justice, funded by assets seized in the framework of criminal proceedings, pecuniary sanctions, and sums advanced from bankruptcy proceedings. Nevertheless, the ministry had to cope with cuts imposed by the cabinet and it reacted by implementing a priority-setting approach under the coordination of the office of direct collaboration with the minister. This approach aimed to ring-fence certain priority projects for modernisation as well as to secure budget items like legal expenses and expenditures for the running of prisons (directly dependent on the ministry in Italy).

In the case of the Ministry of Foreign Affairs, until 2011 cutback management has been implemented by replicating the across-the-board logic percolating from above. Then, in 2012 the ministry faced the major challenge to cut around 250 millions of euros—hardly a limited amount for a ministry whose main asset is its staff; part of it—the diplomatic corps—is protected by a distinctive statutory regime. A committee was constituted to come up with more selective proposals for expenditure reduction. Cutbacks have been focused on the following items: staff working in the network of overseas offices; funds given to international organisations; grants in the field of international development and cooperation programs.

As to the Ministry of Environment, it faced a major spending reduction, more than halving its total expenditure. The reduction ensues mostly from the cut imposed by the cabinet to transfers in favour of subnational authorities for implementing environmental protection measures. Until

Table 5.3 Italy: Tenured Public Employees and Level of Expenditure in Three Selected Ministries (2007–14)

Ministry	2007	2008	2009	2010	2011	2012	2013	2014
Justice								
Total number of employees*	100.030	100.208	98.683	96.365	95.977	94.555	93.348	92.298
Number of tenured public employees	49.267	49.989	48.851	47.840	46.773	45.362	44.489	43.561
Total level of expenditure (000 €)	7.774.178	7.574.741	7.560.741	7.409.616	7.203.882	7.372.564	7.302.133	7.553.228
Foreign Affairs								
Total number of employees**	7.172	7.205	7.226	7.050	6.865	6.754	6.679	6.608
Number of tenured public employees	3.908	3.917	3.825	3.663	3.420	3.294	3.191	3.112
Total level of expenditure (000 €)	2.238.216	2.546.132	2.045.113	2.076.301	1.882.368	1.683.971	1.837.166	1.815.049
Environment								
Number of tenured public employees	640	644	624	605	603	589	580	556
Total level of expenditure (000 €)	1.409.269	1.649.404	1.265.223	737.765	554.381	434.543	468.160	580.519

Source: Ragioneria Generale dello Stato (2010–2015). The three ministries have been subjected to an endless sequence of across-the-board cuts imposed by the cabinet via austerity packages. They have also undergone reorganisation through *ad hoc* regulation of specific offices by the cabinet. It should also be noted that from 2008 until 2015 at least four ministers have succeeded in each ministry; hence, they have operated in conditions of severe political instability.

*Includes prison career, prison police and ordinary judges; **includes diplomats and foreign contractors

2012 cuts had been implemented by senior managers, subsequently the office of direct collaboration with the minister played a central role in the formulation of proposals for expenditure reductions.

Turning to the internal reorganisation processes, cutbacks have been a key driver for reorganisation in the Ministry of Justice where major processes were already underway before the enactment of austerity packages. Cutback management played the role of a catalyst accelerating the revision of the judicial districts that has more than halved the courts on the territory (from 1.589 to 838 offices). The reorganisation has been based on criteria like the offices' workload and the perimeter of their districts. A major reorganisation of the network of offices has also been undertaken by the Ministry of Foreign Affairs: 65 overseas structures, including embassies, consulates, and cultural institutes, have been suppressed in the 2008–15 period; at the central level, five general directorates have been abolished. Moreover, since 2014 inter-administrative centres have been put into operation to achieve savings in procurement. Conversely, the reorganisation of the Ministry of Environment has led to an increase of the number of general directorates.

With regard to the staff, the autonomy of the three ministries under examination has been severely curtailed by the highly frequent and pervasive regulation of the Ministry of Finance. The pace of the sequence of cuts imposed from above made the context of staff reorganisation extremely unstable preventing any coherent assessment of the staff workload. This contextual factor further heightened the well-institutionalised reluctance of the Italian administration of distributing the staff in accordance with the distribution of the workload (Corte dei Conti 2016).

One example of the lack of autonomy is the special plan for recruitment which was devised by the Ministry of Justice as soon as resources became available. It was not approved by the Ministry of Finance which preferred to devote resources to the mobility of staff made redundant by the reorganisation of provinces rather than to the recruitment of new employees. As for the Ministry of Foreign Affairs, it has kept cuts on the diplomatic corps at a minimum. Conversely, new administrative staff has not been recruited since 2008. The lack of tenured staff has been compensated by fixed-term contracts. However, the shortage of staff has persisted since fixed-term employees cannot perform many crucial functions. A major shortage of staff has also been faced by the Ministry of Environment, which has not been allowed to recruit new officials with a specific environmental expertise. This has resulted in an overreliance on external policy experts and advisors.

To sum up, we found that the across-the-board approach has persisted across the three ministries under examination throughout the three stages of the crisis only with regard to staff, an area marked by pervasive regulation and severe shortages as a result of across-the-board cuts. As for the efficiency savings associated to reorganisation processes and the priority-setting of the expenditure, we found that the lower density of regulation in these areas has left room for more selective approaches. We also found that the capacity to implement selective approaches has varied across ministries.

Further, we found that selective approaches have been implemented mostly in the latest stage of the crisis. The phasing of the approaches to cutback management resulted from the managerial need for more selective approaches as further rounds of fiscal packages made cuts more and more painful. Furthermore, since 2012 the institution of an inter-ministerial committee conducting spending review has made the leadership of line ministries aware of the need to adopt less incremental approaches (see Chapter 10 on budget processes). It also facilitated the circulation of good practices, guidelines and methodological tools supporting learning. Thus, the "spillover effect" (Barzelay 2003) from spending reviews to cutback management at the level of line ministries constituted a key interaction between budgetary reforms and fiscal retrenchment.

The Effects of Cutbacks on Public Management

We address the impact of the response to the crisis on four dimensions of public management. First, we assess the effects of cutback management in terms of changing composition of the expenditure side. Second, we analyse how cuts in the domain of public employment have contributed to expenditure reduction. We then focus on patterns of governance in their organisational forms. Finally, we examine how the use of performance management techniques has been affected by cutback management.

Expenditure Reduction

Cutback management has contributed to keep the primary surplus high and stable over the past fifteen years, with 2009–10 as the only exception (Table 5.1). However, the reduction of the debt-to-GDP ratio has been held back by the interest burden, the low inflation and the persisting contraction of the economy. The latter has been prolonged by spending control which generated impressive results at the cost of being growth-adverse. In the period 2007–14, investments have fallen substantially (18%) while the current primary expenditure has grown on average as of 1.5% yearly (Corte dei Conti 2016). As a result, in 2013 public investment amounted to 4.7% of total expenditure while the OECD area average was 7.8% (OECD 2015).

The fall of investments has been particularly sharp at the subnational level: in the period 2009–14, the Regions cut investments by 40%, Provinces by 45.8% and Municipalities by 34.2%; as for current expenditure, it has been reduced by Regions (-8%) and Provinces (-24.7%) while it has grown at the municipal level by 1% (Corte dei Conti 2016). The reduction of spending at the subnational level stems from the reduction of transfers from the central government to regions, provinces and municipalities which contributed to centralise spending responsibility: in the period 2009–14, expenditure of central government decreased from 30 to 29.6% of GDP while expenditure of subnational government decreased from 16.5 to 14.7% (European Commission 2015).

The same period displays a hike in the social security expenditure (from 19 to 20.3% of GDP). The latter is driven by outlays for existing pensioners which cannot be revised as stated by the Constitutional Court (Sentence 116/2013). Combined with the interest burden, pension expenditure constitutes a major constraint on the ability of the government to cut spending as it draws savings potentially for other policies, posing a well-known intergenerational dilemma. Linear spending reductions in other areas of the public budget have penalised in the period 2009–14 sectors like recreation, culture and religion (-22,2%), economic affairs (-12,8%), housing and communities (-12,5%), defence (-14,3%) and education (-10,9%).

Public Employment

The target of containing the public payroll in the short-term has been met. As shown by Table 5.4, the freeze of the public employees' compensation and the significant reduction of the number of tenured officials have greatly contributed to the reduction of expenditure in the 2009–14 period. Concerning the size of public employment, it should also be underlined that the number of temporary employees has been substantially cut, from 304,126 to 203,684 units in the period 2007–13 (Ragioneria Generale dello Stato 2014).

The response to the crisis halted the increase of the payroll as percentage of GDP since 2009. As a result of this trend, since 2012 Italy spends

Table 5.4 Italy: Number of Tenured Public Employees, Average Compensation of Public Employee and Compensation of Employees (2007–14)

	2007	2008	2009	2010	2011	2012	2013	2014
Number of tenured public employees*	3.627	3.596	3.559	3.510	3.459	3.390	3.354	3.333
Average compensation of public employee**	32.221	33.650	34.217	34.662	34.371	34.210	34.296	34.286
Compensation of employees***	10.2	10.4	10.9	10.7	10.3	10.3	10.2	10.1

Source: ISTAT (2015)

Note: *Thousands of persons **Current euros ***Percentage of the GDP at current prices.

on public employment per person less than their counterparts in other EU member countries. Even if compared with the first batch of EU member countries over a longer period, Italy appears successful in keeping a public-sector wage bill under control since in 2014 it was 10.1% of GDP against 10.3% of the European Union at 28 (European Commission 2015).

While being effective in satisfying short-term goals of fiscal consolidation, the response to the crisis risks to affect irreparably the quality of public services in the long run. As revealed by the growth of the public employees' average age (from 43,5 years in 2001 to 49,2 years in 2014) and length of service (from 16,5 years in 2001 to 18,5 years in 2014), the containment of public expenditure came at the price of excluding from public employment younger and potentially more qualified prospective candidates. This implied a severe shortage of skills within the public sector: in 2013 only 18% of public employees were graduate, while 34% did not even finish secondary education (Ragioneria Generale dello Stato 2014). As already highlighted by the analysis of cutback management at the level of line ministries, the shortage of skills has implied the overreliance on external experts and advisors.

Organisational Issues

The level of organisational fragmentation has been left substantially unaltered until the advent of the Renzi government. In the latest stage of crisis management, this government centralised the governance of public sector around the Prime Minister Office as well as reducing organisational fragmentation via merger and streamlining of bodies like port authorities, chambers of commerce, forest rangers, prefectures, state-owned enterprises. At the level of line ministries, across-the-board cuts imposed by the cabinet acted as a catalyst sustaining reorganisation where it was already underway.

Performance Management

On the one hand, cutback management has affected performance management: since 2010 cutbacks dried out resources for the implementation of the new performance management system introduced in 2009. On the other hand, cutback management was affected by the implementation gap of performance evaluation systems introduced before the crisis: the lack of robust performance information implied that cutback management could not be evidence-oriented. This was also due to the focus of the budgetary process on the legalist adherence to rules shielding public managers from any scrutiny of their performance (see Chapter 10 on budget processes).

Prolonged freezing of performance management brought discredit on the prospect of modernisation via performance measurement, which has not been put at the centre of the new wave of public management reform launched by the Renzi government at the end of our period of observation. Rather, the emphasis has shifted from New Public Management–inspired tools like performance measurement to a focus on coordination across the public sector.

Concluding Remarks

In the Italian context, marked by protracted political instability and the implementation gap of previous administrative modernisation efforts, cutback management has been focused on across-the-board cuts at the level of cabinet decision-making. Findings show that the combination of prolonged pressure for fiscal retrenchment, familiarity with severe fiscal crisis since 1992 and endless political instability has defined a pattern of path-dependent change by progressively reinforcing across-the-board cuts. In the latest stages of the crisis, however, the cascading approach typical of across-the-board cuts—meaning that the government adopted a top-down approach in determining how much was to be cut without dictating on how to curb expenditure–has been associated with more selective approaches at the level of line ministries in the context of spending reviews undertaken in the field of budgetary reform.

Across-the-board cuts display two features suiting well a political context marked by fragmentation and instability, that is, high frequency of government turnover (Mele and Ongaro 2014). First, the uniformity of cutback measures kept the level of political conflict at a minimum and was well-received by trade unions as the least threatening approach with regard to their own organisational cohesion. Second, the incremental logic of linear cutback measures enabled governments to adopt an endless sequence of rounds of cuts, progressively adapting the crisis response to ever-increasing fiscal pressures. Yet, cuts triggered conflict in front of the Constitutional Court which constituted a significant external constraint to the government's decisions. Further, the sequential adoption of uniform cuts did not make policymakers aware of the cumulated effects of cutback management.

In terms of personnel policies, the major effect of cutback management has been the exclusion of non-unionised younger candidates from public service. With regard to the composition of the expenditure, the effect of cutback management has been the centralisation of spending responsibility coupled with spending reduction affecting sectors crucial for sustaining economic recovery like education. Concerning performance measurement, a prolonged wage freeze has dried out resources for the implementation of the performance management system introduced in 2009. As for the organisational issues, fragmentation has been reduced only in the latest stages in the context of a new wave of public management reform launched by the Renzi government, which adopted a more experimental and mixed approach in the context of a more confrontational stance vis-à-vis the EU in terms of budgetary flexibility. Whether this might mark a depart from the consolidated pattern hitherto observed remains to be seen.

Acknowledgements

The chapter is the result of a common undertaking. However, the sections 'The Italian Context' and 'Austerity Packages' can be directly attributed to Fabrizio Di Mascio; the section 'Cutbacks in Central Government' to Davide Galli; the section 'The Effects of Cutbacks on Public Management' to Alessandro Natalini; and sections 'Introduction' and 'Concluding Remarks' to Edoardo Ongaro.

References

Barzelay, Michael. 2003. "The Process Dynamics of Public Management Policy Making." *International Public Management Journal* 6(3):251–82.
Cassese, Sabino. 1993. "Hypotheses on the Italian Administrative System." *West European Politics* 16(3):316–28.
Corte dei Conti. 2016. *Rapporto sul coordinamento della finanza pubblica.* Rome: Italian Court of Accounts.
Cotta, Maurizio and Luca Verzichelli. 2007. *Political Institutions in Italy.* Oxford: Oxford University Press.
Derlien, Hans-Ulrich and B. Guy Peters. 2008. *The State at Work: Comparative Public Service Systems.* Cheltenham: Edward Elgar.
Di Mascio, Fabrizio and Alessandro Natalini. 2014. "Italy Between Modernization and Spending Cuts." *American Behavioral Scientist* 58(12):1634–56.
Di Mascio, Fabrizio and Alessandro Natalini. 2015. "Fiscal Retrenchment in Southern Europe." *Public Management Review* 17(1):129–48.
Di Mascio, Fabrizio, Alessandro Natalini and Francesco Stolfi. 2013. "Analyzing Reform Sequences to Understand Italy's Response to the Global Crisis." *Public Administration* 91(1):17–31.
Dunsire, Andrew and Christopher Hood. 1989. *Cutback Management in Public Bureaucracies.* Cambridge: Cambridge University Press.
European Commission. 2015. *General Government Data.* Autumn 2015. Brussels: European Commission.
European Commission. 2016. *Country Report Italy 2016, SWD(2016) 81 Final.* Brussels: European Commission.
ISTAT. 2015. *Sintesi dei conti ed aggregati economici delle amministrazioni pubbliche 1995–2014.* Rome: National Institute of Statistics.
Kickert, Walter and Tiina Randma-Liiv. 2015. *Europe Managing the Crisis: The Politics of Fiscal Consolidation.* London: Routledge.
Mele, Valentina and Edoardo Ongaro. 2014. "Public Management Reform in a Context of Political Instability: Italy 1992–2007." *International Public Management Journal* 17(1):1–31.

OECD. 2015. *Government at a Glance.* Paris: OECD.

Ongaro, Edoardo. 2009. *Public Management Reform and Modernization: Trajectories of Administrative Change in Italy, France, Greece, Portugal, Spain.* Cheltenham: Edward Elgar.

Ongaro, Edoardo. 2010. "The Napoleonic Administrative Tradition." In *Tradition and Public Administration,* edited by Martin Painter and B. Guy Peters, 174–89. Basingstoke: Palgrave Macmillan.

Ongaro, Edoardo. 2011. "The Role of Politics and Institutions in the Italian Administrative Reform Trajectory." *Public Administration* 89(3):738–55.

Pierson, Paul. 2004. *Politics in Time: History, Institutions, and Social Analysis.* Princeton: Princeton University Press.

Pollitt, Christopher. 2008. *Time, Policy, Management: Governing With the Past.* Oxford: Oxford University Press.

Pollitt, Christopher. 2010. "Cuts and Reforms." *Society and Economy* 31(1): 17–31.

Quaglia, Lucia. 2009. "The Response to the Global Financial Turmoil in Italy." *South European Society & Politics* 14(1):7–18.

Ragioneria Generale dello Stato. 2014. *Rapporto sulla spesa delle amministrazioni centrali dello Stato.* Rome: Italian Ministry of Finance.

Ragioneria Generale dello Stato. 2010-2015. *Conto annuale del personale.* Rome: Italian Ministry of Finance.

Ragioneria Generale dello Stato. 2010-2016. *Rapporto sulla finanza pubblica.* Rome: Italian Ministry of Finance.

Raudla, Ringa. 2013. "Fiscal Retrenchment in Estonia During the Financial Crisis." *Public Administration* 91(1):32–50.

Zahariadis, Nikolaos. 2013. "Leading Reforms Amidst Transboundary Crises: Lessons From Greece." *Public Administration* 91(3):648–62.

6 Cutback Management in Denmark

Hanne Foss Hansen and Mads Bøge Kristiansen

Denmark was hit hard by the financial crisis and the attendant international recession in 2009. The recession set in after a boom where both the housing market and the labour market were overheated. In spite of improvement, growth has been modest in Denmark since 2009 and six years after the crisis the Danish GDP per inhabitant is still at a lower level than before the crisis.

(De Økonomiske Råd 2016, 8).

Introduction

Denmark is a small, open economy with a large public sector and, accordingly, high taxation. It is organised as a unitary state with ministerial responsibility and a large degree of decentralisation, where local government is responsible for many functions. As illustrated by the chapter opening quote from a recent report by the independent economic advisory body, the Danish Economic Councils, Denmark was hit hard by the financial crises and growth has been modest ever since. On this background, this chapter focuses on how the Danish government responded to the crisis, concentrating especially on the cutbacks in central government. The chapter addresses the following research questions:

1. How did the crisis evolve and what were the main crisis packages?
2. How were cutbacks implemented in central government in Denmark, which cutback strategies and measures were used, and how can we interpret the decision process?
3. What are the consequences of cutbacks to public management?

The analysis is structured in three main sections. First, we present a descriptive analysis of the economic conditions prior to the crisis, the severity of the fiscal crisis and the adoption of different types of crisis packages at the government level. The focus is on the volume of fiscal consolidation and the content of the main crisis packages, including their size.

Hereafter, we change the level of analysis and move from government decisions on crisis packages to the implementation of cutback requirements in ministries. We focus on an initiative entitled 'Efficient Administration' in which expenses for salaries and operating costs were reduced by 2.5% in 2012 and 5% in 2013. There are two reasons for this. First, Efficient Administration was the biggest cutback initiative launched in the Danish central government for many years. Second, by focusing on an across-the-board cutback initiative, we are able to analyse cutback delegation dynamics. Focusing on one initiative means, however, that it becomes more difficult to examine the stages model of cutbacks. We analyse how the cutback initiative was launched and implemented and investigate the cutback strategies and measures used. This part of the analysis draws on concepts developed in the literature on cutback management presented in Chapter 2 and institutional theories, including goal–means rational, interest-based and garbage can perspectives.

After this, we discuss how the cutbacks have affected public organisation and management. Here, we draw on historical institutionalism, discussing whether the crisis has changed or reinforced pre-crisis reform trajectories. Finally, conclusions are drawn.

Methodologically, the overall analysis of the crisis responses is based on documentary material, including key figures for the economic development, government reports and crisis packages introduced by the government. As publicly accessible material on the Efficient Administration initiative is sparse, this part of the analysis is based primarily on interviews carried out in 15 ministries from January to April 2013. The group of informants included a permanent secretary, several heads of divisions, an agency managing director, and heads of departments and employees in departments with responsibility for financial management, budgets and planning. The respondents were asked to describe how the initiative had been implemented and which strategies and measures were used.

The Crisis and the Crisis Packages

As shown in Chapter 3, Denmark was hit relatively hard by the economic crisis in 2008/2009, GDP growth rates dropping more than the EU average. The Danish economy has recovered very slowly since the recession, and the GDP has yet to return to 2007 levels.

From Overheating to Crisis

Before the crisis, a booming real estate market contributed to an overheated Danish economy. The downturn of the housing market intensified the recession, which resulted in falling housing prices, bankruptcies, a bank crisis, falling export and household consumption figures, and increasing unemployment. Prior to the crisis, the fiscal position had been favourable, with budget surpluses of 5% in 2005–07. As a result of the crisis, the budget in 2009 produced a deficit of 2.8%. The surpluses before the crisis had paved the way for a declining debt-to-GDP ratio, reaching a level in 2007 substantially below the EU average. The debt level increased due to the crisis but remains well below the EU average. During the crisis, Danish fiscal policy was conducted in accordance with the EU Recommendation under the Excessive Deficit Procedure, which included a primary requirement to bring the general government budget deficit below 3% of GDP by 2013 and to improve public finances in structural terms by 1.5% of GDP in total (OECD 2011).

Crisis Responses

The Danish crisis responses included a range of initiatives, including bank packages, consumption stimulation, fiscal consolidation and private job creation. The bank packages were aimed at managing the financial crisis, whereas the purpose of stimulating consumption, creating jobs in the private sector and fiscal consolidation was to manage the economic and fiscal crises. This section investigates some of the major crisis responses and fiscal consolidation initiatives (bank packages excluded) adopted in Denmark in the period from 2009 to the recent change of government in 2015. Table 6.1. gives an overview over the main elements in governmental crisis responses.

Table 6.1 Crisis Packages

Year	Crisis Packages and Their Total Estimated Amount Strengthening Public Finances	Main Elements Included in Crisis Packages
2009	Spring Package (tax reform): €0.7 billion in the long run	Income taxes lowered. Excise duties raised. Public finances estimated to be strengthened mainly due to increase in labour supply
2010	Fiscal consolidation agreement: €3.2 billion	Public consumption held in check 2011–13. Targeted and across-the-board savings in central government reallocated. Welfare scheme reform. Labour market and tax reform
2011	Reform Agenda 2020: €3.2 billion Home-Job Plan: €0.6 billion 2011–13 Budget Bill 2012: €0.7 billion in 2013	Welfare scheme reform (e.g. a retirement reform). Defence cuts Stimulation of private job creation through tax cuts financed by cutbacks (targeted and across the board) Increased excise duties. Ceilings for tax-free allowances to pension schemes lowered

Year	Crisis Packages and Their Total Estimated Amount Strengthening Public Finances	Main Elements Included in Crisis Packages
2012	Tax reform: €0.4 billion/ year in the long run	Lowering income taxes
2013	Growth Plan DK: €1.6 billion 2013–20	Improve conditions for private companies, improve educational attainment and employment, public sector reform and fiscal sustainability (freeing up resources for political prioritisation)
2014	Growth Package 2014	Initiatives to strengthen competiveness in the private sector

In 2009 a *tax reform* was adopted to strengthen public finances over the long term by around €0.7 billion,[1] mainly due to a higher labour supply (Regeringen 2009; 2010a, 6).

A major consolidation initiative was introduced in May 2010 when the government (the Liberal and Conservative parties) and the Danish People's Party agreed on measures to consolidate public finances towards 2013. The *fiscal consolidation agreement* was adopted in order to comply with the EU recommendation mentioned earlier. The agreement was a compound package containing both across-the-board and targeted savings as well as labour market and tax reforms containing consolidation initiatives corresponding to 1.25% of GDP.

The main element was that growth in public consumption (in real terms) was held in check in 2011–13. Relative to previous spending plans, this resulted in savings of €1.4 billion. Within the spending level, the agreement included a switch in spending priorities for a total of €1.3 billion. The budget for welfare services in the municipalities remained unchanged at 2010 budget levels in real terms. In central government, across-the-board savings of ministry operating costs of 0.5% per year in 2011 were implemented. A series of targeted central government savings were also implemented, including certain educational and cultural activities. Development aid was also kept at 2010 nominal levels and child benefits were reduced. The targeted and general savings were reallocated notably towards health, education and initiatives for vulnerable groups (Regeringen 2010b). The fiscal consolidation agreement also included tax reform elements. Finally, the duration of the unemployment benefit period was reduced from four to two years, and requirements for previous employment to be eligible for unemployment benefits were changed (Regeringen 2010b).

The fiscal consolidation agreement was argued to be the first step towards fiscal consolidation. In 2011, *Reform Agenda 2020* followed up on this and presented further initiatives to tackle the remaining part of the challenge to achieve structural fiscal balance by 2020. This package included a proposal for retirement reform gradually abolishing opportunities for voluntary early retirement and postponing old age pension, which was estimated to handle the bulk of the consolidation challenge (€2.4 billion). The package also introduced limitations on student grants, disability pensions and the flex-jobs scheme. The remainder of the challenge was handled by savings in the area of defence from 2015 (€0.3 billion) (Regeringen 2011).

Reform Agenda 2020 also included an initiative aimed at the further stimulation of private job creation financed by central government cost savings, as the government—together with the Danish People's Party, the Social Democrats, the Socialist People's Party and the Christian Democratic Party—agreed on the so-called Home-Job Plan. Planned to run from June 2011 until the end of 2013, it aimed at stimulating renovation work in private homes. The government expected the scheme to cost €119 million in 2011, increasing to €0.3 billion in 2013. When launched, the plan was to be financed largely through savings on costs in the field of active labour market policies, savings on activities in the work environment field, savings related to procurement, and across-the-board cost savings in central government fixed at 2.5% in 2012 and 5% in 2013.

Only a few months after deciding on the Home-Job Plan, a general election was called. In October 2011, a new government headed by the Social Democrats and including the Social Liberals and Socialist People's Party was formed. The new government started by blaming its predecessor that it had irresponsibly used excessive resources on public consumption. In this way, it tried to limit voters' expectations regarding their ability to roll back the former government's fiscal consolidation initiatives. Otherwise, the new government continued most of the former government's initiatives. However, the new government also introduced a fiscal stimulus package aimed at supporting growth and employment in 2012 via *increased investment*. As part of efforts to 'kick-start' the Danish economy, €1.5 billion in 2012 and €1.1 billion in 2013 were agreed upon. Early retirement contributions (to a now defunct scheme) were also released in order to stimulate private consumption. Consequently, the structural budget deficit in 2012 exceeded that which was presented in the 'fiscal consolidation agreement' of May 2010 (OECD 2012), increasing the consolidation effort required in 2013.

Compared to the previous government's consolidation plan, the 2011–15 plan for 2012 and 2013 relied more on increased taxes and excise duties, which were increased permanently with the Budget Bill for 2012 by €0.7 billion (OECD 2012; Regeringen 2012, 34).

In June 2012, an agreement on yet another *tax reform* was adopted, including reduced income taxes (with €1.8 billion towards 2022). The tax cut was financed by targeted savings in central government, reducing the Danish contribution to the EU (€0.1 billion) and adjusting transfer payments (Finansministeriet 2012).

In 2013, *Growth Plan DK* was launched. The key objectives were to strengthen economic growth towards 2020 by €5.3 billion, corresponding to 2% of GDP to create jobs in the private sector and to secure fiscal sustainability (Regeringen 2013a, 11–12; 2013b). *Growth Plan DK* included three reform tracks: *Reform Track 1* included measures to improve the business environment and enhance competitiveness, including a reduction of the corporation tax from 25 to 22%. *Reform Track 2* included initiatives to enhance education attainment and new reforms aimed at increasing structural employment (Regeringen 2014). Reform tracks 1 and 2 were to each contribute €2.6 billion to growth towards 2020. Finally, *Reform Track 3* concerned a 'modernisation' effort. Freeing up €1.6 billion towards 2020 via efficiency gains would render it possible to improve public services in high-priority areas. This effort is equivalent to an annual efficiency improvement of 0.3% in 2013–20 (Regeringen 2013b, 4–6). Numerous well-known initiatives, such as procurement, digitisation and cutting red tape, de-bureaucratisation and rule simplification, were mentioned as means to obtain this efficiency improvement.

Following up on *Growth Plan DK*, a new *Growth Package 2014* containing 89 initiatives was introduced in 2014 in order to strengthen the competiveness of private companies related primarily to *Reform Track 1* but also *Reform Track 2* presented earlier.[2]

The June 2015 general election resulted in a change of government. A new minority government with a cabinet composed solely of the Liberal Party (Venstre) assumed office. This government also started off by blaming its predecessor for not having been economically accountable, which was used as a background for initiating further cutback initiatives.

Summing up, the analysis shows how Denmark met the crisis with a broad range of crisis responses. The crisis packages included reductions of operating costs, but the main element in the estimated long-run consolidation amounts were contributions from the reform of welfare schemes related to retirement, unemployment benefits, disability, student grants etc. Welfare reform aimed at preparing Denmark for a new demographic situation was part of the reform trajectory prior to the crisis, but the crisis provided opportunity to advance and increase the reform intensity. Furthermore, the resources obtained through reforms and cutbacks in the public sector were often allocated to increased public investment, education expenditure (until 2015), lower taxes on labour and business, stimulation of renovation in private homes etc., which was intended to increase the growth potential and strengthen the labour supply. Cutbacks directed towards both central government and local government have included across-the-board savings (cheese slicing), managerial savings (efficiency gains) as well as targeted savings (strategic prioritisations). Although a range of austerity measures have been activated in Denmark during the crisis, many of the measures were also in use before the crisis. The main difference before and during the crisis seems to be that measures have been given another turn; for example, that requirements for across-the-board savings have been significantly increased.

Cutback Management in Danish Central Government

After this presentation of the content of the main crisis packages in central government, we now change the level of analysis and move from government decisions to the implementation of cutback requirements in ministries. As mentioned earlier, the focus is on the Efficient Administration cutback initiative, reducing central government expenses for salaries and operating costs by 2.5% in 2012 and 5% in 2013. In the following discussions, we present the background for this initiative and analyse the implementation process, including the strategies and measures chosen. Finally, we discuss how to interpret the cutback management decision processes.

The Cutback Initiative: Background and Content

The starting point for the initiative initially named 'Focused Administration' was a cheese-slicing strategy presenting every ministry with a common saving requirement. In the description of the initiative, however, it was announced that the ministries had to implement the cutbacks through efficiency gains and prioritisations.

Furthermore, the stage was set for selecting cutback initiatives based on a thorough analytical process. The ministries were ordered to work out action plans and prepare strategies including goals for efficiency improvements and priorities based on a mapping of existing tasks and cost structures (Rigsrevisionen 2013). Finally, the government should take a stand on the specific strategies in the autumn of 2011 (Finansministeriet 2011).

Shortly after the political agreement in May 2011, a general election led to a new government in October 2011. This created ambiguity, as it was unclear whether the cutback plan would be continued. The new government decided to continue the cutback initiative but renamed it Efficient Administration.

The new government made a number of changes to the ministries' respective fields of responsibilities (as is customary in Denmark). This meant that some of the ministries' planned savings could no longer be achieved, as the branches that should have borne substantial parts of them were moved to other ministries. For some ministries, this meant that after the change of government, they almost had to start over again by deciding on their action plan. These delays meant that several ministries did not present their action plans to the government economic committee before February 2012, after which they could implement the specific cutback initiatives, carry out workforce reductions etc.

Although Efficient Administration amounted to considerable cutback requirements, the interview data reveals that these requirements were not in themselves the challenge. The challenge was that Efficient Administration was added to a range of other cutback requirements, including the fiscal consolidation agreement as well as requirements for specific cutbacks related to improving efficiency in procurement and the use of, for example, energy and consultants. Some ministries were also affected by sector-specific cutback requirements and, in some cases, the cessation of temporary appropriations or declining income in areas financed by fees or commercial activities. Finally, it has been usual practice since the 1980s to include a general financial contribution of 2% for reprioritisation in the annual budget. Individually, these cutback requirements do not seem particularly comprehensive; put together and accumulated over time, however, they became considerable. A calculation done by the National Audit Office in 2013 showed that only 45% of the total decline in the ministries' appropriations in 2012 was a consequence of Efficient Administration. The rest was due to other cutbacks (Rigsrevisionen 2013, 37).

While the different cutback initiatives can be distinguished from each other when they are perceived as political initiatives, this is not possible when they are to be implemented. At the organisational level, the requirements melt together; summed up, they were experienced as very challenging. Several of the informants described the situation as standing at the top of 'budget cliffs'.

Implementation: Cutback Strategies and Measures Used

In order to work out action plans, the ministries organised steering committees and working groups to identify the potential for savings and initiatives that might redeem the cutbacks. The reason given for organising in this manner was that the cutbacks were so considerable that they could not be handled using ordinary cheese-slicing measures. The informants experienced a need for a more substantial analysis and described the situation as a window for a different kind of thinking than the typical minor cutbacks.

The processes were managed from the top. The preparation for proposing cutbacks was usually handled by a working group in the budget and financial departments in the parent ministry, which gathered proposals from the agencies, whereas the corporate management usually operated as a steering committee. In some instances, the managing directors in the agencies were asked to deliver cutback proposals. The collection of proposals was organised differently in the various ministries, varying from a relatively closed, top-down managed process to a more open and involving one. Some ministries invited consultants in to identify potential savings (e.g. through the benchmarking of office rental costs or administrative overhead).

This work resulted in a catalogue of cutback proposals containing the total portfolio of various possible initiatives. On this basis, the corporate management or the steering committee prioritised between the initiatives based on criteria, such as technical/practical and political opportunities for implementation.

The civil servants were in charge of the process and the ministers first became involved later. The presentation of the action plans for the ministers only led to adjustments in a few cases, probably because the most politically controversial initiatives were deleted from the action plan before it was presented and because the cutback initiatives were largely presented as efficiency improvements.

Before the action plans were presented in the government economic committee, their content was negotiated between the Ministry of Finance and the line ministries (in some cases between the permanent secretaries of the ministries). These discussions aimed at ensuring that the specific initiatives were clearly specified. As mentioned, the plan was for the government to take a stand on the ministries' specific strategies. If the ambition was for the government economic committee to grant priority to certain strategies, this did not happen. As some of the informants argued, the process became more pragmatic and less political.

In Table 6.2., we have used the typology presented in Chapter 2 (Table 2.2) to categorise the cutback strategies used on a smaller or bigger scale. The empirical data shows how all nine cutback strategies in the typology were used. The ministries used strategies related to a cost-saving logic, a reorganisation logic and a programme logic, and they worked with incremental, managerial and strategic approaches. Efficient

Table 6.2 Chosen Cutback Strategies

Logic of Strategies / Process of Change	Cost-Saving Logic	Reorganisation Logic	Programme Logic
Incremental	1. Cheese-slicing: • Efficient Administration at the start • Hiring freeze	4. Resetting reform elements: • Minor reorganisations as a continuation of previous reorganisation initiatives. e.g. shared-service initiatives	7. Reduction of services, e.g. printing fewer publications, shortening office hours or telephone hours, reducing inspections

Logic of Strategies / Process of Change	Cost-Saving Logic	Reorganisation Logic	Programme Logic
Managerial	2. Assessing potential for savings or efficiency gains through business cases: • Reduced office rental costs • Renegotiation of IT contracts	5. Intra- and inter-organisational reorganisation: • Mergers and shared-service initiatives (to a smaller extent simplification of rules and clearer distribution of tasks)	8. Innovation of inspection routines to become more risk-based
Strategic	3. Substantial savings • Some agencies and organisations	6. Systems redesign • Limited. Some of the agency mergers might, however, appear to be of more strategic character over time	9. Strategic prioritising and cutting away tasks, e.g. shutting down a legal gazette, a smaller museum etc.

Source: Hansen and Kristiansen (2014: 246)

Administration clearly took its point of departure in cell 1, and almost all of the ministries also started by establishing hiring freezes. The main part of the initiative was, however, implemented on the basis of strategies related to other cells. Most initiatives can be placed in cells 2, 5 and 8, which represent the managerial savings.

A range of similarities in the cutback strategies chosen can be identified across the ministries. Of the 15 ministries examined, 12 implemented cutbacks through mergers, 11 through shared-service initiatives in which support functions were centralised in joint corporate units for HR, communication, finance etc., and 11 by savings related to office rental costs. Different kinds of organisational mergers were implemented; big agencies were merged into even bigger ones, smaller institutes were integrated into bigger agencies, and regional units were merged. Mergers provide potential savings on technical structure, support functions and salaries for the higher management levels. Partly due to these reorganisation strategies, approximately 1,000 employees were dismissed in total (Hjortdal and Klarskov 2012). Moreover, unfilled vacancies were frozen and voluntary resignation (e.g. early retirement) was applied.

Several ministries also chose to achieve savings based on the programme logic by 'targeting' their inspections and regulations by introducing more risk-based regulation.

Many of the ministries also reduced service levels in different ways, depending on the nature of their specific operations: fewer publications were printed, opening hours and the number of inspections was reduced etc. Two ministries opted to boost their income by increasing their fee levels as a minor part of their general strategy (however based on an argument related to underfunded fees). Other ministries had considered this strategy but declined, deeming it to be politically unrealistic.

Finally, half of the ministries provided examples of cuts to services and programmes. These typically produced limited savings, such as shutting down a legal gazette produced by the Danish state, closing down a smaller museum and so forth. On a larger scale, numerous diplomatic representations were shut down. This would probably have been implemented irrespective of the cutback requirements in Efficient Administration, as it was part of a comprehensive strategic shift in the Ministry of Foreign Affairs. When Efficient Administration was launched, however, it was possible to include some of the savings related to the closures in the ministry's plan.

In some ministries, the savings derived from the initiatives in the action plan did not sum up to the overall savings requirement. These ministries returned to the cheese-slicer, sending the demand down through the ministerial organisation in order to achieve the remainder of the required savings. This did not necessarily mean that the cutback dynamic ended in cheese-slicing; as some informants argued, it would be transformed locally into a range of specific cutback strategies.

Summing up, the number of initiatives actually cutting away or reducing services is much less extensive than initiatives aiming at efficiency gains through reorganisation. In this manner, savings can be realised without too much pain, as they are presented as less unpleasant and more technical (Pollitt 2010). In practice, however, it is quite difficult to distinguish between efficiency gains and service reductions; that which is said to be an efficiency gain resulting from the implementation of a shared-service initiative might be experienced as a service deterioration and/or reduction. The dismissal of administrative employees might result in other employees having to take care of the associated tasks, thereby leaving less time for core activities.

Interpreting Cutback Management Decision-Making and Implementation Processes

There are several possible interpretations as to why the government decided to finance much of the Home-Job Plan using across-the-board cuts. First, the decision can be interpreted as a path-dependency autopilot reaction, as such strategies had been used repeatedly over the years (e.g. through the annually 2% financial contribution in the annual budget for repriorites). Second, it may be seen as the possible reaction in a situation where a financing solution had to be decided on quickly. One might argue that there was limited time to carry out overall analyses in order to decide on targeted strategies. Third, it may be seen as an appropriate way to delegate cutbacks to each ministry, as Danish central government is based on a 'resort principle' of ministerial government in which ministers are individually accountable to the parliament. Finally, the decision may be interpreted in a blame perspective reflecting how central decision makers, the politicians and probably also the Ministry of Finance were unwilling to take the blame for targeted cutbacks of this magnitude. The use of a general, across-the-board strategy would decentralise unpleasant decisions.

The political decision became an implementation challenge for the ministries. The Ministry of Finance pushed for the implementation of Efficient Administration in line with a rational approach to decision-making in which cutback initiatives in the ministries were to be decided on the basis of a rational-goal model. The solutions with the greatest potential for efficiency improvements and/or being less destructive for the organisations' goal attainment ought to be found. Central informants in the ministries also described their roles as promoting this kind of thinking, establishing steering and working groups and identifying potential savings by mapping existing activities on the basis of which the corporate management group could decide on which initiatives were technically and politically possible for implementation. Due to the Danish labour market model having been built on flexicurity,[3] and with wages determined by collective agreements between employers' associations and unions, hiring freezes and layoffs were the measures possible in relation to employees, whereas pay freezes and pay reductions do not offer legitimate solutions in Denmark in the short run.[4]

Despite this seemingly rational process, the interviews appear to indicate that this kind of thinking was challenged by actors acting to promote their own interests. The cutback exercise started interest games, which were attempts at securing their own tasks and resources, avoid mergers etc. Interest games thrived under the surface.

As shown, similar cutback initiatives were observed in the different ministries. Organisational solutions in the form of mergers, shared-service initiatives and the reduction of office rental costs already in use in some ministries before the crisis were seen as solutions to meet the cutback requirements and seemed to be popular management ideas (Meyer and Rowan 1977; DiMaggio and Powell 1983; Røvik 2007): 'centralisation was something we knew and thought had a potential for savings, and therefore we continued along this path'.

Despite the similarities across the ministries, there were also differences between them, partly reflecting how they dealt with distinct cutback requirements and had different starting points. Inter-ministerial variation can also partly be interpreted as a result of differences in the form of cutback readiness. Some had already carried out analyses of their cost structures, while others had to start more or less from scratch by establishing an oversight over cost structures and activities. Furthermore, some ministries had just concluded a cost-saving drive in which mergers had been implemented. These ministries argued that it was not possible to achieve further savings via this kind of cutback strategy, which was why they were more inclined to cut services. This cutback dynamic might be interpreted on the basis of Jørgensen's (1981, see also Chapter 2) stage-model for cutbacks. As the savings from incremental cutback strategies decline over time, policymakers and managers will tend to move to managerial-style cutbacks. But even these strategies have limits and they will move on to strategic decisions at some point.

Finally, the broader context surrounding the cutback exercise and the rational, interest-based and popular management ideas may be interpreted through a perspective focusing on garbage can decision-making (Cohen, March and Olsen 1972; March 1988). The first accidental coupling of streams occurred when the Home-Job Plan was launched and the decision was made that it was to be partly financed by across-the-board savings in central government. These cutbacks came as a surprise to the ministries, and the informants describe the process as characterised by ambiguity, which was further exacerbated by the general election interrupting it. The general election was followed by changes to the ministerial portfolios, the replacement of permanent secretaries, ambiguity related to the requirements for the presentation of the action plans for the government's economic committee etc. Despite this ambiguity, attempts were made at handling the process in a rational manner in order to bring order to chaos. The ambiguity created a 'window of opportunity' for several ministries to implement changes and for coupling more strategic plans and larger organisational changes to the cutback initiative. As the informants expressed it, all of the good ideas that had been sitting on the shelf were put to use.

Summing up, the decision-making and implementation process would appear to involve a complex interplay of processes that can be interpreted on the basis of different theoretical interpretations. There is path-dependency along with attempts at managing the cutbacks in a rational manner. But the rationale is disturbed and interrupted, and the entire process is characterised by considerable ambiguity. Actors try to promote their own narrow interests to defend their own budget and avoid cutbacks, and ambiguity increases the attention towards popular management ideas.

Consequences of Cutbacks to Public Management

The rise of cutback management has had numerous different consequences for public management. In the following, we discuss the consequences on public-sector development, including personnel policy, organisational restructuring and performance measurement, focusing on whether pre-crisis reform trajectories have been reinforced or changed.

Personnel Policy and Limits to Growth

Overall the cutback initiatives have contributed to bringing the growth of the public sector to a standstill. In Table 6.3, this is illustrated by the development in the number of staff in the public sector after the crisis.

The table shows how the growth in the central government has been slowed and nearly stabilised at 2010 levels. It also reveals how public-sector growth generally continued until 2010 but has since fallen off, indicating that the municipalities have borne the primary drop in staff.

Historically, civil servants have largely benefitted from having special statutory employment protection and special pension rights (*tjenest-emænd*). This tradition has gradually changed over a long period, and the number of civil servants with special protection and rights is now limited and steadily declining, unique to areas such as the police. The public-sector labour market is increasingly coming to resemble the private sector. Cutback management has reinforced this reform trajectory. Dismissals have become a kind of 'new normal' and seem to be used in some areas to renew the workforce, replacing older (expensive) personnel with younger (cheaper) staff. In the wake of the dismissals following the implementation of Efficient Administration, some of the unions claimed to be able to document an overrepresentation of senior staff among the dismissed (e.g. Bøgelund and Arre 2016). Moreover, in the wake of the crisis, agreements concerning working conditions have been changed in some areas, giving management greater flexibility to organise working hours more individually with staff. The public employers appear to be taking a tougher stance than previously (Hansen and Mailand 2013).

Organisational Restructuring: Recentralisation and Integration

On the organisational dimension, the solutions chosen in cutback management, such as mergers and shared-service initiatives, have increased centralisation and integration, which reinforces the pre-crisis reform trajectory (Hansen 2011; Hansen and Andersen 2011). As centralisation initiatives accumulate over time, however, it has become ever clearer in recent years that this is a rather dramatic change compared to the 1980s and 1990s, where organisational autonomy under responsibility in line with the NPM doctrine was a key concern. In this manner, the increased vertical and horizontal integration can be interpreted as quite different compared to prior reform trajectories.

With the most recent Danish government, however, this logic has shifted once more. The efficiency-through-centralisation administrative policy strategy driven by the civil servants has become challenged by a governmental relocation plan, moving some 4,000 central government jobs out of the Copenhagen area. As all ministries must deliver to this

Table 6.3 Number of Staff in Central Government and the Public Sector in Total (Full Time Equivalents, 1st Quarter)

	2008	2009	2010	2011	2012	2013	2014	2015	2016
Number of staff in central government	165,320	170,308	173,551	174,956	173,333	174,200	173,831	173,432	173,940
Number of staff in public sector in total	712,502	730,185	745,559	738,483	725,979	723,309	724,659	722,873	716,048

Source: Statistics Denmark (2016).

agenda, a number of the former merged agencies are now being split up. Moreover, some of the merged agencies have already been divided again in order to enhance attention to special tasks. Thus, the pendulum (Aucoin 1990) may already start swinging back towards more tightly focused, specialised organisations.

Performance Measurement: Benchmarking as a Strategy for Improving Efficiency

During the implementation of Efficient Administration, decision makers in the Ministry of Finance found that managers in several ministries lacked information and transparency concerning cost structures. Consequently, a central government performance measurement system has been established introducing cross-cutting key performance indicators that benchmark agencies and ministries on items such as rental costs, administrative costs and wage costs. This has been intended to improve transparency and the basis for internal priorities in measures targeting efficiency and productivity. Benchmarking is hardly a new phenomenon in administrative policy, but a new institutional layer has been added to the existing systems in central government trying to force ministries and agencies to adapt to the best performers.

Conclusion and Discussion

This chapter has cast light on how the Danish government responded to the crisis through crisis packages, including growth initiatives and cutbacks. Numerous different fiscal consolidation measures and cutback initiatives have been used, including the reform of income transfers and cash benefits and increased excise duties. Savings on public expenditure have also been an important austerity measure, including general savings (cheese slicing), managerial savings (efficiency gains) and targeted savings (strategic prioritisation). While many different austerity measures were activated during the economic and fiscal crisis, most of them were already in use prior to the crisis; they were simply used more in the wake of the crisis.

The analysis of the Efficient Administration cutback initiative revealed that the cutbacks overall were decided as cheese-slicing initiatives. But when cutback requirements were delegated to lower levels, they became implemented through efficiency gains and strategies giving priority to core tasks. Cutbacks were implemented via mergers, shared-service initiatives and reduced office rents, which also involved the layoff of civil servants.

The political decision to make across-the-board cuts may be interpreted as a path-dependent reaction but also as a way to delegate and avoid blame for unpleasant decisions. Attempt was made to implement the cutbacks on the basis of clear goals–means rationality, but decisions were influenced by what was viewed as technically and politically feasible. At the same time, uncertainty, interest games and the stream of popular management ideas influenced cutback decisions.

The cutbacks had an impact on public management institutions. Personnel management has become tougher. Centralisation increased as both vertical and horisontal integration have been strengthened. Budget guardians gained power, intensifying centralisation in the hierarchy of delegation. Economic management has come to the forefront. New benchmarking practices have been established and have added to the existing performance measurement systems. Although the analysis reveals a range of changes to public management institutions, the pattern of change is primarily reinforcements and further layers added to the pre-crisis reform trajectories. Especially the changes towards further integration appear rather radical compared to the decentralisation reforms in the 1980s and 1990s, but it has been a slow and gradual pattern of development moving in the direction of a higher degree of centralisation and integrated public management.

Generally speaking, the consequences of crisis responses and cutback initiatives have been that public-sector growth has been slowed down and stabilised. According to the government, the plan is to stick to this policy in the coming years (Finansministeriet 2016). The government therefore seems to have little leeway unless it is able to release funds for new priorities, which is why budgets are being 'vacuumed' in order to establish space for political prioritisation and new initiatives. This has recently resulted in cutbacks in education, research and development aid together with the implementation of an effectiveness programme for local government. Cutback management appears to have come to stay.

Notes

1   All amounts have been calculated using the exchange rate of 13 July 2016 (€100 = DKK 756.79).
2   One example of an initiative related to Reform Track 2 was the introduction of a general model for dimensioning higher education programmes according to labour market demands, which is expected to result in cuts to higher education in the coming years.
3   Flexicurity refers to a welfare state model that combines labour market flexibility and employee security, meaning that it is rather easy for employers to dismiss staff (also in the public sector) and that the unemployment benefits covering the transition period between jobs has historically been favourable compared to many other countries.
4   However, the development in real wages has been negative for some years due to a regulation mechanism linking the development in wages in the public sector to the development of wages in the private sector. This mechanism can be said to have worked as a hidden austerity measure (Mailand and Hansen 2016, 235).

References

Aucoin, Peter. 1990. "Administrative Reforms in Public Management: Paradigms, Principles, Paradoxes and Pendulums." *Governance* 3(2):115–37.

Bøgelund, Eva and Mikkel Arre. 2016. "De Ældste Djøfere Ryger Først Ud." *DJØF Bladet* (6), 29 March 2016.

Cohen, Michael D., James G. March and Johan P. Olsen. 1972. "A Garbage Can Model of Organizational Choice." *Administrative Science Quarterly* 17(1):1–25.

Det Økonomiske Råd. 2016. *Dansk Økonomi, Forår 2016.* Copenhagen: De Økonomiske Råd.

DiMaggio, Paul J. and Walter W. Powell. 1983. "The Iron Cage Revisited: Institutional Isomorphism and Collective Rationality in Organizational Fields." *American Sociological Review* 48(2):147–60.

Finansministeriet. 2011. "BoligJobPlan: Fradrag for Hjælp og Istandsættelse i Hjemmet." www.fm.dk/nyheder/pressemeddelelser/2011/05/20110518-bolig jobplan/~/media/Files/Nyheder/Pressemeddelelser/2011/05/BoligJobplan/Bol igJobplan aftale.ashx.

Finansministeriet. 2012. "Aftale om Skattereform." June 2012. www.fm.dk/ nyheder/pressemeddelelser/2012/06/endelig-aftale-om-skattereform.

Finansministeriet. 2016. *Økonomisk Redegørelse.* May 2016. Copenhagen: Rosendahl a/s.

Hansen, Hanne F. 2011. "NPM in Scandinavia." In *The Ashgate Research Companion to New Public Management*, edited by Tom Christensen and Per Lægreid, 113–29. Farnham: Ashgate.

Hansen, Hanne Foss and Mads Kristiansen. 2014. "Styring af besparelser." In *Offentlig Styring: Forandring i krisetider*, edited by Caroline Howard Grøn, Hanne Foss Hansen and Mads Kristiansen, 227–56. Copenhagen: Hans Reitzels.

Hansen, Morten B. and Vibeke N. Andersen. 2011. "Denmark." In *Government Agencies: Practices and Lessons From 30 Countries*, edited by Koen Verhoest, Sandra van Thiel, Geert Bouckaert and Per Lægreid, 212–22. Basingstoke: Palgrave Macmillan.

Hansen, Nana W. and Mikkel Mailand. 2013. "Public Service Employment Relations in an Era of Austerity: The Case of Denmark." *European Journal of Industrial Relations* 19(4):375–89.

Hjortdal, Marie and Kristian Klarskov. 2012. "Regeringen Gennemfører Historisk Massefyring." *Politiken*, August 26. http://politiken.dk/indland/politik/ ECE1732343/regeringen-gennemfoerer-historisk-massefyring/.

Jørgensen, Torben B. 1981. *Når Staten Skal Spare: Et Studie i Politiske og Administrative Problemer Med at Fordele Besparelser.* Copenhagen: Nyt fra Samfundsvidenskaberne.

Mailand, Mikkel and Nana W. Hansen. 2016. "Denmark and Sweden: The Consequences of Reform and Economic Crisis for Public Service Employment Relations." In *Public Service Management and Employment Relations in Europe: Emerging From the Crisis*, edited by Steven Bach and Lorenzo Bordogna, 218–43. New York: Routledge.

March, James G. 1988. "The Technology of Foolishness." In *Decisions and Organizations*, edited by James G. March, 253–65. Oxford: Basil Blackwell.

Meyer, John W. and Brian Rowan. 1977. "Institutionalized Organizations: Formal Structure as Myth and Ceremony." *American Journal of Sociology* 83(2):340–63.

OECD. 2011. *Restoring Public Finances, 93–97.* Paris: OECD Publishing.

OECD. 2012. *Restoring Public Finances,* 2012 Update, 102–107. Paris: OECD Publishing. http://dx.doi.org/10.1787/9789264179455–12-en.

Pollitt, Christopher. 2010. *Public Management Reform During Financial Austerity.* Stockholm: Statskontoret.

Regeringen. 2009. "Forårspakke 2.0." The Danish Government, February 2009.

Regeringen. 2010a. "Denmark's Convergence Programme 2009." The Danish Government, February 2010.

Regeringen. 2010b. "Fiscal Consolidation Agreement: English Summary", October 2010.

Regeringen. 2011. "Denmark's Convergence Programme 2011." The Danish Government, May 2011.

Regeringen. 2012. "The National Reform Programme. Denmark 2012." The Danish Government, April 2012.

Regeringen. 2013a. "Vækstplan DK: stærke virksomheder, flere job." The Danish Government, February 2013.

Regeringen. 2013b. "Convergence Programme: Denmark 2013." The Danish Government, April 2013.

Regeringen. 2014. "Convergence Programme: Denmark 2014." The Danish Government, April 2014.

Rigsrevisionen. 2013. *Beretning til Statsrevisorerne om Revisionen af Statsregnskabet for 2012.* Copenhagen: Rigsrevisionen. www.rigsrevisionen.dk/media/1943109/rs-2012.pdf.

Røvik, Kjell A. 2007. *Trender og Translasjoner, Ideer som Former det 21. Århundrets Organisasjon.* Oslo: Universitetsforlaget.

Statistics Denmark. 2016. "Statbank Denmark." www.statistikbanken.dk/stat bank5a/default.asp?w=1680.

7 Cutback Management in Ireland in the Wake of the Financial Crisis

Muiris MacCarthaigh and Niamh Hardiman

Introduction

Ireland was one of the European states most severely affected by the financial crisis. A number of official reports into the causes of that crisis (Honohan 2010; Regling and Watson 2010; Independent Review Panel 2011; Nyberg 2011; Houses of the Oireachtas 2016) have pointed to a combination of domestic contributing factors, including weak regulation of financial institutions, weak state capacity and pro-cyclical fiscal policies adopted by successive governments from the late 1990s. The crisis resulted in one of the world's largest ever state-backed bank guarantees and a subsequent 'bailout' loan from the Troika of the IMF, EU and ECB in late 2010. Also as a consequence of this crisis, the 2008–15 period was defined by an unprecedented series of cutbacks in the Irish public service, as part of a broader strategy to reassert control of the state's finances.

The political choices and ideological debates surrounding the trajectory of administrative reforms undertaken during this period, are considered elsewhere (Hardiman and MacCarthaigh 2016). Instead, this chapter unpacks the Irish cutback management response to the financial crisis using a public management lens in order to identify a number of distinctive cutback phases over 2008–15. The chapter analyses the main features of the governments' strategic orientation to fiscal retrenchment and presents the wide range of reforms introduced to work patterns and terms and conditions of public-sector employment. The chapter concludes that the crisis can be viewed as a critical juncture in the state's trajectory of public management reform. Furthermore, the contention is that budgetary retrenchment followed an 'orthodox' line more heavily based on spending cuts than on tax increases. And while this might have been expected to generate widespread resistance and protest, the Irish government combined a strategy of tough budget management with broad-based efforts to secure consent, or at least quiescence, from the key target groups affected by budget measures.

Central to the Irish story has been the careful management of industrial relations between government and trade unions, and the consolidation of reform efforts in a single ministry—the Department of Public Expenditure and Reform (DPER)—over the 2011–16 period. The creation of the department provided a distinctive critical juncture in the Irish experience of cutback management. The data used to inform this chapter comes from official as well as academic sources, complemented by information derived from a set of 61 semi-structured interviews undertaken by MacCarthaigh with senior civil servants over the 2013–15 period for a fellowship project on the work of DPER.

The chapter proceeds as follows. The next section presents contextual data concerning the size and cost of the Irish administration, before and during the period of the crisis. Following this, the strategies used to manage the cutback process are identified by phase: emergency responses (2008–10), strategic cuts (2011–13) and stabilisation and development (2014–15). The final section collates the main findings and suggests lessons from the Irish case of cutback management.

The Crisis, Austerity and Cutbacks in Ireland

The Irish economy grew rapidly in the decade prior to and including 2007, with very positive year-on-year GDP growth rates. Boyle and Mulreany (2015) note that while improvements in productivity and competitiveness defined the Irish economic growth during the 1990s, much of the growth between 2001 and 2007 was fueled by credit flows between the banking and constructions sectors. This in turn led to a sharp collapse in GDP arising from a combination of domestic financial, banking and economic crises triggered by the wider global crisis profiled in Chapter 1.

During the pre-crisis decade, government revenues consistently exceeded government expenditure, due in large part to a construction sector-led economic expansion. Pro-cyclical fiscal policies facilitated annual public expenditure growth of around 10%, with much of the growth consumed by a growing public sector in the form of rising pay and increasing personnel. Transfer spending on a range of welfare benefits also increased steadily during this period. Between 2000 and 2008, the numbers working in the public service had increased by 30% (Department of Public Expenditure and Reform 2014a, 5). The cost of the public service had in large part increased due to pay increases successfully negotiated by trade unions in the context of triennial 'social partnership' agreements with government. These increases affected all parts of the public service, and contributed to wage rises in the private sector also.

The subsequent economic slowdown from 2007 was not mirrored by a commensurate reining in of public expenditure, leading to a large structural deficit opening up from this period. As Figure 7.1. illustrates, the rapid growth in public spending continued into 2009, before entering a period of retrenchment. As the gap quickly opened up between revenue

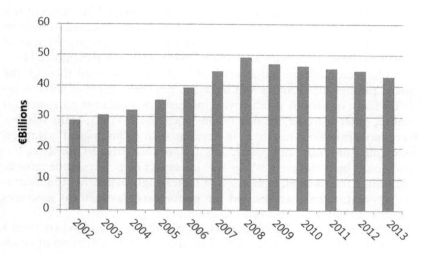

Figure 7.1 Current Government Spending (Pay and Non-Pay, Gross), 2002–13

and expenditure, the government was forced to look to international bond markets to fund its immediate current spending needs.

Consequently, the two Irish governments which held office over the period of retrenchment (from 2007–11 and 2011–16, respectively) drove a programme of 'shrinking' the state. The following section outlines the backdrop against which they did this.

Cutback Management in Irish Central Government

On the eve of the crisis, the OECD published a final report in its review of the Irish administrative system, which had begun in late 2006, and which contained a suite of recommendations for reforms (OECD 2008). The OECD noted that the Irish state is a unitary parliamentary system (in the Westminster/Whitehall mode), with the 15 departments making up the Irish civil service at the heart of the wider public service. What was anomalous, though, was the scale of the diverse population of state agencies (referred to as 'public agencies and bodies'), which had grown rapidly in tandem with the economy from the mid-1990s, and which provided the venue for much of the extra recruitment and spending that had been taking place during the preceding years. These agencies added considerable capacity, but also complexity, to the bureaucracy (MacCarthaigh 2012).

In respect of reforms, prior to the crisis the Irish administrative system had proven itself largely impervious to significant change. There had been little significant reduction in its size or the distribution of tasks between levels of government during previous economic downturns in the 1950s and 1980s. And it was not until the 1990s that New Public Management ideas came to Irish shores in the form of the 'Strategic Management Initiative'. Ultimately, these were translated in a much weakened form from those witnessed in the New Zealand and UK cases, with little by way of sanctions for underperformance (Hardiman and MacCarthaigh 2011).

Public-sector reform initiatives had long been managed through the 'social partnership' process and linked to pay increases. But there is little evidence of serious productivity increases or fundamental structural change, other than the creation of new agencies. In effect, many reforms were modernisation initiatives in keeping with technological advances, following European (and particularly UK) norms. Prior to the crisis, Ireland could be considered a 'laggard' in respect of public-sector reform, featuring a fragmented, complex and increasingly expensive administrative apparatus that had resisted the performance assessment measures common to NPM reforms (OECD 2008).

By the end of 2014, however, the Irish public service had experienced a 21% reduction in the annual wage bill, through a combination of headcount reduction of some 10% as well as significant reductions in pay and allowances. By any scale this was a major contraction in the size and cost of running the state. And unlike equivalent experiences in other Eurozone states during the crisis, it occurred in the absence of widespread industrial action by public service unions.

In order to explore and understand the strategies adopted during these cutback years, and the factors influencing the choices made, we can distinguish between three phases: emergency responses (2008–10), strategic cuts (2011–13), and stabilisation and development (2013–15). As Table 7.1. identifies, for each phase, the strategies can be examined by theme: Key expenditure control tools, approach to cuts, dominant public service reform objective, industrial relations framework, organisational changes and the primary source of reform.

Table 7.1 Phases of the Irish Cutback Management Approach

	Emergency Responses 2008–10	*Strategic Cuts 2011–13*	*Stabilisation and Development 2014–15*
Key expenditure control tools	Emergency budgets, 'stock-taking'	Troika 'bailout', comprehensive review of expenditure, performance budgeting	Multiannual spending
Approach to cuts	Cheese-slicing cuts dominant	Targeted cuts dominant	No cuts, targeted expenditure increases

	Emergency Responses 2008–10	Strategic Cuts 2011–13	Stabilisation and Development 2014–15
Dominant public service reform objective	Emphasis on employee numbers reduction, pay cuts	Ongoing emphasis on numbers and pay, plus new reform measures	Securing productivity increases and reform implementation
Industrial relations framework	1st pay agreement with unions	2nd pay agreement with unions	3rd pay agreement with unions
Organisational changes	Agency terminations dominant	Agency mergers dominant, new rationalisation/ centralisation measures	Agency mergers, regulation of agency-department relationships
Primary source of reform	Department of Finance	Department of Public Expenditure and Reform	Department of Public Expenditure and Reform

Phase 1: Emergency Responses 2008–10

As a growing public finance deficit began to cause concern during 2008, a first round of cuts to the cost of running the state were introduced by the then Fianna Fáil–led coalition government. Specifically, they were introduced by the Department of Finance, which held responsibility for fiscal and budgetary policy. They amounted to 3% of administrative budgets, with discretion devolved to public service managers across the public service as to how savings could be secured in their organisations. At the time, the cuts were quite a shock to a bureaucracy that had experienced year-on-year growth for a decade. The cuts were, however, insufficient to restore stability to the state's finances.

As the scale of the collapse in the Irish construction industry became clear the economic crisis spread to the banks as investors grew concerned about their exposure to property investment (Whelan 2014). Irish banks found it difficult to borrow on bond markets, and two weeks after the collapse of Lehman Brothers, the Irish government issued its extraordinary guarantee of all bank liabilities in September 2008. Controversially, it made Ireland the only Eurozone member-state to protect bank creditors and bondholders.

Immediately following this, an 'emergency' budget for 2009 was published which resulted in the Department of Finance taking a more direct approach to departmental spending plans, refusing to sanction any spending increases and identifying programmes to be cut by departments. An early feature of the Irish response to the crisis was this rapid centralisation of decision-making, and primarily to the Department of Finance. However, as managing the financial, economic and banking crisis consumed ever more of the limited resources in that department, the issue of public service cutbacks became a secondary issue, and with a focus on cutting costs rather than productivity increases or wider reform issues such as those suggested by the OECD.

The Department of Finance introduced a pay freeze for the whole public service in October 2008 (a recruitment embargo had been in place since 2007), which was followed by a pay cut[1] totalling 6% of gross pay per annum in early 2009. This was legislated for by means of a number of 'Financial Emergency Measures in the Public Interest' (FEMPI) Acts. With one minor exception from the 1930s, these pieces of legislation provided for the first permanent cut in public service pay rates in the history of the state, and provided for graduated cuts such that higher rates were applied to higher earners. Incentivised career breaks, voluntary redundancy and early retirement schemes were also introduced, but no compulsory redundancies were sanctioned.

A new centrally devised 'Employee Control Framework' (ECF) was also introduced at this time, which was designed to manage public service numbers by organisation. Each government department was given a target number of staff, lower than it then had, and which it was expected to achieve through a combination of retirements, mobility of staff to other organisations, and incentivised career breaks. Each department in turn presented a target number to agencies under its remit to achieve such that all public service organisations had an ECF staffing number.

Notwithstanding these early interventions, public spending continued to rise (due to prior commitments) during 2009 before peaking, after which time there were what one official referred to as 'massive' cuts. These cuts were informed by a 'stock-taking' report undertaken by a prominent academic economist on 'Public Service Numbers and Expenditure Programmes'. The final report recommended cuts amounting to some €5 billion and a reduction of 17,000 in the public service headcount (or 5%). Portrayed as excessive if not extreme at the time, by 2014 the cuts introduced exceeded €20 billion and a reduction of some 32,000 personnel (10%). Following the report, there was a further comprehensive pay cut for all public servants in January 2010, which yielded savings of approximately 8% of gross pay that year.

In early 2010, with enormous changes to the terms and conditions of public service employment having occurred and some isolated strikes beginning to take place,[2] the government began to negotiate with public service unions on a new pay deal, the first since 2006. An early wave of public-sector protests, concentrated on 'front-line' emergency staff, healthcare workers and teachers, had brought demonstrations on to the streets during 2009 and 2010. Politically, the government did not want to see any continuation or escalation of mass industrial unrest, and was keen to avoid compulsory layoffs if at all possible. The tripartite social partnership pay-setting process had collapsed at the end of 2009, not least because government had lost confidence in the capacity of the process to yield cost savings on the scale required through productivity increases alone. But within a short period of time, government had initiated a new round of consultations with the public-sector unions alone—the private sector unions and employers were not part of the talks at all. The bilateral government—public-sector unions negotiations represented a sort of truncated social partnership process, albeit this time focused entirely on concession bargaining, that is, focused on securing agreements on pay cuts in exchange for stability in future budgetary provisions governing public-sector pay. It is quite remarkable that this process was initiated and finalised so quickly; the preceding phase of over twenty years of social partnership had undoubtedly built the foundations for making such a deal possible for government and plausible to the unions.

The new deal was to include a common framework for reducing the cost of the public service that did not involve redundancies. This first crisis-era agreement was popularly referred to as the 'Croke Park Agreement' after the venue for the negotiations, and was due to run for the period 2010–14. Key features of the final agreement included:

- No further public service pay cuts
- Significant cost-saving reform measures to be implemented across all parts of the public service
- A reduction in public service staff numbers in 2010
- No compulsory redundancies but flexible redeployment arrangements to be introduced
- Creation of a single public service labour market
- An industrial peace clause to be put in place to avoid strikes

The creation of a single labour market was particularly important for the movement of workers not only within sectors of the Irish public service (e.g. local government, civil service), but also across these sectors. The absence of such cross-sectoral mobility had been identified by the 2008 OECD review, and was now an essential ingredient in the reallocation of staff according to ECF guidelines.

As the Irish economy continued to experience negative growth (tax revenues fell by 22% between 2008 and 2010), however, these measures still delivered insufficient savings. When the cost to the Irish government of borrowing money on bond markets grew to prohibitive rates arising from wider Eurozone issues, the government reluctantly agreed to an external 'bailout loan' in December 2010 of some €67 billion provided by the EU and IMF. As part of the loan programme, the Troika approved a set of financial management reform proposals and targets for further reductions in public service numbers to the end of 2015.

The final aspect of this first phase in the Irish cutback management approach involved a broad-based initiative of organisational rationalisation, and in particular a reduction in the number of state agencies at national and local levels. With the exception of a 1969 report on the organisation of the Irish administrative system which had suggested a reduction in the number of 'state-sponsored bodies' (Public Service Organisation Review Group 1969) little attention had been given to the issue of state agencies until the OECD's eve-of-crisis report (OECD 2008). The review noted the variety in governance and accountability arrangements in play across the agency sector and made various reform suggestions. The issue of agency reform quickly gave way to agency termination in the context of the crisis in the public finances, and in the 'emergency' budget for 2009, the Minister for Finance announcing a plan to reduce the number of national agencies by 33 through a process of mergers, dissolution, abolitions and recentralisation of functions (MacCarthaigh 2014b).

The stock-taking report in 2009 suggested further reducing the number of agencies by 43 by means of mergers and abolitions, including privatisations (Special Group on Public Service Numbers and Expenditure Programmes 2009). And a 2010 review of the myriad of local and regional agencies also led to plans for reductions totalling over half the number of almost 250 prior to the crisis (MacCarthaigh 2013, 25), mainly through mergers and functional 'upscaling' to the national level.

The implementation of these agency terminations was devolved to the 'parent' departments, but progress on achieving the envisaged number of terminations was slow. Early terminations were mainly of agencies comprising small staff numbers and minimal budgets, and it became apparent that other agency mergers required time-consuming bespoke legislation. In the event, it was only after 2011 that many mergers announced in 2009 actually took place and, interestingly, no privatisations of commercial state-owned enterprises occurred.

Phase 2: Strategic Cuts 2011–13

Phase 2 of the Irish cutback management process followed a seismic general election of February 2011, in which the incumbent government suffered a heavy defeat and a coalition of the center-left Labour Party and center-right Fine Gael formed a government with the largest parliamentary majority in the state's history. Both parties in the new administration had campaigned on the theme of political and administrative reform and, upon taking office, split the Department of Finance to create a new Department of Public Expenditure and Reform (DPER). This new department provided an institutional focus for a new phase of public service cutbacks as it assumed responsibility for expenditure, industrial relations, and public service reform combined. What was left of the

Department of Finance was concerned with revenue-raising and management of the Irish banking sector. Importantly, the fiscal approach of the new administration was consistent with its predecessor, such that two-thirds of budgetary adjustments fell on the expenditure side, with the remainder coming from revenue-raising measures.

As it held the 'purse strings', DPER wielded considerable authority over the other government departments and interviews identify that in its early years, it was successfully able to link reform implementation with funding allocations to government departments. This phase of cutbacks was strategic in the context of identifying and prioritising new areas for reform, and setting a strict and realisable series of timelines for implementation. It was assisted politically by a new cabinet subcommittee on public service reform, which provided the necessary authority to overcome any barriers to reform. It was also represented in a new powerful decision-making forum within the cabinet known as the Economic Management Council (EMC). The EMC consisted of the Taoiseach (PM), Tánaiste (Deputy-PM), Ministers for Finance and Public Expenditure and Reform, respectively, as well as their top officials and economic advisers. The EMC's role was to manage the Troika loan programme-related reforms, and to provide for faster executive decision-making. The EMCs approval of DPER's public service reform agenda as part of the national response to the economic crisis gave it further political authority for implementation.

As Chapter 12 on Irish budgetary management shows, DPER became the focal point for negotiations with other 'line' departments concerning budgetary allocations. In its first years, DPER adopted a 'case management' approach whereby administrative reforms and budgets were linked together when it negotiated with departments. If departments could not make their required savings, DPER was able to draw on its own reviews of departmental spending (see the following) to identify areas for cuts.

In respect of the implementation of its reform plans, DPER created a 15-member 'Reform Board' comprising a representative from each government department to oversee and coordinate a government-wide reform agenda. An internal website was also developed to monitor each specific reform across the public service against agreed timelines, with progress reports being reported to the 'Reform Board'. As well as directly engaging with parts of the public service where reforms were proving difficult to implement, DPER paid third-party consultants to assist departments with their reform efforts.

One of the first initiatives of the new Department of Public Expenditure and Reform was to engage in a new 'stock-taking' exercise, known as the Comprehensive Review of Expenditure (CRE), to provide an updated account of public service spending since the 2009 review. (This process was repeated in 2014 and measures passed to ensure a CRE would take place every three years thereafter.) The report that emerged from the 2011

CRE placed considerable emphasis on prioritisation of key reform objectives, as well as a focus on more targeted spending cuts. The department's subsequent publication of a new 'Public Service Reform Plan' (DPER 2011) was heavily influenced by the findings of the CRE, and specified a series of strategic measures that would lead to efficiency savings, and with associated deadlines for their implementation. These strategic measures included new modes of collaboration and efficiency-savings by means of organisations sharing resources and personnel, as well as centralisation of issues such as procurement and property management.

Work began on these strategic measures, but by the beginning of 2012 it became increasingly clear that the public service pay bill was still too large to achieve the targets set by the Troika. Informal discussions began between the department and trades unions before formal negotiations between the government and licensed trade unions took place in January 2013. The ensuing *Public Service Stability Agreement 2013–2016* (popularly known as the Haddington Road Agreement) was signed by both parties in May 2013 and superseded the Croke Park Agreement. As part of the new agreement, a third and final piece of FEMPI legislation was passed by parliament, which included graduated cuts (ranging from 5.5 to 10%) to those on higher salaries (over €65,000) in order to secure savings of a further €1 billion by 2015. In contrast with the Croke Park Agreement, which had envisaged a global savings target, the Haddington Road agreements had a more defined set of reform measures, each with associated target savings.

As Figure 7.2. identifies, the combination of a recruitment embargo, voluntary redundancy and early retirement schemes, managed by organisational targets through the ECF, brought public service numbers down by almost 30,000 over the six years between 2008–14, and the Troika target of 282,500 was comfortably surpassed by end-2014.

In parallel, towards the end of 2012 DPER had initiated an examination of all 'drivers' of the pay bill, including overtime and additional pay arrangements with a view to reducing them. And in order to facilitate greater mobility across the various parts of the public service, which formed part of the new pay agreement, DPER also initiated legislation to provide for greater standardisation of terms and conditions of employment in the Irish public service. This included establishing consistency in annual leave and sick leave arrangements, as well as introducing a new pensions systems for all new recruits to the public service.

Further agency closures were also envisaged and a review of existing agencies was proposed by DPER, again to be organised by each department, which would report back on potential for further agency rationalisations. It had become apparent that a politically driven 'bonfire of the quangos' would not yield much savings, and so the focus moved towards maximising the number of agency mergers and reabsorptions of agencies back into departments. Plans were also initiated to 'share' and centralise

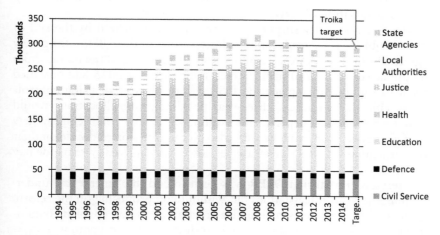

Figure 7.2 Irish Public Service Numbers by Sector 1994–14 (Including 2014 Target Agreed with Troika in 2010)

Sources: Department of Public Expenditure and Reform 2016; Government of Ireland 2010, 64.

a number of corporate support functions across the public service, including HR, payroll and procurement services.

Finally, as noted in Chapter 12, a new performance-budgeting regime came into being during this phase, with government departments required to produce performance budget statements to link spending with public services. More performance information was presented to the parliament along with the annual budget, and a public-facing 'Irelandstat' (www.irelandstat.gov.ie/) website went live, presenting progress against agreed public service delivery targets. In December 2013, Ireland formally exited its loan programme and reassumed full control over its budgetary and fiscal powers, albeit within the context the new European Stability and Growth Pact and the associated budgetary semester process.

Phase 3: Stabilisation and Development 2014–15

Finally, we consider the period during which the Irish public finances stabilised and key economic indicators such as unemployment and GDP indicated a turnaround in fortunes. The focus of the Department of Public Expenditure and Reform turned away from strategic cuts towards securing the productivity measures agreed with unions in the previous two pay agreements, introducing mechanisms to control increases in public spending, as well as introducing a series of new efficiency- and accountability-related reforms. A new public service reform plan (Department of Public Expenditure and Reform 2014a) was published, which sought to switch the reform focus towards service outcome improvements, including greater digitisation of services.

The first budgetary surplus in seven years was secured by the end of 2014. Public service trades unions began to voice their desire for a new agreement that would restore public service pay and end the moratorium on public service recruitment. In fact, the budget for 2015 had provided for a new policy to replace the ECF system. Instead of using controls by specific staff numbers, three-year pay budgetary allocations would now be provided to departments within which they could employ new staff as needed. Departments were also given discretion to decide on their recruitment and promotion strategies, albeit within fixed systemwide pay structures.

Interviews reveal that DPER was keen to end the 'emergency' underpinning the FEMPI legislation, but without compromising on the reform agenda, as the reforms struck under previous deals had enabled containment of payroll costs and increased productivity. Once again, it is striking that a new agreement with unions was secured within days. Titled the *Public Service Stability Agreement 2013–2018* (and nicknamed the 'Lansdowne Road Agreement', again after the location of the negotiations), it began the process of unwinding the provisions of the financial emergency (FEMPI) legislation, and allowed pay increases, or rather pay restoration, as it was termed, to be awarded in a phased basis to lower- and middle-income earning public servants.

Meanwhile, the aggregate number of agencies had been reduced between 2008 and 2013, but savings had been modest, and DPER turned toward regulating rather than reducing agency numbers from 2013 onwards. As Dommett, Hardiman and MacCarthaigh (2016) show, rules were introduced to make it more difficult to create new agencies, ranging from the requirement for a stronger business case for the establishment of new agencies, to the use of performance agreements between agencies and departments, to 'periodic critical reviews' of agencies and their missions (Department of Public Expenditure and Reform 2014b). All told, the new environment for agencies was a more regulated one, but one which involved more negotiation than hierarchical governance than heretofore between agencies and departments.

Furthermore, a number of 'shared service centres' came into operation across the public service (MacCarthaigh 2014a). The idea of shared services had been floated in the OECD's 2008 report, but no action was taken until they appeared in DPER's first reform plan in 2011 (discussed earlier), where considerable attention was given to their potential for efficiency savings. Shared services became commonplace in the private sector since the 1980s. The practice involves independent organisations amalgamating certain corporate or 'back office' support functions in areas such as HR, payroll and finance into a third-party organisation, which in turn offers the service to a number of user organisations at reduced cost. During 2012, recruitment to a new National Shared Service Office took place, and the first shared service centre—for civil service HR and pensions—opened in 2013. By 2015, a number of other shared service centres had opened, concerned with civil service payroll, local government payroll, and pensions and business services in the health sector, respectively. The consolidation of transactional operations across the public service into shared service centres represented an important departure for the Irish administrative system, not only through the creation of new single-purpose organisations but also the separation of 'front-office' from 'back-office' functions.

In parallel with the development of shared service initiatives, a major project on consolidating all public service procurement activity into one national office came to fruition in early 2014 with the opening of the 'Office of Government Procurement' (OGP) The primary organising principal for the OGP was to give the state 'one voice to the market' and to eliminate efficiencies that had developed through decentralised procurement. The OGP devised a new system for data gathering on procurement across the public service, and its early consolidation work involved the centralisation of procurement activities in relation to cleaning, catering, ICT and professional services. The NSSO and OGP both encapsulate key features of the final stage of the cutback management process identified here, particularly the search for greater standardisation across the bureaucracy, and introduction of new productivity-supporting practices—in effect, a rebureaucratisation of key functions.

Consequences of Cutbacks to Public Management

In total, the scale of the Irish budgetary cutbacks and administrative reforms were significant and involved the use of a variety of retrenchment measures and policy tools over several years that cumulatively point to a critical juncture in the Irish experience of administrative reform. The two Irish governments that held office over the period of retrenchment (2007–11 and 2011–16) followed a largely consistent budgetary formula that prioritised expenditure cuts over taxation increases. Common to the government strategies adopted over three phases discussed in this chapter was a centralisation of control, greater monitoring and oversight of expenditure, and the search for improved performance measurement. This was achieved through a two-pronged approach. On the one hand, we note a consistently tough drive from the centre, particularly after the establishment of the Department of Public Expenditure and Reform. On the other, successive governments negotiated stable agreements with key public-sector unions, which made it possible to pursue their retrenchment and restructuring drive without inciting overt protest and opposition.

The reforms introduced over this period including sweeping changes to personnel policies, and mainly the terms and conditions of public service employment, including pay reductions. Considerable energy was expended on harmonising terms and conditions of employment across all sectors of the bureaucracy, as well as reducing variety in leave arrangements. A significant part of the public budget was composed of a substantial public service pay and pensions bill. Reducing this bill and avoiding significant industrial unrest entailed three separate phases of negotiation between government and unions between 2010 and 2015. Each represented important milestones in the Irish response to the financial crisis. They enabled the introduction of productivity reforms that had previously proved problematic to implement. When combined with pensions reform and related measures, these efficiencies (such as increased teaching, policing and nursing shift hours) had positive productivity effects.

It is well established that crisis leads to a centralisation of budgetary and management controls as they provide the most efficient means to manage cutbacks (Levine 1979). This has certainly been the case in Ireland, with the Department of Finance and latterly the Department of Public Expenditure and Reform taking strong central roles in managing the cutback strategies. In particular, the Department of Public Expenditure and Reform achieved considerable success in managing public expenditure and securing two agreements with public service trade unions. However, it may be argued its work was most successful in the core civil service, whereas in the large and extensive health and justice (policing) sectors, attempts at reform were much more limited. Spiralling operational costs and weak management continued to bedevil the government.

Among other reforms introduced under the umbrella theme of 'openness, transparency and accountability' we may note a greater public availability of data on the performance of public service bodies, and more performance-focused publications as part of the budgetary process (see Chapter 12). Departments were also required to set out multiannual spending plans, though adherence to the associated spending limits remained problematic in practice as the economy began to improve. Thus, in the search for better information on the use of expenditure, a considerable volume of new information was generated as part of the annual budgetary and performance measurement process. The crisis period can therefore be pointed to as the catalyst for a new era of performance measurement in Irish government.

Although political power was now divided between three departments rather than two (with the addition of DPER to the Finance and Taoiseach's Departments), the intense focus on correcting the public finances led to centralisation of authority in the EMC. Local authorities were not immune from this centralisation, with budgets being cut and a host of small subnational agencies being amalgamated or closed, with their functions absorbed into local authorities. Some local authority mergers also occurred and the lower tier of Irish local government—a network of 80 small municipal town and borough councils—ceased to exist after 2014. In total, the 114 elected subnational authorities that existed prior to the crisis had been reduced in number to just 31 by 2015.

Organisational reform at the national level saw a series of agency terminations particularly affecting advisory and service delivery bodies. And although the core organisational shape of the public service did not change, and there was not a radical reduction in the number of agencies, the crisis certainly arrested the proliferation of agencies that had developed relatively unchecked prior to 2008. Agencies remain a feature of the Irish administrative system, however, and notwithstanding the extensive programme of mergers and absorptions of agencies back into core departments, a number of new and often large agencies emerged during the crisis, demonstrating the resilience of this institutionalised form of delegated governance. And as noted earlier, the attempts to standardise relationships between ministries and agencies in the state agency sector inadvertently led to a more regulated and 'negotiated' agency-department environment. The agencies that survived termination were quite successful in negotiating a more partnership approach to replace the 'parent-child' model that had initially informed the cutback management process (Dommet, MacCarthaigh and Hardiman 2016).

The crisis provided for enhanced vertical coordination within Irish government through centralisation of financial controls in the first instance as the crisis unfolded, and latterly also through the management of a reform agenda. Horizontal coordination across government was also important in driving the reform agenda. Specifically, management and implementation of reform was coordinated by DPER through such means of various forums populated by officials with responsibility for reform in their departments and policy sectors, as well as virtual mechanisms such as an online reform monitoring portal. Interviews also suggest, however, that the integration of reform efforts with the allocation of expenditure to departments by DPER was a challenge for much of the 2013–15 'stabilisation and development' period. A number of officials suggested there was scope for better coordination within DPER of its various relationships with other departments. In other words, notwithstanding the centralisation of authority for implementing reform that occurred with the creation of DPER, the challenge of ensuring cross-government reform coordination and coherence remained.

Conclusions

The pattern of change in Ireland was consistent with the expected experience of countries hit hardest by the crisis. Bringing together the three phases identified here, the Irish case featured widespread and deep budgetary cutbacks over the 2008–15 period, and a wide range of reforms to work patterns and terms and conditions of public-sector employment.

The crisis can be viewed as a critical juncture in the state's trajectory of public management reform.

The character of the changes underlying the reform agenda, occurring as it did alongside a deep period of budgetary adjustment, resulted in centralisation of control across the public service and the re-emergence of efforts at standardisation and rationalisation. Departments reined in discretionary financial autonomy from agencies as they sought to meet cutback targets. Final authority over spending decisions shifted to the new Department of Public Expenditure and Reform, which provided the institutional basis for coordinating and implementing cutbacks alongside reform measures. Organisational mergers meant that many public service bodies became even more diverse in the range of their functions.

The Irish case of cutback management from 2008 was heavily informed by the motto that one should 'never waste a crisis'. In the process, a series of reforms that may previously have been considered unlikely were introduced by two successive governments, backed by strong and sustained political commitment and enabled by a rhetoric that consistently stressed economic imperatives and diminished scope for budgetary choice. This was in large part assisted by the loan programme agreement with the Troika, which bridged the change of government in 2011. The loan agreement set a cascading series of targets. But it is important to note here that the programme was extensively drafted by national policymakers, not by the lenders. National political 'ownership' of the reform agenda was extensive from the outset, and was taken over virtually wholesale in 2011 by the incoming government from its predecessor. The agreement of public service unions to adhere to the reforms, and not to engage in industrial action, is a critical part of the Irish reform story.

When surveying the 2008–15 crisis period, it is also important to consider the reforms that might have been expected to materialise in a state under extraordinary fiscal pressure, but which did not happen. In the first instance, although cutbacks were widespread, there was little evidence of complete state 'exit' from the delivery of public services in any specific sector of activity. This was particularly noteworthy in respect of welfare provision where the main payments were largely protected and welfare budget insulated from deep cuts experienced elsewhere, particularly by the arts and transport.

There was also very little by way of privatisation of state assets, even though a range of potential state divestments formed part of the loan programme agreement with the Troika, and an agency called New Era was established to manage a privatisation programme. Interviews reveal that the fact that the key Minister for Public Expenditure and Reform came from the social democratic Labour Party was significant in limiting the prospects of such a programme. By 2015, only the state's gas company had been sold, but not the gas distribution network's infrastructure, and as economic fortunes improved privatisation fell off the political agenda altogether.

Finally, there was little functional decentralisation to local authorities' experienced in Ireland. This is perhaps less unexpected, as previous crises have demonstrated that functional upscaling from local to national levels is a common response by governments seeking to exert control on public spending. Nonetheless, it is important to note that while the crisis provided a window of opportunity to introduce many long-standing reform measures at the national level, long-standing calls for local authority empowerment were largely ignored.

In conclusion, the Irish experience of cutback management over the 2008–15 period was substantial for a state that had not been known for radical or swift public service reforms. The scale of the economic crisis both necessitated and provided the impetus for cutbacks and parallel reform measures that led to a smaller but more productive public service. The single most striking features of cutback management featured a consistent centralisation and drive from the centre to achieve the required targets, and a sustained approach to defusing public-sector protest and resistance. The details of the measures adopted varied across time. By examining the cutbacks according to three phases—emergency responses (2008–10), strategic cuts (2011–13) and stabilisation and development (2014–15)—the interplay between a variety of cutback strategies and administrative reform measures in Ireland is more clearly understood.

Notes

1 The formal term for this pay cut was a 'pension-related deduction', devised on the basis that public sector pensions enjoyed a state guarantee that was not available to those in the private sector.
2 In March 2010, staff in passport offices engaged in strike action over pay cuts.

References

Boyle, Richard and Michael Mulreany. 2015. "Managing Ireland's Budgets During the Rise and Fall of the 'Celtic Tiger'." In *The Global Financial Crisis and Its Budget Impacts in OECD Nations: Fiscal Responses and Future Challenges*, edited by John Wanna, Evert A. Lindquist and Jouke de Vries, 284–308. Cheltenham: Edward Elgar.

Department of Public Expenditure and Reform (DPER). 2014a. *The Public Service Reform Plan*. Dublin: Department of Public Expenditure and Reform.

Department of Public Expenditure and Reform. 2014b. *Report on the Implementation of the Agency Rationalisation Programme*. Dublin: Department of Public Expenditure and Reform.

Department of Public Expenditure and Reform. 2014c. *The Civil Service Renewal Plan*. Dublin: Department of Public Expenditure and Reform.

Department of Public Expenditure and Reform. 2016. *Databank*. Dublin: Department of Public Expenditure and Reform. www.per.gov.ie/en/databank/.

Dommett, Kate, Muiris MacCarthaigh and Niamh Hardiman. 2016. "Reforming the Westminster Model of Agency Governance: Britain and Ireland After the Crisis." *Governance* 29:.535–552.

Government of Ireland. 2010. *National Recovery Plan 2011–2014*. Dublin: Stationery Office.

Hardiman, Niamh and Muiris MacCarthaigh. 2011. "The Un-Politics of New Public Management in Ireland." In *Administrative Reforms and Democratic Governance*, edited by Jon Pierre and Jean-Michel Emeri-Douzans, 55–67. London: Routledge/ECPR Studies in European Political Science.

Hardiman, Niamh and Muiris MacCarthaigh. 2016. "State Retrenchment and Administrative Reform in Ireland: Probing Comparative Policy Paradigms." *Journal of Comparative Policy Analysis*, forthcoming in print, can be retrieved electronically: http://dx.doi.org/10.1080/13876988.2015.1103432

Honohan, Patrick. 2010. *The Irish Banking Crisis Regulatory and Financial Stability Policy 2003–2008*. Dublin: Central Bank.

Houses of the Oireachtas. 2016. *Report of the Joint Committee of Inquiry Into the Banking Crisis*. Dublin: Houses of the Oireachtas.

Independent Review Panel. 2011. "Strengthening the Capacity of the Department of Finance (Wright Report)." www.finance.gov.ie/documents/publications/reports/2011/deptreview.pdf.

International Monetary Fund (IMF). 2013. *Ireland: Fiscal Transparency Report*. Washington, DC: International Monetary Fund.

Levine, Charles H. 1979. "More on Cutback Management: Hard Questions for Hard Times." *Public Administration Review* 39(2):179–83.

MacCarthaigh, Muiris. 2012. "From Agencification to De-Agencification: The Changing Irish Bureaucratic Model." In *Governing Ireland: From Cabinet Government to Delegate-d Governance*, edited by Eoin O'Malley and Muiris MacCarthaigh, 128–51. Dublin: Institute of Public Administration.

MacCarthaigh, Muiris. 2013. 'The Changing Structure of Irish Sub-National Governance'. *Local Government Research Series* (No. 4) Dublin: Institute of Public Administration.

MacCarthaigh, Muiris. 2014a. "Shared Services in Ireland." In *Organizing for Coordination in the Public Sector: Practices and Lessons From 12 European Countries*, edited by Per Laegreid, Külli Sarapuu, Lise Hellebø. Rykkja and Tiina Randma-Liiv, 54–65. Basingstoke: Palgrave Macmillan.

MacCarthaigh, Muiris. 2014b. "Agency Termination in Ireland: Culls and Bonfires, or Life After Death?" *Public Administration* 92(4):1017–37.

Nyberg, Peter. 2011. *Misjudging Risk: Causes of the Systemic Banking Crisis in Ireland: Report of the Commission of Investigation Into the Banking Sector in Ireland*. Dublin: Department of Finance.

OECD. 2008. *Ireland: Towards an Integrated Public Service*. Paris: OECD.

Public Service Organisation Review Group. 1969. *Report of the Public Service Organisation Review Group* (The Devlin Report). Dublin: Stationery Office.

Regling, Klaus and Max Watson. 2010. *A Preliminary Report on the Sources of Ireland's Banking Crisis*. Dublin: Stationery Office.

Special Group on Public Service Numbers and Expenditure Programmes. 2009. *Report of the Special Group on Public Service Numbers and Expenditure Programmes*. Dublin: Stationery Office.

Whelan, Karl. 2014. "Ireland's Economic Crisis: The Good, the Bad, and the Ugly." *Journal of Macroeconomics* 39(B):424–40.

8 Cutback Management in Estonia During the Crisis of 2008–10 and Beyond

Riin Savi, Tiina Randma-Liiv
and Ringa Raudla

Introduction

Commitment to fiscal discipline has characterised Estonian governments for more than two decades, since regaining independence in 1991 (see Raudla and Kattel 2011). Also, after the outburst of the recent economic crisis when Estonia witnessed severe recession, the government pursued fiscal consolidation. The Estonian government was among the first in Europe to apply immediate and radical expenditure cutbacks in response to the crisis as early as 2008—by implementing three negative state budgets within two years. As a result, Estonia recorded the third lowest crisis-time budget deficit in the EU and a low government debt rate (OECD 2012). It also became a new member of the Eurozone despite the crisis.

The radical and successful cutback management received attention all over the world, and the Estonian government was praised for making 'hard decisions', 'applying aggressive austerity' and 'being resolute' (see e.g. Åslund 2012). The current chapter investigates how the expenditure cuts materialised, how the cutbacks decisions were met and implemented, and what have been the implications of cutting back.

The chapter demonstrates that cutbacks posed extensive burdens to the central government and the operational measures of single government organisations. The cutback era contributed substantially to the centralisation of decision-making through the increase in the power of politicians and budgetary institutions as well as to centralised political decisions. Still, achieving the urgent solutions was strongly facilitated by decentralised decisions at the organisational level and intensive engagement of the civil servants. It is concluded that cutback management did not alter the existing reform paths; however, the general retrenchment environment helped the government to carry out reforms that had been turned down earlier.

The empirical study is based on extensive document analysis—memoranda and explanatory notes of the Estonian Ministry of Finance and the cabinet of Ministers, verbatim records of the parliamentary sessions and transcripts of legislative committee meetings, official press releases of state institutions and OECD reports on budgetary retrenchment. In addition, 33 in-depth, semi-structured interviews were conducted with budget department heads from line ministries, civil servants from the Ministry of Finance engaged in the cutback decision-making and street-level bureaucrats engaged in implementing the cutback decisions.

The Crisis, Austerity and Cutbacks

Economic Conditions Prior to the Crisis

Prior to the recent crisis Estonia enjoyed years of remarkable economic growth with a yearly average of circa 8% from 2000 to 2007. In 2008 and 2009, the GDP growth turned negative, reaching –4.2% and –14.1%, respectively. In terms of budget balance, Estonia had run fiscal surpluses since the early 2000s (mainly resulting from conservative fiscal policy and windfall tax revenues) but experienced a deterioration of fiscal balance from a surplus of 2.5% in 2006 to a deficit of 2.9% in 2008. General government debt was steadily around 4% in the pre-crisis area but rose to 10.1% of GDP by 2013. The unemployment rate was around 5% prior to the crisis but underwent an extensive increase by reaching an exceptional 16.7% in 2010, and it did not reach the pre-crisis level even four years later in 2014 (Eurostat; OECD 2011, 98–100).

Stages of the Crisis

The Estonian government was among the first in the world to implement immediate and radical expenditure cutbacks right after the outset of the fiscal crisis as early as 2008 (instead of postponing the cuts) (OECD 2011, 99). Estonia did not face the banking crisis that forced numerous EU member states to save national banks (Kickert 2012), since the Estonian banking sector had come to be dominated and operated by Nordic banks (the foreign-owned banks held 92% of the market in 2007). Although the dramatic fall in the GDP indicates that Estonia faced a serious economic crisis in 2008–09, the government did not engage in borrowing or applying any other measures for stimulating the economy despite remarkably low government debt (see Table 8.1). Instead, to cope with the fiscal stress, it decided to go for fiscal consolidation (see Table 8.2). The decision to opt for fiscal tightening can mainly be explained by the Estonian government's political priority to join the Eurozone. This goal tied the government to a target to keep the public deficit below 3% of GDP and government debt under 60% of GDP, as stipulated in the Maastricht Treaty. This way the adoption of the euro turned into a focal point orchestrating the government's action during the crisis management and retrenchment (OECD 2011, 99; Raudla 2013).

Table 8.1 Main Macroeconomic Indicators of Estonia 2007–12

	2006	2007	2008	2009	2010	2011	2012	2013	2014
GDP growth	10.1	7.5	−4.2	−14.1	2.6	9.6	3.9	1.6	2.9
Budget balance	2.5	2.4	−2.9	−2	0.2	1.2	−0.3	−0.2	2.5
State debt (% of GDP)	4.4	3.7	4.5	7.1	6.7	6.1	9.8	10	4.4
Inflation	4.4	6.7	10.6	0.2	2.7	5.1	4.2	3.2	0.5
Unemployment rate	5.9	4.7	5.5	13.8	16.7	12.3	10.0	8.6	7.4

Source: Eurostat.

Table 8.2 Major Cutback Measures 2009–15

Measure	Budgetary Impact (% of GDP)			
	2009	2010	2011	2012–15
Expenditure Measures	854.5 (6.2)	331.1 (2.3)	111.1 (0.7)	0.0
1. Operational measures (including personnel expenditures)	100.7	57.8	–	–
2. Programme measures	454.5	113.5	111.1	–
2.1. *Pensions*	163.6	71.4	79.1	–
2.2. *Social security*	115.1	–	–	–
2.3. *Defence*	30.9	10.1	–	–
2.4. *Construction*	52.1	–	–	–
2.5. *Transfers to local governments*	38.3	–	–	–
2.6. *Lending to local governments*	32.0	32.0	32.0	–
2.7. *Environmental investments*	22.4	–	–	–
3. *Other initiatives* (e.g. overall spending limits, expenditure freeze at central government level)	299.3	159.8	–	–

Source: The structure of the table is adopted from OECD (2012). Figures on actual consolidation measures in Estonia have been obtained from the Ministry of Finance.

The Adoption of the Austerity Packages

As a response to the crisis, the Estonian government imposed fiscal discipline by applying several consolidation measures across three negative supplementary budgets within two years (the first in 2008, two more in 2009) and several one-off measures, thus improving the budgetary position by circa 9% of GDP in 2009, circa 6% of GDP in 2010, circa 3% of GDP in both 2011 and 2012 (OECD 2012, 112). In 2009, the consolidation measures concentrated on reducing the expenditures through operational and programme cuts, whereas the consequent measures increasingly focused on strengthening the revenues (see Table 8.2.). All three negative supplementary budgets applied extensive cuts in operational measures at the central/government level.

Major Consolidation Measures in 2008–15

In the 2008 June austerity package, nearly half of the expenditure reduction concerned operational cuts. The governmental operational expenditures were decreased by applying across-the-board cuts—proportional 7% cuts for all policy areas (only defence, education and internal security were cut less or left untouched) (Jõgiste, Peda and Grossi 2012, 189). Operational cuts were predominantly achieved by curtailing personnel expenditures in central/government bodies–ministries, agencies and constitutional institutions. As a consequence, the central government abolished circa 3,000 positions and laid off circa 1,000 civil servants in 2008. For example, the Government Office, the Ministry of Finance and the Ministry of Environmental Affairs laid off 16%, 11% and 17% of their respective workforces (Peters, Pierre and Randma-Liiv 2011, 22), and the two ministries abolished 25% and 10% respectively of their positions. In 2009, the government applied additional cuts to operational expenditures by using across-the-board cuts—7% in February and 8% in June. In 2009 the share of dismissals was smaller than in 2008, but civil-service salaries were further sliced back. Also expenditure freeze and limits to overall spending at the central/government level were set (see Raudla 2013). All in all, the cuts in government operational expenditure contributed strongly to the improvement of the budgetary position in 2009 and 2010. After 2010, operational costs were not targeted during the cutbacks.

While the first negative supplementary budget adopted in 2008 amounted to budgetary retrenchment with extensive cuts on the government wage bill and postponing strategic investments, the subsequent budgets introduced substantial cuts to programme measures. Concerning the social security, the planned increase in unemployment insurance benefits was not enacted, the expenditures of the Health Insurance Fund were reduced, and the sick-leave compensation scheme was altered (by shortening the period covered by sick-leave benefits). The rise in old-age pensions was decreased (5% rise instead of 14%), and state-funded contributions to the mandatory pension fund were temporarily suspended. Transfers to local governments were reduced, their lending conditions were restricted, and several allocations to local governments (e.g. school lunch, living allowance) were cut. In addition, investments in road construction and environmental investments were curtailed. Also the state defence expenditures were targeted (reduction of 0.2% of GDP), which made Estonia one of the few OECD countries where curbing defence expenditures substantially added to consolidation (OECD 2011, 46). See the overview of cutback measures in Table 8.2.

Principal changes on the revenue side of the budget were only established with the third negative supplementary budget in June 2009 by numerous tax increases: 2 percentage point increase of the VAT rate (from

18% to 20%) and increase of the lowered (exceptions) VAT rate (from 5% to 9%), additional excise duties on alcohol, tobacco (5% increase), fuel (up to 12% increase) and environmental fees (20% increase of pollution fees). In addition, a sharp increase was imposed on the unemployment-insurance contribution rate (from 0.9% to 4.2%) and the social-tax obligatory minimum. The government also relied strongly on non-tax revenues (compared to other countries) by selling state-owned real estate and land, and taking out additional dividends from state-owned enter-prises (OECD 2012, 112).

In addition, to improve the budget position, some of the ear-marked revenues were untied from foreseen expenditures (e.g. abolishment of fixed proportions of revenue to local governments from the accrual of the fuel excise) to achieve greater budgetary flexibility. See the overview of major revenue measures in Table 8.3.

As the Estonian government started substantial front-loaded consol-idation already in 2008, measures focusing on the expenditure reduc-tion were applied in 2008, 2009 and 2010, with a slight spillover effect also in 2011. Though the Estonian government did not introduce an official consolidation plan after 2010, it continued a conservative fis-cal policy. This is also a reason why the main focus of this chapter is on the period from 2008 to 2010. From 2010 onwards the overall size of the consolidation measures driven by the revenue side reflects mainly the effects of tax and excise-rate increases decided upon in 2009 (OECD 2012, 109).

In 2016, eight years after the first round of cutback measures were taken, several austerity-era effects are still present. Concerning public administration and the cuts in operational expenditures, hiring freeze has been gradually abandoned and public-sector wages gradually restored as of 2011. Still several 'symbolic cuts' that enabled curbing operational measures (e.g. optimising travel costs, minimising costs related to office administration etc.) and the general goal of bigger cost-effectiveness have remained in place. The fiscal consolidation also strongly affected the social-security and pension system—the raise in pensions was decreased and the retirement age was raised during the early years of the crisis. Though the state-funded contributions to the mandatory pension fund have been restored and also the old-age pensions have constantly risen (the latest rise 6.3% in 2016), the pensions have not yet witnessed the growth rate pledged before the crisis. Public-sector investments approached the pre-crisis level quickly after the first consolidation measures. The Esto-nian government curtailed those parts of capital budgets that were not financed from EU funds and accelerated spending on EU-financed invest-ments. Still, the stipulations in legislative acts that abolished the fixed proportions of expenditures to the state budget are still valid. Also, most of the revenue side measures decided upon in 2009 are still in force and have a strong effect for the state budget.

Table 8.3 Major Revenue Measures for Consolidation 2009–15

Measure	Description	Budgetary Impact (% of GDP)						
		2009	2010	2011	2012	2013	2014	2015
Revenue Measures		417.3 (3.0)	578.3 (4.0)	484.4 (3.0)	523.6 (3.1)	561.6 (3.1)	571.0 (3.0)	526.4 (2.6)
1. VAT	Increasing VAT rate from 18% to 20%	51.1	111.8	119.9	128.4	136.8	145.0	154.8
	Increasing the lowered VAT rate	21.1	21.9	23.5	25.1	26.8	28.4	30.0
2. Personal income taxes	Abolishing additional basic allowance for the first child	–	46.1	45.3	45.3	45.3	45.3	45.3
	Excluding labour-union fees and study-loan interest from income deductions	–	–	3.0	3.0	3.0	3.0	3.0
	Creation of the investment account	–	–	–	–4.2	–4.2	–4.2	–4.2
	Excluding educational costs from the list of fringe benefits	–	–	–	–2.1	–2.1	–2.1	–2.1
3. Social-security contributions	Raising unemployment-insurance tax from 0.9% to 4.2%	50.2	112.7	124.7	133.7	142.4	150.4	161.2
	Increasing the social-tax obligatory minimum to 100% of the minimum wage	21.0	23.0	23.0	23.0	24.0	25.0	27.0
4. Excise duties	Increasing excise on alcohol, tobacco, fuel, gas and electricity	33.2	103.9	111.1	149.1	161.4	167	175.1
5. Dividends	Additional dividends from state-owned enterprises	108.6	82	32	–	–	–	–
6. Property	Sale of real estate and land	75.9	64.9	–	–	–	–	–
7. Other	Other revenues	56.1	2.0	2.0	22.1	23.2	24.2	24.4

Source: The structure of the table is adopted from OECD (2012). Figures on actual consolidation measures in Estonia have been obtained from the Ministry of Finance.

Cutback Management in Central Government

In this chapter, we first give an overview of the implementation of cutbacks in the Estonian central government (with a specific focus on operational expenditures). We proceed by examining the shifts in decision-making processes during the cutback era: increased power of politicians and budgetary institutions, changes in organizational arrangements, and increased responsibility of individual civil servants.

Implementation of Cutbacks (Operational Expenditure)

For reducing the government operational expenditure, the cabinet of Ministers opted for across-the-board cuts by insisting on an equal share of cuts from most policy fields and occupational groups. The cuts were implemented in three rounds—7% in June 2008, 7% in February 2009 and 8% in June 2009. In principle, the across-the-board cuts delegated the right and power to decide how to achieve the set level of cuts to individual government organisations. Still, the 'room for manoeuvring' for the managers was limited, as the amount of cuts to be reached was big, had to be achieved in a tight timeline and addressed operational costs that entail only few flexible budget lines (Savi and Randma-Liiv 2015). Further, the room for 'manoeuvring' differed from one organisation to another, as it strongly depended on the budget and expenditure structure of each specific government organisation and the share of 'waste eliminated' before the crisis period (Savi 2014).

All in all, the decentralised nature of the cabinet's cutback strategy led to somewhat different cutback strategies and methods in single government organisations (see also Savi 2014).

Although downsizing the government's operational costs was seen as a combination of cutting the pay fund and administrative costs, cuts were predominantly achieved by curtailing personnel expenditures. A mix of measures such as layoffs, pay and salary cuts, unpaid leave, decreased work time and hiring freeze were combined in all government organisations. In addition, in most organisations civil servants faced a cut in benefits when additional pay funds, training funds and one-time support schemes (e.g. compensation for health-related activities) were significantly reduced or even abolished.

Most commonly a combination of layoffs, pay cuts and hiring freeze was used; still, the proportion (%) of pay cuts and the duration of hiring freeze differed between individual organisations. In some cases, the civil servants even inside one organisation faced different degrees of wage loss and work-related rearrangements. For example, the Ministry of Social Affairs applied two rounds of cuts: in the first, an equal pay cut of 7% was applied to the entire staff, in the second, the civil servants had the opportunity to choose between an additional pay cut of

9%, 12 days of unpaid leave or decrease in work load. In the Ministry of Justice, in addition to an 11% cut in wages, pay for performance was abolished. The Ministry of Economic Affairs avoided cuts in basic salaries but severely curbed other items of the pay fund (e.g. pay for performance and extra pay).

To achieve the centrally set amount of cuts in operational expenditures, remarkable cuts in administrative and maintenance-related expenditures also occurred in Estonia. Spending limits on utilities, supplies, equipment, travel and communications were most common (see also Raudla 2013). Also, cosmetic cuts such as 'no free coffee' and 'no colour printing' were introduced widely (Savi and Cepilovs 2016). At the agency level, cuts in maintenance-related expenditures were significant and deprived the civil servants of their habitual amenities. For example, at the Estonian Tax and Customs Board, switching off the heating system in the office during the weekend and optimising lighting in offices whenever possible occurred (Savi and Cepilovs 2016). This indicates that cuts in non-personnel expenditures can also have strong implications for civil servants as they put further pressures on the work environment.

The case of Estonia demonstrates that different types of cutback strategies were applied at the organisational level to implement the centrally imposed cutback targets, mainly combining across-the-board and targeted cuts. In most of the government organisations, the across-the-board strategy was further applied when curbing the salaries and, as a rule, civil servants in one organisation faced the same share of cuts. There were also some exceptions. For example, at the Estonian Tax and Customs Board, non-managerial positions were cut less (3–5%) than managerial positions (15%), and in the Labour Inspectorate, subunits implementing projects co-financed from the EU structural funds suffered less than the others in salary cuts. Targeted cuts occurred mainly in programme-related expenses and touched upon specific public services either financed or provided by government organisations (e.g. abandoning the state-covered home delivery of pensions and cancelling the financing of a counselling helpline) (Savi 2014).

The Estonian government's response to the fiscal crisis constitutes a unique case, because instead of denying the need for and postponing cuts, it was among the first European countries that implemented immediate and radical cutbacks after the outset of the crisis as early as 2008. What makes the Estonian case interesting is that the fiscal tightening was motivated by the government's political priority to join the Eurozone. This provided a very specific context for the entire fiscal consolidation exercise. Joining the euro area had been a long-standing aspiration in Estonia, widely shared by the population at large. It was not only rooted in the economic logic, but euro adoption was seen as yet another step towards closer integration with Western Europe, in a similar vein as joining the European Union, NATO, the OECD and the Schengen zone.

The euro was seen as the key to securing financial and political stability, a dominant objective after a turbulent history. The prospect of joining the Eurozone made the political actors more willing to go ahead with the austerity measures, in the hope that the arrival of the euro would compensate the painful measures in the eyes of the citizens (Raudla and Kattel 2011).

In order to qualify for the euro, Estonia had to fulfil the Maastricht criteria. This tied the government with a target to keep the public deficit below 3% of GDP, low inflation (calculated on the basis of inflation rates in other EU member states) and the government debt under 60% of GDP, as set in the Maastricht Treaty. Pre-crisis efforts to join the Eurozone were hindered by high inflation, meaning that Estonia did not comply with the price-stability criterion of the Maastricht Treaty. As the deflationary pressures during the recession were expected to lead to a drop of inflation, meeting the inflation criterion was suddenly within reach. The window of opportunity opened in early 2009, when it became clear that by year end the 12-month inflation rate could be below the reference level for the first time in five years. This way the deficit limit of 3% became the main priority in discussions over fiscal policy. In fact, the size of austerity measures in Estonia was calculated with reference to the 3% deficit criterion (Raudla and Kattel 2011).

A comparative study of European governments (Kickert and Randma-Liiv 2016) showed that general elections in all but Estonia's case resulted in a defeat of the incumbent government that had taken steps towards fiscal consolidation. The Estonian government's perceived success in joining the Eurozone overshadowed radical cutbacks in the general elections of 2011. It can be argued that the cabinet's well-calculated perspective of joining the Eurozone and a broad public support for the euro made the radical cutback decisions and their speedy implementation possible in Estonia.

Another intriguing fact about Estonia, when compared to international practice, is that despite the wage cuts and layoffs, the majority of civil servants showed loyalty and commitment to the cabinet decisions, and there was no systematic resistance to cutbacks by civil servants. Several rounds of cuts were even regarded as reasonable, as the civil servants believed that the successive (rather than one-off) rounds of cuts provided them time to adjust. This can be explained by the Estonian civil servants' adherence to the prevalent political ideologies and general beliefs: belief and trust in the euro, in cutting back and in fiscal discipline (Kattel and Raudla 2013). The public acceptance of fiscal austerity may have occurred because the budget in Estonia was usually in balance and people had come to expect this outcome at all times. In addition, the missing tenure in the civil-service regulation, combined with relatively underdeveloped civil society and unions, supported the government when it was looking for possibilities for personnel cuts.

Thus, the social acceptability of cutback decisions can be explained by the supportive public opinion to fiscal discipline, by the simple polity with a marginal role for unions, social partnerships, constitutional veto players, corporatist structures in the policy process and widely shared expectations related to joining the Eurozone (Kattel and Raudla 2013). The struggle towards fiscal discipline and the subsequent austerity measures were primarily driven by the government's goal to qualify for the adoption of the euro. This was a clear and straightforward sign for everyone and, by being accepted to the Eurozone, the government justified the necessity of its decisions.

The Decision-Making Process

The cutback era contributed substantially to the centralisation of decision-making, after the cabinet realised the need for retrenchment and decided in favour of immediate radical cuts. The crisis decision-making was characterised by an increase in the power of politicians, the empowerment of budgetary institutions and centralised political decisions. Still, achieving the urgent solutions was facilitated by decentralised decisions at the organisational level and intensive engagement of the civil servants.

Increase in the Power of Politicians

More centralised decision-making occurred due to the increase in the power of politicians (especially the members of the cabinet) during the crisis. The power position of politicians was enhanced by the establishment of ad hoc working groups and 'super-committees' made up of a handful of influential politicians to enable fast and flexible coordination between coalition partners in order to speed up consensus-finding at the political level and reach the cutback decisions. The domination of the political elements in the decision-making process led to overriding the habitual practices of legitimisation and shook the established roles and power positions of state institutions, politicians and civil servants. For example, policy decisions were enforced despite clear expressions of discontent from both formal policy actors (legal chancellor, opposition parties) and other stakeholders (such as entrepreneurs or unions). Most remarkably, the adoption of the negative supplementary budget in the parliament was linked to a vote of confidence to the government in power in order to bypass the lengthy procedure for passing the budget. The supremacy of political elements is also confirmed by the fact that the minority government was able to push through the cutback measures (Savi and Randma-Liiv 2015).

Increase in the Power of Budgetary Institutions

In Estonia, the centralisation materialised first of all in the increase in the power of the Ministry of Finance, which became the central mediator between the cabinet and the line ministries when reinforcing top-down budgeting. The increased power of the Ministry of Finance is illustrated by the following. First, the Ministry of Finance was responsible for providing the cabinet, but also the ad hoc workgroups, with background materials and estimates about the influence of alternative cutback measures on the budgetary position. As a rule, these estimates were based on information gathered, systemised and summarised by the civil servants of the Ministry of Finance. In many cases, the information remained technical and numerical in form, treating ministries and agencies in a standardised form as 'budget holders'. Second, the Ministry of Finance directly orchestrated the cutback related processes in line-ministries by allocating duties and setting deadlines. Namely, working out the saving proposals was not left in the hands of line ministries (except cuts in operational measures) but the Ministry of Finance, which requested line ministries to forward all possible (financial) data to the Ministry of Finance to provide information on the cutback proposals (Jõgiste, Peda and Grossi 2012, 193). Third, the cabinet decided to apply complementary centralisation measures for strengthening fiscal control by appointing the representatives of the Ministry of Finance to the management boards of the state foundations and state-owned enterprises that did not yet have representatives from the Ministry of Finance (e.g. North Estonia Medical Centre; Welfare Services Ltd.). The aim was to improve control over budgetary decisions, especially loan-taking by these bodies—to achieve that, a clause requiring the consensus of the management board in case of loan-taking was imposed. Fourth, the local governments' borrowing procedures were restricted by the central government through binding loan-taking to permission from the Ministry of Finance. In many occasions, the Ministry of Finance served as an extension of the cabinet in the relations with line ministries (see Chapter 13 in this book for further details).

Also on the organisational level a shift of power between line and budget departments was detected. During the crisis the budgetary departments received a stronger position as they were, more than ever before, engaged in reviewing the content of proposed budget amendments (proposed by line departments). The budgetary departments looked at the entire policy field as a whole and were expected to propose cutbacks for the top management or even directly to the Ministry of Finance). As a result, cutback management empowered the budget units and often subjected various policy fields to the budget policy, because the lack of time (and information and expertise) did not allow thorough impact assessments and negotiations.

Organisational-Level Decision-Making and (Re)arrangements

In ministries and agencies, the top management made the principal decisions concerning the cutbacks in operational measures. The degree of employee inclusion and participation in decision-making differed: in some organisations, the decisions met at the top management level were simply forwarded to the department heads, who obtained the role of the messenger; in others, the department heads were consulted in several rounds; and in some cases the whole staff could participate in open informative meetings led by the secretary general. Still, on rare occasions the detailed cutback propositions were left to the department heads and programme specialists, as the budgetary offices in line ministries tried to avoid further across-the-board cuts.

The existing structures and venues of decision-making within ministries and agencies remained in place during retrenchment. As a rule, no ad hoc working groups were established, organisational structures and work processes were formally not changed, but habitual organisational structures and measures were exploited more extensively. Hence the civil servants were subject to a more intense workload (shorter deadlines, longer working hours), impelled mainly by the constant and urgent need for information concerning the possible cutbacks. Some degree of deviation from the habitual processes was brought about by the time constraint, because as a rule, there was not enough time to provide detailed explanations, evaluations and analyses (Savi and Randma-Liiv 2015).

In Estonia the reorganisation of service provision at the organisational level occurred rarely, especially when taking into account the overall centralised setup of cutback management. Concerning the public-service delivery, though, due to the shrinking workforce and prevalent urgency, civil servants had to assume new tasks, non-routine duties and also new responsibilities. As a rule, the changes in service provision were not formalised and no specific guidelines were given in the changed work environment from the top management (Savi and Cepilovs 2016). With these *non-decisions* and *non-actions* (e.g. by formalising guidelines, setting procedural rules), the top management 'delegated' the search for further solutions to the individual level. Thus, the organisation-based reorganisations were ad hoc and temporary rather than systematic efforts to use reorganisations as a cutback strategy.

Increased Responsibility of Individual Civil Servants

Although at the 'aggregate' level, the power and authority of the decision makers in 'higher' levels increased, the responsibility of individual civil servants in Estonia also increased in the decision-making process during the crisis. Civil servants acquired more autonomy and a more important role as the main source of technical expertise and the 'last link' in the chain making the final decisions and delivering public services. For example, due to the lack of time, information and general urgency, civil servants in ministries faced important decisions concerning the cutback targets based on their 'gut feeling'. The time constraints on in-depth analysis and the sheer scope of cutback decisions rendered impossible the usual practices related to budget preparation in line ministries and in the Ministry of Finance. When faced with asymmetrical (or even absent) information and the urgency to formulate budget evaluations, civil servants from the Ministry of Finance often left areas not well known to them untouched, whereas the others suffered more in downsizing (Savi 2014; Savi and Randma-Liiv 2015).

Also at the service-delivery level, increased responsibility of individual civil servants occurred. It was visible in the different coping strategies adopted by street-level bureaucrats when working overtime, fulfilling new tasks and trying to find more efficient ways to deliver the services to a maximum number of citizens. In many cases the street-level bureaucrats developed a stricter and more impersonal attitude towards the customers to speed up service delivery. For example, civil servants consciously limited information normally provided to customers and expected them to look up information themselves. In addition, stereotyping of the clients occurred: customers that were seen as the most 'needy' were serviced first in order to achieve the policy outputs (e.g. register the unemployed). Therefore, the civil servants had a great influence on who received the public services when and how quickly during the crisis (Savi 2014).

Paradoxically, in Estonia the empowerment of civil servants in public policymaking did not result from strategic steering and the inclusion of the managerial level, but rather from non-decisions at the managerial level and from being left 'on their own'. It was the crisis context that empowered them when the course of events impelled by the fiscal crisis resulted in a situation where an increasing amount of work had to be done under more intense time pressure in a more complex working environment.

Consequences of Cutbacks to Public Management

In Estonia, the already existing reform paths were not substantially altered during fiscal retrenchment; the prevailing goal was 'more cost-efficiency', which had been the leitmotif of public-administration reform since the early 2000s (and continued to be one of the aims of reform even during the years of economic boom). This has to do with prevailing 'anti-state' attitudes among the citizens, partly inherited from Soviet legacy and partly fuelled by consecutive right-wing governments. Hence, no path-breaking changes to public administration were introduced. As the cutbacks were carried out in the context of urgency at the very beginning of the global financial crisis, and given that there was very little organised resistance to cutbacks, there was no need to use systematic reorganisations as a cutback strategy.

However, some public-sector reforms and changes were carried out during the years of acute crisis, but these were only indirectly triggered by the fiscal crisis.

First, the most influential public-management reform during the years of cutbacks addressed public-personnel policies. The environment of general retrenchment helped the parliament to pass a new Public Service Act in 2012 that had been rejected already twice before, in 2002 and 2009. According to the new act (implemented in 2013), a quarter of civil servants (e.g. staff in the IT, personnel, accounting and public relations departments) lost their civil-service status and became employed according to the private sector Employment Act. Seniority pay and public-service pensions were abandoned, and the existing (limited) job security was equalled with that in the private sector. Although this reform had been prepared before the crisis hit and was politically motivated, first of all, it can be argued that the crisis situation paved the way for its approval within the coalition and in the parliament, since it carried values such as cost-efficiency and flexibility in personnel management that were also strongly emphasised during the years of cutback management.

Second, the crisis only indirectly affected the ongoing changes in organisational structures, such as the establishment of shared service centres, mergers of government agencies (nine mergers took place at the peak of the crisis in 2008–10) and the government policy to amalgamate local government units. The cabinet was looking for opportunities to reduce operational costs of the public sector, and mergers of organisations as well as consolidating support services were expected to be one possible option for achieving significant cost-savings. All these changes—like the public financial management and budget reforms described in Chapter 13—reflect the more general direction in the Estonian public administration: steps towards greater centralisation.

Third, although the general goal of the Estonian government over the past decades has been to move towards performance management and performance-informed budgeting, the fiscal crisis had a negative effect on the use of performance information in the Estonian government. During 2008–10, the amount of performance information submitted by the line ministries to the Ministry of Finance decreased, as witnessed by shorter performance documents and less focus on performance indicators in the State Budget Strategy (Raudla and Savi 2015). During the crisis, preparing the strategic-planning and performance-budgeting reform was not a priority for the government as its focus was on maintaining fiscal discipline and achieving cutbacks. Consequently, the experience of the crisis appears to have slowed down the performance-budgeting reform.

In terms of more general changes in administrative practices, the Estonian case demonstrates that several shifts in habitual decision-making processes during retrenchment were ad hoc and did not get formalised—as a consequence, they ceased to exist once the immediate fiscal stress was over. On the other hand, the Estonian case study also provides evidence that the impact of crisis on administrative practices may be prolonged, as several changes regarding both cutback measures and the decision-making process initiated during the peak of cutbacks have persisted over time.

Namely, the crisis context caused some formal changes in the legislation concerning the governmental decision-making processes, which provides evidence of a longer-term (if not permanent) effect of the crisis. For example, the crisis brought about several new practices: the Ministry of Finance started to collect and publicly launch monthly reports on the dynamics of macroeconomic indicators and the fulfilment of the state budget; the crisis-time budget formulation contributed to bigger transparency of the budgetary process, especially when considering the visibility of the process to the wider public; civil servants from the Ministry of Finance still belong to the management boards of the state agencies, and local governments still have to consult with the Ministry of Finance when taking loans; and the budget negotiations between line ministries and the Ministry of Finance are still strongly based on top-down budgeting principles (versus reversing the trend of increasing bottom-up elements in budgeting before the crisis). Although these changes were made with a view to specific short-term conditions, they provide for a long-term change towards the centralisation of decision-making. Thereby the crisis context left its footprint on the coordination practices within the central government with a shift from practices based on market and network to hierarchy.

All in all, in the case of Estonia, the dominance of across-the-board cuts and quick administrative fixes addressing the immediate symptoms (short-term fiscal targets) rather than the underlying causes of crisis and structural modernisation provide evidence of an incremental change (versus large-scale structural reforms).

Conclusion

This chapter investigated the response of the Estonian government to the recent fiscal crisis. It has been demonstrated that after the outburst of the crisis the government undertook radical and straightforward cutback measures both on the expenditure and revenue side of the budget, repeatedly introducing negative supplementary budgets. Noteworthy cuts at the expenditure side put an extensive burden on the central government and the operational budgets of individual government organisations. As an unprecedented case in Europe, there was systematic resistance to cutbacks neither by civil servants nor by general public. The government's well-calculated perspective of joining the Eurozone and a broad public support for the euro and fiscal discipline, combined with underdeveloped civil society with a marginal role for unions, made the radical cutback decisions and their speedy implementation possible in Estonia.

In Estonia the radical and quick cutback decisions were facilitated by combining both the centralisation and decentralisation of governmental decision-making procedures, though the former prevailed over the latter. Although the current case study clearly supports the existing theoretical arguments towards more extensive centralisation of decision-making during the cutback management, it vividly demonstrates the complexity of the centralisation-decentralisation dilemma. In the case of Estonia this complexity has been mostly a function of the decentralised across-the-board cuts in the generally centralised decision-making environment as well as the crisis-led empowerment of civil servants and street-level bureaucrats in the urgent decision-making and implementation process.

We conclude that although the budget cutbacks were extensive and directly burdened government organisations and civil servants, the cutback era did not serve as a critical juncture paving the way for novel patterns of public management. The crisis intensified the pressure to reform public management to some extent, but these pressures did not translate into large-scale structural reforms and/or specific reform trajectories in Estonia. Instead, the crisis and general retrenchment environment enabled the government to justify and carry out reforms under the slogan of 'more cost-efficiency'. Thereby reforms that had been postponed or turned down earlier were implemented in personnel management and organisational structures.

Overall, the Estonian case indicates an indirect link between the crisis and public-management reform as the government's response to the crisis displayed elements of continuity rather than change. Therefore, the Estonian case provides evidence for path-dependent rather than path-breaking changes in public management during the cutback era.

References

Åslund, Anders. 2012. "Southern Europe Ignores Lessons From Latvia at Its Peril Crisis." *Policy Brief, Peterson Institute for International Economics,* June: 12–17.

Jõgiste, Kadri, Peeter Peda and Guiseppe Grossi. 2012. "Budgeting During Austerity: The Case of Estonian Central Government." *Public Administration and Development* 32(2):181–95.

Kattel, Rainer and Ringa Raudla. 2013. "The Baltic Republics and the Crisis of 2008–2010." *Europe-Asia Studies* 65(3):426–49.

Kickert, Walter. 2012. "How the UK Government Responded to the Fiscal Crisis: An Outsider's View." *Public Money & Management* 32(3):169–76.

Kickert, Walter and Tiina Randma-Liiv. 2017. "The Politics of Cutback Management in Thirteen European Countries: Statistical Evidence on Causes and Effects." *Public Management Review* 19(2): 175–193. doi:10.1080/14719037.2016.1148193.

OECD. 2011. *Public Governance Reviews. Estonia: Towards a Single Government Approach.* Assessment and Recommendations. Paris: OECD.

OECD. 2012. *Restoring Public Finances: 2012 Update.* Paris: OECD.

Peters, Guy B., Jon Pierre and Tiina Randma-Liiv. 2011. "Global Financial Crisis, Public Administration and Governance: Do New Problems Require New Solutions?" *Public Organizational Review* 11:13–27.

Raudla, Ringa. 2013. "Fiscal Retrenchment in Estonia During the Crisis: The Role of Institutional Factors." *Public Administration* 91(1):32–50.

Raudla, Ringa and Rainer Kattel. 2011. "Why Did Estonia Choose Fiscal Retrenchment After the 2008 Crisis?" *Journal of Public Policy* 31(2):163–86.

Raudla, Ringa and Riin Savi. 2015. "The Use of Performance Information in Cutback Budgeting." *Public Money & Management* 35(6):409–16.

Savi, Riin. 2014. "Public Policy Making in Time of Crisis: The Responses of the Street Level Bureaucrats in Cutback Management in Estonia." *Halduskultuur— Administrative Culture* 15(1):100–17.

Savi, Riin and Aleksandrs Cepilovs. 2016. "Central Decisions, Decentralized Solutions: Comparing the Implications of Central Cutback Policy for Agency Level in Estonia and Latvia." Forthcoming in *Journal of Comparative Policy Analysis.*

Savi, Riin and Tiina Randma-Liiv. 2015. "Decision-Making in Time of Crisis: Cutback Management in Estonia." *International Review of Administrative Sciences* 81(3):479–97.

Part III

Budgetary Reforms in Times of Austerity

9   New Fiscal Rules and Budgetary Reforms Supporting Fiscal Turnaround in Germany

Jobst Fiedler and Juliane Sarnes

Introduction

This chapter focuses on the most important budgetary reform in Germany: the introduction of a second-generation fiscal rule requiring structurally balanced budgets and its impact on the federal (*Bund*) and subnational government (*Länder*) levels. The analysis centres, thus, on two main questions:

1. Did the introduction of the German 'debt brake' have a centralising effect on public management in Germany, resulting in power shifts within and between the different levels of government?
2. What fiscal policy responses were triggered by the constitutional, balanced budget requirement on the Länder level? More specifically, is there a correlation between the level of fiscal stress and the tightness of the fiscal rules?

To answer these questions, this chapter is structured as follows: after briefly recounting the years preceding the crisis and the crisis responses in Germany, budgetary reforms in times of austerity are discussed by: (1) describing the window of opportunity presented by the crisis in 2009 which paved the way for the introduction of the binding fiscal rule in the constitution; (2) analysing the essential elements of this reform as well as the changes in budgeting practices it engendered, with a special focus on expenditure ceilings set in a top-down manner (top-down budgeting); and (3) commenting on the impact of these reforms thus far, improving allocative efficiency and effectiveness in the German public sector. We then explore and typify the variety of approaches chosen by the 16 Länder, implementing new fiscal rules and changing budgetary processes in response to the debt brake and highlight the impact of the debt brake on fiscal results and public administration. We conclude by tracing the potential effects of the debt brake on German fiscal governance in future years.

The analysis is based on a multiyear research project on changes to fiscal governance changes and the fiscal strategies of German subnational

governments between 2010 and 2016. A total of 35 interviews were conducted: three each in ten of the 16 Länder and five in the federal Ministry
of Finance.[1]

Budgetary Institutions and Reform Trajectories Preceding the Crisis

Germany spent the first decade of the new millennium battling the repercussions of national reunification in 1990: deficit-funded fiscal stimuli,
rising debt-to-GDP ratios, stalling economic growth together with persistent, double-digit unemployment figures. The situation was aggravated
by the unintended side-effects of a larger tax reform in 2001, which
weakened government revenues considerably. Between 2002 and 2005,
Germany's overall fiscal deficit rose above 3.0% of GDP, breaching the
Stability and Growth Pact (SGP), a largely German creation aimed at
safeguarding the single currency against fiscally irresponsible decisions
among the Eurozone members; the *Economist* famously referred to Germany as 'the sick man of Europe' (*The Economist* 1999, Siegele 2004).

German governments implemented a range of austerity measures:
between 2000 and 2008, over 430,000 public administration jobs were
cut. In parallel, the German labour market and social systems underwent a fundamental overhaul, also known as the 'Hartz Reforms'. In
hindsight, it becomes apparent that there was actually more austerity
and more substantial reforms in the decade preceding the financial crisis
than in the years after. Aided by the economic recovery from 2006 and
an increased VAT tax rate, these efforts resulted in a close-to-balanced
budget for Germany just before the global crisis hit the country again
after 2008.

Thus preoccupied, the federal and some Länder governments did not
prioritise budgetary reforms, such as initiatives to introduce accrual
accounting and performance budgeting, in the years preceding the crisis.
Budgetary institutions in Germany remained largely as they had been for
decades.

In 2006, however, inspired by similar developments in Switzerland, the
federal Ministry of Finance laid the conceptual groundwork for a macro-
budgetary reform: a German 'debt brake'. This process was accompanied
by increasing debate among academics and experts on the deficiencies of
the 'golden rule' in the German constitution, which had proven ineffective in preventing substantial debt-taking on both the federal and Länder
levels. Over the 40 years it was in place, politicians had creatively pushed
the boundaries of this fiscal rule, which permitted net borrowing up to the
amount of gross investment and in situations of 'macroeconomic imbal-
ance'. In addition, German fiscal federalism grants the Länder almost no
income autonomy but allows leeway with regards to borrowing. Thus,
bailout expectations among the weak Länder had started to undermine

fiscal discipline. Consequently, there was a notable increase in public debt, especially at the federal and Länder levels, reaching about 69% of GDP in 2009, up from about 20% over a 20-year period from the 1950s to the early 1970s (Federal Ministry of Finance 2015, 6).

The Crisis and Government Responses in Germany

In Germany, the financial crisis led to the deepest recession since 1949. The dramatic decline in global trade in 2009 hit the export-driven economy harder than the EU-28 average, export figures plummeting by 18% and investments in plants and machinery by 28%. Overall, the GDP contracted by 5.6% in real terms. The government, a grand coalition of the centre-right Christian Democratic Union (CDU) and the Social Democratic Party (SPD), responded with a comprehensive recovery programme focused on three main areas:

1. Stabilising the banking sector;
2. Keeping up employment via short-term work, cutting taxes and employer contributions to alleviate pressure on companies; and
3. Shoring up domestic demand through two sizeable fiscal stimulus packages totalling 3.1% of GDP, including a 'cash for clunkers' programme to support the German automobile industry.

Consequently, the rise in unemployment was well contained. Aided by the reform efforts of the preceding decade, the German economy bounced back rapidly in 2010 with over 4% real GDP growth. In fiscal terms, however, the year 2010 was not quite so rosy. Falling revenues combined with steeply rising expenditure left federal and Länder governments with a deficit totalling €65 billion (federal: €44.3 billion, Länder: €20.8 billion).

Budgetary Reform in Times of Austerity

The decision to adopt the debt brake coincided with the climax of the economic crisis in Germany—fiscal crisis looming on the horizon. This confirms the view of the crisis as a 'critical juncture' in which the failure of existing institutions became apparent, creating an 'open space' for the establishment of new institutions (Thelen and Steinmo 1992) or a 'window of opportunity' (Kingdon 2003) for a 'paradigm shift' (Hall 1993) in German fiscal policy.[2]

When first proposed in 2008, the debt brake met strong resistance from two sides: Keynesian economists and some members of the co-governing SPD criticised its limited scope for fiscal stimuli in times of economic crisis, while several financially weaker Länder regarded it as a 'straitjacket' that would leave them even worse off in light of the widening infrastructure gaps and the challenges arising from demographic change. With the onset of the crisis, however, the concept of a German debt brake quickly gained traction. Suddenly, fiscal discipline ranked much higher on voters' agendas, and the country's longer-term fiscal sustainability shifted into broad public focus.

Several other factors also played an important role in the adoption of the reform:

1. It took 'a Nixon to go to China' to overcome the political opposition from the SPD: the main promoter of the debt brake, then-Finance Minister Steinbrück, was a member of this party which traditionally favours expansionary fiscal policy in times of crisis. The design of the debt brake, which allowed for cyclical adjustments, also proved helpful.
2. The grand coalition had already established a Commission on Fiscal Federalism involving the Länder. This forum became a suitable arena for debate before the debt brake was brought to a vote in the *Bundesrat*, the second chamber of parliament formed by the leaders of the German Länder. Consequently, several of the Länder's concerns were taken into account:

   a. A comparatively long adjustment period of ten years (2010–19) was intended to give financially weaker Länder enough time to reduce their high deficits.
   b. A sizable financial assistance programme totalling €7.2 billion— co-financed equally by the federal and Länder levels—was drawn up to support the weakest Länder on their path to compliance with the new fiscal rule.
   c. The CDU refrained from pushing for the further tax reductions initially proposed in its election manifesto, which would have had repercussions for Länder revenues.

The grand coalition was thus able to secure the necessary two-thirds majority in the German parliament (*Bundestag*) and the Bundesrat to make the constitutional amendment introducing the debt brake.

The German Debt Brake: Building Blocks of a Macro-Budgetary Reform

The following sections take a closer look at Germany's new fiscal rule: type, legal basis, coverage and supporting arrangements of the reform as well as the changes in budgeting practices it engendered.

Constitutional Amendment of a Flexible Fiscal Rule

From 2010 onward, the constitutional requirement of having (structurally) balanced budgets at the federal and Länder levels replaced the previous 'golden rule' in German fiscal legislation (Article 109a of the Basic Law). Since its reference point is the 'structural deficit'—a result net of one-off and short-term factors—the German debt brake is a second-generation fiscal rule (Schick 2010). It is essentially a countercyclical limit, allowing for more expenditure and potential deficits in bad times and less expenditure in good times. The cyclical adjustments are complicated, partly contested and the final figures are only available ex post for the fiscal year in question. Despite these drawbacks, cyclical adjustment renders the debt brake more resilient than a static fiscal rule, which might easily come under pressure in an economic downturn. Exceptions from the new rule are possible for emergency situations, such as natural disasters. But deviation from the debt brake requires a parliamentary majority of 50% of the Bundestag members plus one together with a binding amortisation plan of all new debt incurred.

Binding Targets for the Structural Deficit and Initial Deficit Reduction

As of 2016, after a transitional five-year period, the federation's structural deficit is limited to 0.35% of GDP. For the Länder, structural deficits will not be permitted after a 10-year transitional phase ending in 2019. Imposing a constitutional rule to the Länder is a considerable shift in German fiscal federalism, as it enables the Bund for the first time to limit the amount of debt the Länder are allowed to take on. All entities that are ascribed to the government subsector under the European budgetary rules must also be included in the borrowing limits set by the debt brake. Former regulations exempting special funds from central government debt have been rescinded in order to prevent a shift of borrowing to off-budget entities.

Since the initial fiscal deficits were very high for both levels of government in 2010, drastic deficit reduction was necessary before the debt brake would come into effect in 2016 and 2020. For the federation this process was legally codified: by 2016, the deficit had to be reduced to zero in equal steps. The Länder remained free to choose their own path to deficit reduction, since budgetary decisions fall under the jurisdiction of each federal state and cannot be stipulated by the national constitution. Some Länder passed subnational fiscal rules during the transitional period, albeit with large variation concerning their strictness. Others postponed such changes to the subnational fiscal framework to later years (see the following).

Enhanced Surveillance Through a Fiscal Stability Council

In order to ensure Bund and Länder governments' compliance with the debt brake and prevent future budgetary emergencies, a Fiscal Stability Council was established.[3] This joint body consists of representatives from the finance ministries of the federation and the 16 Länder and reflects the substantially increased centralisation of the cooperative structure of

German federalism. While the Stability Council monitors the budgets of all German governments, Länder receiving financial consolidation assistance are more closely scrutinised. These Länder have to report on their progress and, in the event of non-compliance, their annual financial assistance can be withdrawn.

Budgeting Changes on the Federal Government Level

At the federal level, the adoption of the debt brake has triggered significant changes in budgeting procedures. The breakthrough of the constitutional debt brake was used to also switch to

1. A top-down approach in establishing the annual budgets that break down the maximum allowable expenditure into departmental expenditure ceilings; and
2. An extension of the timeframe beyond the annual budget, i.e. medium-term budgeting frameworks (MTBF) with a binding effect.[4]

Top-Down Budgeting and Binding MTBFs

Inefficiencies in the traditional bottom-up budgeting process involving line-item scrutiny by the Federal Ministry of Finance and lengthy multitier negotiation processes were not unknown to German public managers. But a window of opportunity was needed to make the necessary reforms possible. Remarkably, these path-breaking reforms were implemented without encountering much resistance. In their inaugural year, the State Secretary in the ministry, a key promoter of these reforms, immediately made use of them to incorporate the cuts foreseen in the government consolidation programme of 2011 in the annual and medium-term ceilings for the departments.

Since 2011, key steps in the new budgetary procedure have included:

1. In February, the Ministry of Finance sends its proposal for the departmental ceilings. They are derived from the medium-term framework that is based on the limits set by the debt brake, but mandatory changes and programmes approved by cabinet resolution are incorporated.
2. The departments then have four to six weeks to question the premises of certain assumptions made by the Ministry of Finance and, after brief negotiations, the departmental ceilings are brought to a cabinet decision.
3. This is followed by a two-month period during which departments draw up their budgets accordingly.
4. In early July, the cabinet ministers decide on the federal budget draft.
5. Parliament adopts the budget in mid-December.
6. Budget execution is continuously monitored in order to adjust, if needed, expenditure to revenue forecasts in order to avoid a breach of the debt brake.

Interviews reveal how, compared to the previous time-consuming, bottom-up budgeting processes, this change led to the centralisation in the relation between the Ministry of Finance and line departments. During the last five years, the binding nature of the departmental expenditure ceilings allocated in a top-down approach was respected by all ministries. While negotiation on certain issues still occurs, the budgeting process is now much more straightforward than the bottom-up process practiced the previous 60 years. According to our interviews, top-down budgeting has strengthened the Ministry of Finance's power, as the multistage bargaining of the past is now largely limited to the first step of setting the departmental ceilings. Our interviewees reported that these negotiations were usually held in a consensus-oriented, calm atmosphere. Where departmental ceilings necessitated reprioritisation and expenditure shifts, top-down budgeting also increased the demand to centralise budgetary decisions within the concerned line ministries. For most line departments, however, the new top-down regime did not result in increased budget pressure, largely because fiscal conditions were improving rapidly after 2010. Moreover, centralisation has paradoxically increased the line ministries' scope of action; as long as they remain within the stipulated expenditure ceilings, they have more freedom to set their departmental budgets, because not every single line item is subject to negotiation. But the Ministry of Finance still scrutinises department estimates for planned savings or additional expenditure. Interviews show, however, that only a few ministries have already made extensive use of their enhanced managerial flexibility given the very favourable financial development in recent years, which has made expenditure shifts largely unnecessary.

Performance Aspects of the Budgetary Process

The federal budget can still be characterised as a detailed input budget, the budget document being about 3,000 pages and containing some 6,600 line items. A budget modernisation initiative (MHR) had already been developed before the crisis but stalled in mid-2010 due to lacking parliamentary support related to an unwillingness to abandon its detailed, line-item-based control. The initiative intended, among other things, to

- replace the present budget chapters with one or more 'products' with a maximum of 1,000 'products' for the whole federal government.
- specify non-financial output measures for each product.
- introduce non-binding accrual-based accounting for ex post reporting to the budget and cash-based accounting.

There has been limited appetite for output measures within a number of line departments, as the Länder are responsible for the execution of a large share of federal expenditure and output. Today, the Ministry of Finance is pursuing a more modest reform agenda, trying to enhance at least the transparency of the budget by adding a foreword to each ministerial budget indicating the performance elements to be tracked. The use of performance information in the budget process thus remains underdeveloped relative to other OECD countries. At best, this moderate reform can result in a modest form of 'presentational performance budgeting'.

The introduction of much-needed spending review processes remains in its initial phase. Binding budget targets and a top-down approach to resource allocation require the ability to confront the resulting challenges of budget prioritisation more directly and systematically. According to our interviews, there are several reasons why progress in this direction is slow:

- The Ministry of Finance was disappointed by a previous large-scale review of all family-related expenditure, starting in 2012, which had yet to be implemented for political reasons.
- The necessary shift in the focus and capabilities within the budget division is met with internal resistance from the so-called mirror units (each unit mirroring one line department).
- Given the large current budget surpluses, there is little appetite for questioning the running programmes of line departments and their clientele so close to the next general election.

Critical reviews of the effectiveness of spending programmes will most likely gain support when it will become more difficult to keep expenditure within the budget limits of the debt brake during the next five years. While a government-wide spending review process has yet to gain support, two large line ministries stand out with internally conducted, comprehensive reviews of their organisation as well as of their running investment or transfer payments programmes—the Ministry of Defence and the large Labour Agency belonging to the Ministry of Labour and Social Affairs. Apart from these two exceptions, administrative reforms on the federal level progressed only incrementally during the post-crisis years.

Fiscal Rules and Budgetary Reforms in the 16 Länder

As one leading German economist has written: 'It is the Länder level where the debt brake and new budgeting procedures come to a real test' (Fuest and Thöne 2013). This is because the Länder and the municipalities that are fiscally dependent upon them make up over 40% of total public expenditure. They employ almost 85% of all public employees and are, due to their role in the second chamber of parliament (the Bundesrat), a powerful player in German politics. The analysis of changes in fiscal rules and budgeting in Germany must therefore go beyond the federal level.

In 2010, the Länder were confronted with a combined financial gap of €30 billion—including €20 billion in deficits and €10 billion in revenue losses due to the discontinuation of certain transfer payments in

2019[5]—which needed to be covered in the ten years until 2020. This seemed a very challenging task for most Länder at the time, as they could not anticipate how increases in tax income and simultaneously falling interest rates would alleviate this task later on. Moreover, deficit reduction is more difficult for the Länder than for the federal government; while the latter can implement changes in tax legislation, reduce the costs of unemployment by lowering benefit levels or by scrapping major subsidy programmes, the former are subject to serious budgetary constraints:

1. Limited autonomy over their major tax revenues—most taxes can only be changed jointly with the federal level;
2. Constrained expenditure flexibility, as about half of their expenses consist of personnel costs, which can only be reduced by voluntary or age-related exits as German law excludes the dismissal of civil servants and public employees for all practical purposes;[6] and
3. High political pressure to increase expenditure, especially in the policy areas for which the Länder are responsible (e.g. schools, universities, courts, police).

In addition, the Länder are characterised by great disparity regarding their economic and fiscal strength. This is only partly mitigated by the consolidation aid received by some of them and the horizontal fiscal equalisation mechanism in place. Consequently, the burden of the task to close the financing gap was not equally distributed among the Länder. Figure 9.1. illustrates how the crisis from 2008, while deteriorating the financial situation in most Länder, significantly increased the disparity between them.

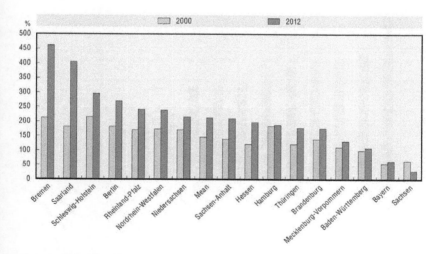

Figure 9.1 Länder Debt as Share of Their Revenues (2000, 2012)[7]
Source: OECD 2014, 33.

The 16 Länder offer a broad field for analysing the variation between them and how they implement fiscal rules and budgetary reform. They are comparable in their tasks and the general constitutional and administrative framework in which they work, but they differ largely in terms of economic and fiscal situation. The following section explores the question as to whether there is a correlation between the level of fiscal stress and tightness of the fiscal rules and the degree to which budgeting institutions and procedures have changed in the different Länder.

Fiscal Rules

In order to comply with the constitutional debt brake in 2020, most Länder have adopted additional fiscal rules applying for the transitional years until 2020. Our research project scrutinises this diverging set of legal requirements among the Länder, analysing their effects on reducing expenditure growth and deficits. In Fiedler and Maderspacher (2014), we developed an index measuring the strength of these special legal rules. The index was developed in 2014 according to an ideal fiscal rule, which was then adjusted to the German Länder during the transition period. It contains categories such as 'strength of legal basis', 'defined deficit reduction steps', 'flexibility regarding economic cycle and extraordinary events', 'share of overall budget covered' and 'corrective mechanisms and sanctions'. Consequently, the index considers issues such as legal quality (constitutional or ordinary legal basis), the majorities needed to use the escape clause, the chosen method for cyclical adjustments as well as specifics of the control account. Figure 9.2

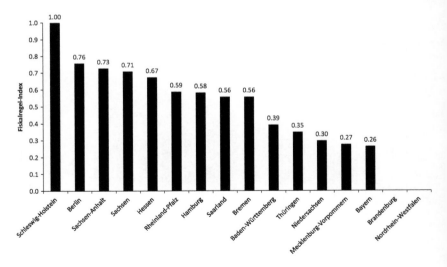

Figure 9.2 Fiscal Rules Index of Federal States (Länder)

Source: Fiedler and Maderspacher 2014, 280.

ranks all 16 Länder according to this index (cp. Fiedler and Mader-spacher 2014, 280).

At first glance, the strength of the fiscal rules for deficit reduction during the transition period until 2020 differs widely between the Länder. While some have put on themselves a restrictive fiscal corset of constitutional rules or contracts, others have only weak or no formal rules preceding 2020, entrusting compliance with the debt brake to the political process or a prevailing culture of fiscal discipline. Comparing and interpreting the results of the two rankings in Figures 9.1. and 9.2., we can distinguish between **four groups** of Länder responses:

A **first group** of five Länder: Bremen, Saarland, Schleswig-Holstein, Berlin and Sachsen-Anhalt. They all have high debt levels and are constrained by tight fiscal rules to reduce their deficits until 2020 based on their contracts with the federal government in exchange for the annual assistance they receive. In addition, most of the Länder in this group have installed additional fiscal rules on top of that.

A **second group** of Hamburg, Baden-Württemberg, Hessen and Sachsen rank low in debt levels but high in the fiscal rules index.[8] Their rules reflect the ambitions of their governments to secure fiscal discipline.

A **third group** of West German Länder (Nordrhein-Westfalen, Niedersachsen, Rheinland-Pfalz) rank high in debt and also in running deficits; apart from Rheinland-Pfalz,[9] however, they have installed only weak or no fiscal rules governing the transitional period.[10]

A **fourth group** of some East German Länder (Brandenburg, Thueringen, Mecklenburg-Vorpommern) rank lower in debt but face the continuing reduction of their post-reunification subsidies until 2020. As fiscal discipline ranks high in their political culture, they do not rely on tight fiscal rules but rather on defending the balanced budgets they have achieved since 2013.

Budgetary Reform

The first steps towards budgetary reform taken by the 16 Länder correspond almost entirely to their fiscal-rules ranking discussed earlier.

The five Länder in the **first group** have all introduced departmental expenditure ceilings set in a top-down manner for their annual and mid-term budget in the first years after the crisis. These were based on a 'contract' approach to centralised budgeting by their cabinets or government coalition (see e.g. Hagen 2007 for the distinction between contract and delegation approaches to centralisation). They chose not to rely further on bottom-up budgeting for reaching the fixed target of no structural deficit by 2020.

In the **second group**, with lower fiscal stress, political entrepreneurs have centralised the budgetary process; in three cases by contract in their cabinet and governing coalition to install top-down budgeting, in Sachsen by delegation to a strong finance minister.

In the **third group** of other West German Länder, cabinet decisions to support a switch to top-down budgeting could not be reached or, in the case of Niedersachsen, could only be reached late in 2015.

The **fourth group** of East German Länder chose a different route, continuing with bottom-up budgeting except for their multiyear binding targets of personnel reduction, which had already been introduced before the crisis. Only Brandenburg also introduced top-down budgeting.

Even among the Länder in groups 1 and 2, some did not install top-down budgeting as consistently as did the federal government. Some still allowed for a parallel bottom-up procedure for the line departments' budget proposals. Some raised their expenditure ceilings substantially once the fiscal situation had improved. Half-hearted implementation was also due to resistance within the central budget offices of the ministries of finance, which were reluctant to give up control over line items.

To conclude: there is no consistent link among the 16 Länder between the fiscal stress metric (Länder debt as a share of their revenues) and the tightness of the chosen fiscal rules. But there is a clear link between the fiscal rules chosen to safeguard against the deficit bias going along with the political process and decisions in cabinet not to rely further on bottom-up budgeting, choosing instead a top-down approach. As Hallerberg stated, this contract approach functions better for coalition governments consisting of two or three parties. Given that multiparty coalitions in almost all German Länder will persist, once the constitutional debt brake is operative in 2020 more Länder can be expected to switch to a top-down approach guarded by cabinet contract.

As on the federal government level, significant changes in budgeting that support improved performance are rare on the Länder level.

By 2012, most of the Länder were moving towards extending cash-based budgeting, reflecting widely held reservations against the superiority of an accrual accounting system over the alternative of enhancing the traditional cash accounting system by adding accrual data.[11] Only one-quarter of the Länder—Bremen, Hamburg, Hessen and, most recently, Nordrhein-Westfalen—decided to implement accrual accounting. This process was led by German city-states such as Hamburg and Bremen, which are simultaneously local and regional governments. The same is true for entering performance information into the budgetary process. The four Länder that decided to introduce accrual accounting are also first-movers when it comes to performance budgeting. While Bremen and Hamburg have already defined a comprehensive set of performance indicators and targets, Hessen and NRW are still in the process of doing so.

Fiscal Results and Broader Effects on Public Management

The following sections trace the potential impact of the debt brake on fiscal results and public administration, taking external developments such as favourable economic growth trends and high inmigration in 2015 into account.

Fiscal Results

As federal and state governments share all major tax revenues, both levels of government benefitted equally from the very favourable economic and financial conditions in Germany between 2010 and 2014, which are continuing to date. As a result, the high deficits of 2010 could be almost completely eradicated (Länder) and turned into a surplus (federal) in a much shorter time span than could have been expected during the financial crisis. This rapid deficit reduction was strongly facilitated by the successful resistance of the ministries of finance at the federal and Länder levels against the demands for tax reform, which would have lowered tax revenue by about €30 billion. The Länder especially based their resistance on their need to comply with the debt brake. This very positive fiscal result was aided by two very favourable economic conditions in Germany during this four-year period:

- Employment increased by about four million people, resulting in a strong, continuous increase in tax income. Between 2010 and 2014, revenue has thus been rising by a CAGR of 3% (federal) and 4.8% (Länder).
- The growth of expenditure was significantly alleviated by plummeting and even negative interest rates that reduced interest payments in 2014 by about €35 billion (€20 billion federal, about €12 billion Länder). This amount would otherwise have to be paid if the 2008 4.3% average interest rate had persisted and, thus, debt would have increased in parallel. This windfall effect has multiplied, as maturing bonds are being refinanced.[12]

The growth of expenditure on the Länder level shows: the remarkable amount of deficit reduction was based much more on these revenue-boosting effects than on a strong limitation of primary expenditure. Cutbacks in back offices were largely offset by additional demands for expenditure in education, social affairs or youth issues directly visible to the public (public employment increased until 2014 by about 90,000 jobs). This resulted in a compound annual expenditure growth (CAGR) of 2.6%.

The numbers also show large differences in the growth of expenditure among the Länder: very limited growth in group 1 (tight fiscal rules) and, in most Länder, in group 2 as well as in group 4 consisting of East German Länder defending their balanced budget in the face of receding federal subsidies. In group 3 (most West German Länder), expenditure growth was much less curtailed in the hope that balanced budgets could be reached through the extraordinary effects of high tax growth and strongly reduced interest rates persisting for most of the period until 2020.

On the federal level, expenditure has fallen slightly, by a CAGR of 0.6%.[13] This was facilitated by the tight fiscal rules and top-down imposed expenditure limits. But it was also assisted by low infrastructure investment, unemployment being down to 5.0% and the high crisis-related expenditure in 2010 running out in the subsequent fiscal years.

Since the surplus in the federal budget in 2015 has exceeded €10 billion, German Finance Minister Schäuble took a rather unprecedented step. He raised the bar and promoted an even more ambitious goal for the years to come: to attain and maintain a fully balanced budget without any cyclical adjustments. In the fall of 2015, the federal surplus proved to be very helpful for an unexpected reason: the high influx of refugees in Germany in 2015 leading to an additional estimated annual expenditure of €15 billion from 2016 for the federal government—including assistance payments to the Länder and local level. These costs can now be financed by the surpluses of 2015 and the subsequent years.

For the Länder, the high remaining amount of €10–15 billion annual net costs for refugees, which are not reimbursed by the federal government, led to a setback in reaching their deficit reduction goals faster than previously planned. But the fortunate revenue and interest rate development continues to be very supportive, meaning that most Länder can still reduce deficits in the steps required by their fiscal rules in 2015 and 2016. Bremen, though, claimed in 2016 that the refugee influx and its costs represented an 'extraordinary emergency' according to the law allowing for exemption from the debt brake rules. The Fiscal Stability Council did not accept this view.

Impacts on Public Management

The potential effects of the new fiscal rules and top-down-imposed departmental ceilings on German public management are quite strong. Unless the limits set by the debt brake will be largely circumvented in the future, its constraints will increasingly put pressure on public administrations, leading to a 'centralisation cascade'. In the first years after the crisis, this has not yet materialised because of the very favourable economic conditions in Germany. As described in greater depth in chapter 4, 'Germany: An Outlier in Terms of Fiscal Consolidation', administrative reforms have thus far remained incremental and generally path-dependent with Germany's cautious approach to NPM-style reforms. In the future, increased budget pressures putting much stronger limits on expenditure would necessitate the deeper reform of processes and structures in public administration.

Impacts on Fiscal Federalism

In October 2016, the German federal and state governments reached agreement on changes to the horizontal and vertical fiscal equalisation system post-2020. Key elements of this reform agreement, which will still have to be entered into the constitution, are:

1. The federal level has committed itself to new annual payments of €5.5 billion to Länder and their local governments, thereby especially helping the financially weaker Länder to be able to comply with the debt brake from 2020 on.
2. This large vertical federal transfer compensates the financially weak Länder for a reduction of the existing horizontal fiscal equalisation system between the Länder. The four financially strong Länder had lobbied heavily to lower their payments. Thereby, all Länder receive a substantial improvement of their revenue from 2020 on.
3. In return, the Federal government will expand its policy remit in certain fields, necessitating stronger cooperation across the Länder (e.g. *Autobahn* development and maintenance). Most importantly, the Fiscal Stability Council's mandate and capacity will be enlarged to monitor compliance with the debt brake.

These changes must be seen in the context of the debt brake and will further increase the centralisation and coordination within the system of German cooperative federalism. On the one hand, this package further strengthens the principle of solidarity between the government levels. This becomes most obvious in the rule-setting paradox that the Federal level is now financially assisting the Länder to comply with the fiscal rules it had previously 'imposed' on them. On the other hand, the focus on vertical equalisation (transfer payments substituting for the reduction of the horizontal fiscal equalisation between the Länder) plus the enlarged powers conferred to the federal government clearly strengthen the role of the federal level and further centralise cooperation within German federalism.

Conclusion

The crisis and a very favourable political context have allowed for a critical juncture in German fiscal governance. While the crisis was brief in Germany, sharply rising fiscal deficits in mid-2009 opened a window of opportunity for installing a tight fiscal regime, pushing through comprehensive budgetary reforms that previously encountered much resistance.

While these reforms are path-breaking in terms of the implied spending trajectory, they are in keeping with—if not a reinforcement of—legalistic traditions in German public administration. The debt brake turned the budgetary process, which is essentially an economic and political process,[14] into a tight, rule-based procedure. Only the cyclical adjustment component of the rule allows for (necessary) macroeconomic stabilisation. The detailed constitutional provisions, which can only be abolished or changed by new two-thirds majorities, are of special significance in a country where the constitution and especially the constitutional court has been held in high regard during the last six decades. Thus, the political cost of future non-compliance would be quite high. It remains to be seen if these new fiscal rules will hold and instil a new and lasting administrative culture.

Given the very favourable economic and fiscal conditions in Germany seemingly continuing until 2017/2018, the new fiscal governance has yet to be exposed to a severe test. This especially concerns the prescribed methods to calculate the cyclical adjustments needed for the structural balance prescribed by the debt brake. The method determined by the EU Commission (applied by the federal government and some Länder) is an issue of contention among economists (Claeys, Darvas and Leandro 2016). The criticism is manifold: it regards an overestimation of the 'output gap' in the case of Germany as well as doubts as to whether it will work in the symmetrical manner as envisioned. In addition, the Länder have been free to choose cyclical adjustment methods individually, with some of them choosing variations on an approach based on tax revenue change. Consequently, Germany might end up with 16 different debt brakes by 2020 that are difficult to monitor and evaluate.[15]

Most of all, however, this rule-based reform in budgeting has led to a more centralised budgetary process, which extends to many management decisions impacting on budget execution. This centralisation has affected the relations of the ministries of finance with the line ministries on the federal and Länder levels alike. The centralisation impact was strongest when top-down set expenditure ceilings had been introduced, but centralisation also worked in some cases by delegating more power to a strong finance minister (Raudla et al. 2015). The centralisation effect has been weak in some of the West German Länder, as top-down budgeting has not been chosen nor have the respective finance ministers been strengthened. Between 2010 and 2014, the same can be observed in the line ministries. In the light of very favourable fiscal developments, the centralisation effect only became weaker in recent years.

Notes

1 More detailed results from the Jobst Fiedler and Juliane Sarnes study will be published in 2017. The research project is co-financed by EUFP 7 funds as well as by two foundations. Juliane Sarnes has been a doctoral student working on the project since 2014; the research assistants Max Osterheld and Quirin Maderspacher preceded her. Intermediate results are published in: Fiedler, Osterheld and Maderspacher (2014) and Fiedler and Maderspacher (2014).
2 Kingdon's concept of a window of opportunity is especially fitting in the German case, as the crisis allowed several necessary conditions (problems, concepts and actors) to unite at a single point in time.
3 Following the European Fiscal Compact, the Stability Council was enlarged by a group of independent experts.

4 Both changes have not yet been entered legally into the federal budget code. The MTBFs are not decided by parliament, but are only binding within government.

5 In 2010, East German Länder received €9 billion in special subsidies, which will be digressively reduced to 0 by 2019. The annual financial assistance received by the five weakest Länder will have been phased out in 2019.

6 In comparison, personnel costs account for less than 10% of federal government expenses.

7 OECD 2014, "Budget Revue Germany," p. 33.

8 Only Baden-Württemberg ranks somewhat lower because of the tight fiscal rule proposed by the government, which could not be entered into the constitution because of purely party political objections raised by the opposition.

9 Loopholes have now appeared in their fiscal rule, which is thus weaker than indicated in the index.

10 Bavaria as one outlier was not included in this group, as it has been in substantial surplus since 2012.

11 With regards to accrual accounting, the greatest reform efforts were made on the local level, but with mixed results to date. Whether this shift to accrual accounting will result in stronger performance-orientation remains to be seen.

12 This sum was calculated by contrasting the reduced interest rates in 2014 with a scenario where the 4.3% interest rate of 2008 would have continued until 2014. See Spiegel Online: 'Bundesbank: Staat spart 120 Milliarden durch Niedrigzins'. In: httpp://www.spiegel.de/wirtschaft/soziales/bundes bank-staat-spart-milliarden-durch-niedrige-zinsen-a-985575.html.

13 Whereas primary expenditure has increased slightly.

14 Quite a few non-German economists have been critical about such a rule-based approach, but Germany managed to enter the rule-based approach into the European fiscal compact of 2012, which was then signed by all but two European countries.

15 A Land could well be able to consider itself compliant under its own regulations while it would be breaking the debt brake under those of another. It remains to be seen whether the Fiscal Stability Council will develop into an effective fiscal watchdog that either enforces some form of harmonisation of debt brake regulation at Länder level or, more likely, translates Länder results into one common monitoring system and ensures compliance with the help of its yet-to-be-defined power to impose sanctions after consolidation assistance expires.

References

Adam, Berit. 2013. "The Need for Harmonised, Accruals-Based European Public Sector Accounting Standards from a German Perspective." Presentation held at the Conference "Towards Implementing European Public Sector Accounting Standards", May 29–30, 2013, EU Commission, Brussels.

Baumann, Elke and Jürgen Schneider. 2010. "Die neue Regel des Bundes." In *Die neuen Schuldenregeln im Grundgesetz*, edited by Christian Kastrop, Gisela Meister-Scheufelen and Margaretha Sudhof, 89–120. Berlin: Berliner Wissenschaftsverlag.

Claeys, Grégory, Zsolt Darvas and Alvaro Leandro. 2016. "A Proposal to Revive the European Fiscal Framework." *Bruegel Policy Contribution*, Issue 2016/2017. http://bruegel.org/wp-content/uploads/2016/03/pc_2016_07.pdf. Accessed on 19th of December 2016.

Economist. 1999. The Sick Man of the Euro, *Economist*, June 5th, Special Section, Retrieved from www.economist.com

Fichtner, Ferdinand, Simon Junker, Guido Baldi, Jacek Bednarz, Kerstin Bernoth, Franziska Bremus, Karl Brenne, Christian Dreger, Heller Engerer, Christoph Große Steffen, Hendrik Hagedorn, Katharina Pijnenburg, Kristina van Deuverden, Alexander Zaklan. 2013. "Wirtschaftspolitik im Zeichen der Krise." *DIW-Wochenbericht* 80(1/2):39–48.

Fiedler, Jobst and Quirin Maderspacher. 2014. "Die deutschen Bundesländer vor der Schuldenbremse: Wirkungen einer veränderten Fiscal Governance über neue Fiskalregeln und Budgetprozesse." *Zeitschrift für Staats- und Europawissenschaften*. Nomos Verlagsgesellschaft 12(2-3):272–299.

Fiedler, Jobst, Max Osterheld and Qurin Maderspacher. 2014. "Wirkungen der Schuldenbremse auf die Governance und Strategien der Defizitreduzierung in deutschen Bundesländern." Zwischenbericht, M.S. Hertie School of Governance, July 2014. www.hertie-school.org/fileadmin/images/Downloads/research_projects/Schuldenbremse_FiscalGovernance_deutschenBundeslaendern.pdf. Accessed on 19th of December 2016.

Fiedler, Jobst, Max Osterheld and Qurin Maderspacher. 2014. "Wirkungen der Schuldenbremse auf die Governance und Strategien der Defizitreduzierung in deutschen Bundesländern." Zwischenbericht, M.S. Hertie School of Governance, July 2014. www.hertie-school.org/fileadmin/images/Downloads/research_projects/Schuldenbremse_FiscalGovernance_deutschenBundeslaendern.pdf. Accessed on 19th of December 2016.

Fuest, Clemens and Michael Thöne. 2013. *Durchsetzung der Schuldenbremse in den Bundesländern*. Köln: Finanzwissenschaftliches Forschungsinstitut an der Universität zu Köln. http://m.stmwmet.bayern.de/fileadmin/user_upload/stmwivt/Themen/Wirtschaft/Dokumente_und_Cover/Schuldenbremse_Bundeslaender_April-2013.pdf.

Hagen von, Jürgen. 2007. "Budgeting Institutions for Better Fiscal Performance." In *Budgeting and Budgetary Institutions*, edited by Anwar Shah, 27–52. Washington, DC: World Bank.

Hall, Peter. 1993. "Policy Paradigms, Social Learning and the State." *Comparative Politics* 25(3):275–96.

Kingdon, John Wells. 2003. *Agendas, Alternatives, and Public Policies*. New York: Longman.

OECD. 2014. "Budget Review Germany." *OECD Journal of Budgeting* 14(2): 1–79.

Paetz, Christoph, Katja Rietzler and Achim Truger. 2016. "Die Schuldenbremse im Bundeshaushalt seit 2011: Die wahre Belastungsprobe steht noch aus." *IMK Institut für Makroökonomie und Konjunkturforschung*. IMK Report 117, September 2016.

Pollitt, Christopher and Geert Bouckaert. 2004. *Public Management Reform: A Comparative Analysis*. New York: Oxford University Press.

Raudla, Ringa, James W. Douglas, Tiina Randma-Liiv and Riin Savi. 2015. "The Impact of Fiscal Crisis on Decision-Making Processes in European Governments: Dynamics of a Centralization Cascade." *Public Administration Review* 75(6):842–52. doi:10.1111/puar.12381.

Schick, Allen. 2010. "Post-Crisis Fiscal Rules: Stabilising Public Finance While Responding to Economic Aftershocks." *OECD Journal on Budgeting* 2:1–18.

Schneider, Stefan and Busso Grabow. 2015. *KfW-Kommunalpanel 2015*. Frankfurt Am Main: KfW Bankengruppe.
Siegele, Ludwig. 2004. "Germany on the Mend", *Economist* Nov 17th, Berlin, Retrieved from www.economist.com.
Spiegel Online. "Bundesbank: Staat spart 120 Milliarden durch Niedrigzins." www.spiegel.de/wirtschaft/soziales/bundesbank-staat-spart-milliarden-durch-niedrige-zinsen-a-985575.html.
Thelen, Kathleen and Sven Steinmo. 1992. "Historical Institutionalism in Comparative Politics." In *Structuring Politics: Historical Institutionalism in Comparative Analysis*, edited by Sven Steinmo, Kathleen Thelen and Frank Longstreth, 1–32. Cambridge: Cambridge University Press.

10 Italy

Centralisation of Budgetary Processes as a Response to the Fiscal Crisis

Fabrizio Di Mascio, Alessandro Natalini, Edoardo Ongaro and Francesco Stolfi

Introduction

As highlighted in chapter 5 on cutback management, Italy is character-ised by the combination of political and fiscal crises, in the context of the broader Eurozone crisis. The goal of this chapter is to investigate the impact on the budgetary process of the peculiar form of crisis (combined political and fiscal) faced by Italy. The budgetary process has been sub-jected to an intense reform activity, combining long-standing calls for mod-ernisation (which had already resulted in a series of interventions since the 1990s) with fiscal discipline, so as to meet ever-increasing fiscal require-ments imposed by the membership of the European Monetary Union.

By applying an historical institutional approach (Pierson 2004), our research addresses the interaction between the legacy of budgetary reform and the pressures of the sovereign debt crisis in the context of the EU framework for fiscal surveillance. Our findings reveal that the response to the crisis has reinforced the legacy of previous budgetary reforms: while the control of the fiscal aggregates by the executive has been further strengthened, the capacity to identify priorities and imple-ment efficiency gains has remained rather weak.

The empirical analysis is based on research carried out between March 2012 and July 2016: data collated are based on statutory and reg-ulatory sources, secondary literature and 12 semi-structured interviews conducted face-to-face in Rome with experts knowledgeable about pub-lic budget from a variety of backgrounds, from senior civil servants to policy advisors in apical posts in public entities endowed with authority over formulating or implementing the state budget (Ministry of Finance, Spending Review Units, Parliamentary Budget Office). The interview protocol includes four themes corresponding to four sets of factors (insti-tutional legacy, changing patterns of political competition, fiscal pres-sures, EU pressures) identified as significant in shaping the response to the fiscal crisis.

This chapter unfolds in three sections. The first sets the stage for the post-crisis developments by briefly describing budgetary reforms in the period leading to the crisis; the thrust towards a more top-down approach to budgetary decision-making is highlighted. In the second section we review the reforms after the onset of the crisis (from 2009 on), focusing on the initiatives of the Berlusconi, Monti and Renzi governments. The key point that emerges from this account is the progressively enhanced influence of the EU on decision-making in Italy, as the financial crisis unfolded and financial market operators were raising concerns regarding the sustainability of the Italian government public debt. Combined with the domestic political context (large and non-cohesive government majorities), this set of circumstances has led reformers to focus overall spending control over any other goal, and notably over the improvement of the efficiency of public administration and the effectiveness of public policies. Furthermore, and contrary to the findings of the literature on cutback management (Raudla, Savi and Randma-Liiv 2015), we do not find evidence of a move from across-the-board to targeted cuts ('priority-setting') as the crisis deepened. We also discuss the use of spending reviews, which began well before the 2008 crisis and have continued afterward: as we will show, their goal of improving the effectiveness of government spending has largely failed. The final section discusses findings providing a summary of our research arguments.

Budgetary Institutions and Reform Trajectories Preceding the Crisis (1992–2008)

The Italian budgetary process used to display a bottom-up approach. At the formulation stage, the overall expenditure was the resultant of the sum of the requests by all spending ministers, with the finance minister acting as the moderator curbing as much as possible the requests coming from spending ministries: a former finance minister portrayed the role as that of a modern-day Saint Sebastian pierced by the darts thrown by the spending ministers (Pisauro and Visco 2008). The government budget did not reflect a coherent, agreed-upon government program. Rather, each ministry used to act as a 'fiefdom' (Hallerberg 2004); a largely autonomous spending centre controlled by the minister's party (or often the minister's faction).

The budgetary process was incremental and fragmented (De Ioanna and Goretti 2008). Budget decisions were made in a piecemeal way, so that until the late 1970s the government budget reflected the simple accretion of the revenue and spending decisions of the line ministries plus the uncontrolled creep of past spending decisions. The broad thrust of the reforms carried out since the late 1970s has been to move from a bottom-up to a more top-down budgetary process. At the core of a top-down budgetary process lies the centralisation of the budget's formulation and the decentralisation of its implementation (Kim and Park 2006).

In particular, centralisation at the formulation stage means that government expenditure is set and allocated to the line ministries based on the government's policy priorities as the first step in the budget process, while decentralisation at the implementation stage means endowing managers in the spending ministries with autonomy over resources to make the most efficient and effective usage of them for attaining the assigned goals ('letting managers manage'). While Italy has achieved a substantial centralisation of the budget formulation process, it has, at the end of the observation period, substantially missed the goal of effective decentralisation of spending responsibilities.

A first step towards centralisation was a new legal instrument, the finance bill (*legge finanziaria*), introduced by Law 468/1978, which brought together decisions on both spending and taxation into a single document subject to parliamentary approval. However, this did not impede spending to accrue beyond the set ceilings, thus contributing to the deteriorating fiscal conditions of the country over the 1980s. A new budget system was established by Law 362/1988, which introduced the medium-term expenditure framework (MTEF) that sets aggregate fiscal targets that the finance bill cannot trespass. This reform strengthened the position of the executive, yet the process for keeping up with MTEF prescriptions has proved frail, as frequently forecasts beyond the first year have proved mutable and baselines modified. Further, new supplementary provisions could be 'linked' to the finance bill beyond the overall limit set by the MTEF.

Reform efforts intensified after 1992 along two connected reform threads: one affecting the budget process so as to modernise public management as well as pursuing efficiency gains; the other aimed at centralising the control of spending through the empowerment of the executive and in particular of the Ministry of Finance, which was merged with the treasury (Stolfi, Goretti and Rizzuto 2010).

With regard to the 'modernising' reform paradigm, Law 94/1997 changed the structure of the budget in the attempt to make public administration more managerial (Gualmini 2008; Ongaro 2011). The number of line-items in the budget was reduced as they were aggregated into units (*unità previsionali di base*) assigned to the responsibility of public managers after the authorisation of programs (*funzioni-obiettivo*) by the parliament. However, neither greater transparency of the budget nor greater orientation to outputs and political accountability of public managers was attained by the implementation of the reform, because the new classification was interpreted in a formalistic fashion, as revealed by the lack of targets and indicators which weakened the connection between budget and programs (Ongaro 2009). A lack of objective yardsticks made it impossible to assess the success of public managers in achieving the policy goals (themselves often vague and ambiguous) mandated by the political decision makers.

Whereas public management reforms in terms of modernisation and efficiency savings have displayed an implementation gap (Ongaro and Valotti 2008), the control of fiscal aggregates by the executive has been progressively effected. Law 208/1999 adapted the budgetary process to the new demands of fiscal surveillance at the EU level by further regulating the finance bill and the linked provisions to ensure the coherence with the overall fiscal targets. However, the fragmentation of the parliamentary majority in a context of perfect bicameralism made it difficult for the executive to limit micro-distributive amendments. Under ever-increasing pressures from EU fiscal surveillance, since 2003 the executive has curbed amendment powers via the progressive consolidation of the 'maxi-amendment' technique: this consists of proposing an amendment while the examination of the finance bill is about to be concluded, which completely replaces the bill in question and the proposed amendments. The maxi-amendment is covered by the confidence vote and this secures the swift approval by stifling parliamentary debate at the expense of the overall transparency of fiscal choices emerging from the budget process (De Giorgi and Verzichelli 2008).

The executive has also adapted the fiscal framework to the devolution of powers to subnational levels of government which started in 1997 before being consolidated by the 2001 constitutional reform. Since 1998 a Domestic Stability Pact (DSP) has provided the framework to make all levels of government co-responsible for the respect of the EU Stability and Growth Pact. The DSP has been enforced by the State General Accounting Department (*Ragioneria Generale dello Stato*, or RGS) within the Ministry of Finance.

The RGS is the body conducting budget execution whose powers have been gradually strengthened under the pressure for tighter expenditure control imposed by the EU level. The taming of expenditures has been secured by introducing cash flow management (Stolfi 2010) and the so called 'expenditure-cut' mechanism, meaning that the Ministry of Finance is authorised to unilaterally and discretionarily limit the expenditure during the fiscal year whenever the deficit grows in an unforeseen manner.

These developments have further centralised budget execution around the RGS, which assumes many of the roles typically located in line ministries in other countries (Blondal, Trapp and Hammer 2016). Notably, the RGS has its units in each ministry enacting expenditure control in a legalistic fashion (privileging compliance with budgetary and accounting regulations to substantive results orientation), often prioritising control over minute disbursements rather than focusing on the output-oriented use of resources. RGS units are also responsible for the budget formulation requests to the Ministry of Finance, meaning that there are no budget units within the line ministries able to and responsible for negotiating with the Ministry of Finance, which has a virtual monopoly of the process. Thus, there is little incentive for the use of performance information in ministry-wide prioritisation and program evaluation, circumstances which provide leeway for the use of across-the-board cuts by the RGS as the main tool of expenditure reduction.

Budgetary Reforms in Times of Austerity (2009–15)

The broad thrust of budgetary reforms has been one of centralisation. Key events (the 1992 currency crisis, the 2008–12 phase of the Eurozone fiscal crisis) seem to have acted as path breaking episodes: the 1992 response to the crisis has been one of centralisation to the executive and the Ministry of Finance, as well as one of redesign along a top-down logic the budgetary process, reversing the traditional bottom-up approach characterising the budgetary process in Italy since at least World War II. The control of aggregates, rather than allocative effectiveness and operational efficiency, has progressively consolidated as the main thrust.

This section focuses on the 2009–15 period, which has seen a dramatic strengthening of the influence of the EU on the budgetary process. In part to respond to EU requirements, the budget process also became more transparent. Three of the four governments that have succeeded each other after the start of the crisis have each tackled budgetary reform. The analysis in this section is organised around them and summarised in Table 10.1. Alongside the influence of EU-induced requirements, governmental interventions on the budget process have in part been affected by the evolution of market confidence in the sustainability of the Italian debt (see chapter 5 on cutback management).

Table 10.1 Italy: Budgetary Reforms (2009–15)

Berlusconi Government (2009–11)	Law 42/2009	Fiscal Federalism
	Law 196/2009	Budget Reform
	Law 39/2011	Alignment of planning documents with the European semester
Monti Government (2011–13)	Constitutional Law 1/2012	Introduced balanced budget provisions and established a fiscal council to uphold the principle of the 'balanced budget'
	Reinforced Law 243/2012	Detailed the principle of balanced budget, set up the Parliamentary Budget Office (PBO), increased the scope of the budget law
Renzi Government (2014–15)	Legislative Decree 54/2014	Implementation of EU Six Pack (Directive 2011/85)
	Law 208/2015	Shift from Internal Stability Pact to balanced budget

Source: Authors' own elaboration.

Berlusconi Government (2009–11): Adaptation to the
European Semester and Stop-and-Go Fiscal Federalism

A new reform of public finance and accounting was enacted with Law 196/2009 so as to increase the coherence of the budget process as well as to adapt the regulatory framework to the EMU requirements and to the new institutional set up designed by Law 42/2009 implementing fiscal federalism. The latter was a late consequence of Constitutional Law 1/2001 which had introduced a quasi-federal institutional framework.

The budget reform did not entail the modernisation of accounting instruments, as it mandated the changeover to a cash-basis budget only, but it revitalised an incomplete process of federalisation by holding subnational governments accountable for resource use, expenditure control, and assessment of results. Consequently, Law 196/2009 provided for the harmonisation of accounting systems at all levels of government and the reform of the financial planning cycle as essential prerequisites for greater involvement of subnational governments in setting budget objectives. However, delays in the adoption of the implementing legislation hindered the institutionalisation of fiscal federalism. In the meantime, the Ministry of Finance has centralised the governance of the expenditure using the constraints set by the Domestic Stability Pact on the subnational governments' freedom to spend (Di Mascio, Natalini and Stolfi 2013).

Law 196/2009 oriented financial and budgetary planning to the medium term (three years) and to an improved transparency and openness of the budget process, consistent with the transparency requirements of top-down budgeting. However, the need to get bills approved quickly and without too many amendments led to maintaining the established practice of forcing the budget through parliament. Most of the austerity packages (see chapter 5 on cutback management for an overview of their trajectory in the period 2009–15) have been spelled out in law decrees (decrees issued by government in cases of necessity and urgency without any prior authorisation by the parliament) that have been later converted into law through the already discussed technique of the 'maxi-amendment' covered by the confidence vote.

Law 196/2009 was amended by Law 39/2011 to ensure the coherence of domestic budget planning within the framework of the European Semester which had introduced the ex ante coordination of member states' economic and fiscal policies as well as reinforced multilateral fiscal surveillance.

Monti Government (2011–13): Stricter Fiscal Rules in
the Context of the Fiscal Compact

As revealed by a leaked confidential letter sent by the present and future heads of the European Central Bank to Prime Minister Berlusconi in the midst of the debt market crisis of late summer 2011, European institutions dictated a reform agenda to the Italian government including stricter fiscal rules with a view to achieving a balanced budget in the short term. However, the collapse of the Berlusconi government prevented the adoption of a reform proposal aimed at introducing the balanced budget in the Italian Constitution—an initiative that was taken up by the successor of Berlusconi.

To gain the confidence of markets about the credibility of its reform efforts, the Monti government opted for the more binding constitutional amendment rather than ordinary legislation. It was adopted in April 2012 (Constitutional Law 1/2012) so as to be applied in the financial year 2014. The amendment introduced the new balanced budget principle ('taking into account the positive and negative phases of the economic cycle', article 81 of the Italian Constitution) and the rules to pursue the new budgetary objectives. In particular, it stated that the whole government sector must have a balanced budget (article 97) and that the harmonisation of public accounts is an exclusive legislative competence of the central government (article 117). These provisions further reinforced the subnational governments' responsibility to share the burden of fiscal adjustment imposed by European requirements (in the meantime further strengthened through the 'Six Pack') on the central government.

Until the application of the new constitutional framework, the Domestic Stability Pact was the domestic counterpart of European fiscal rules. However, under the Monti government the Domestic Stability Pact was reinforced by a number of spending reductions and constraints on subnational governments that went beyond Italy's obligation with the EU as stressed by sentence 129/2016 of the Constitutional Court. The latter declared as illegitimate spending reductions and limits that were imposed on subnational governments by the Monti government in 2013 without negotiating with the representatives of lower levels of government.

The constitutional amendment stated that the violation of the balanced budget rule is allowed only when there are negative effects on the economic cycle or there are exceptional circumstances. In line with the Fiscal Compact providing for the need to adopt a 'reinforced law' to establish the maximum deviation from the parameters of equilibrium in the budget, Law 234/2012 has been adopted in December 2012 by a qualified majority (absolute majority of the members of each House) to define the exceptional circumstances and the corrective mechanisms in case of significant deviations from fiscal targets. This law is reinforced since it may be repealed, modified or waived only by a subsequent law passed by the same special majority. Law 243/2012 also addressed another element of top-down budgeting, namely the comprehensiveness of the budget process (Ljungman 2009), since it aimed to curb the current widespread use of off-budget funds and mandated a new structure based on missions and programs corresponding to public policies

Also with a view to improving the transparency of the budget process and the meaningfulness of the policy choices made through it, law 243/2012 mandated a single budget law, which would cover both the financial implications of new policies and the spending forecast based on preexisting legislation, at the moment approved with two separate laws, respectively the 'stability law' and the budget law. The problem with this arrangement is that the political process, including the decision by parliament, was focused on marginal changes to overall government spending (2% of primary spending in 2014–15; 4.5% for 2015–16), which moreover were impaired by allocative changes made throughout the year by the executive outside the budget process (Camera dei Deputati 2015). The merger of the 'stability law' and the budget law into the new single budget law, due to come into effect from 2016 (budget for 2017), aimed to clarify the allocative choices made by the executive and the parliament and increase flexibility by making a large section of spending based on current legislation open to reassessment (Ministero dell'Economia e delle Finanze 2015).

Finally, Law 243/2012 defined the structure and the functions of the new fiscal council, the Parliamentary Budget Office (PBO), to implement the requirement of the Fiscal Compact to establish an independent fiscal council. It is an independent body, composed of a three-member board appointed by the presidents of the two houses, responsible for monitoring public finances and compliance with fiscal rules and for assessing macroeconomic projections, as well as macroeconomic effects of major legislative packages and public finance sustainability. The political independence of the PBO should ensure, among other things, that the calculation of the structural balance, the reference value for the Fiscal Compact, is not unduly influenced by the government

The introduction of the PBO represents a significant enhancement of the analytical capacities available to the parliament for budget scrutiny in a context that has been marked throughout the period under investigation by a more and more centralised control of the executive over the budget process. The latter has been implemented through emergency law decrees and votes of confidence curtailing transparency and parliamentary debate. Centralisation occurred mainly in the direction from spending ministries to the Ministry of Finance, with the exception of the Monti government, and partially of the Renzi government, in which the process was kept mainly in the hands of the prime minister (it should be noticed Monti initially took also the office of finance minister). Overall, the PBO may be interpreted as a way of retilting the balance in the budgetary process towards some form of (constrained) repoliticisation and offsetting the extensive role of the RGS.

Renzi Government (2014–16): In Search of Flexibility

EU requirements have become more pervasive after the adoption in spring 2013 of the "Two Pack" Regulation which was aimed at balancing the interdependence of economies with a greater degree of information sharing and coordination. The Renzi government adopted Legislative Decree 54/2014 implementing the EU Directive 2011/85 which constituted one of the components of the Six-Pack. This legislative decree aligned the fiscal framework with the EU rules providing for public accounting systems covering all areas of income and expenditure; fiscal planning based on realistic macroeconomic and budgetary forecasts; a medium-term budgetary framework including a three-year fiscal planning horizon.

With regard to the budget process within the parliamentary arena, the PBO started assessing the forecasts of the executive, strengthening the credibility and transparency of the fiscal policy. However, the independent body faces the challenge of priority-setting given its limited resources. Moreover, the PBO's full access, in a timely manner, to all relevant information in the Ministry of Finance, including methodology underlying the budget and macroeconomic projections, is yet to be guaranteed. Nonetheless, at the time of writing, autumn 2016, the PBO for the first time has criticised as too optimistic the GDP growth forecast underpinning the government's proposed budget.

While implementation of the budget has remained under the strict control of the Ministry of Finance, in the Renzi government, as already occurred under the executive led by Monti, the control over budget formulation has to some extent shifted from the Ministry of Finance to the prime minister. Renzi has exploited the mounting public intolerance of EU fiscal rules to ask EU institutions to allow for derogations in order to make room for pro-growth measures. The advocacy of the prime minister led the EU to accept in 2015 and 2016 temporary deviations from the Stability Pact on the condition that Italy would comply with the EU requirements in 2017.

The strengthening of the role of the prime minister in budget formulation represents a departure from the delegation model of fiscal governance, with a concentration and formulation and implementation powers in a strong finance minister that has taken hold in Italy since the mid-1990s. However, in this book the 'centre of government' encompasses both the Prime Ministerial Offices and the Ministry of Finance, hence this relative shift of power does not alter the picture of centralisation characterising the Italian trajectory of budgetary reform under conditions of fiscal crisis and consolidation.

The rising importance of the prime minister, it should be noted, has not however implied the sidelining of the Ministry of Finance. In particular, the position of the Ministry of Finance has been buttressed by the European Semester, as the ministry acts as the linchpin connecting the line ministries with the commission, a role that has almost been thrust upon it by the chronic lack of analytical skills in the ministries.

With regard to the fiscal relations between central and subnational governments, until 2015 these were based on the Domestic Stability Pact. This mainly represented a way of transmitting nationally (and often for a significant part internationally, that is, mandated by the EU) constraints to subnational governments. One trait of this tool and the way it was actually used was its uniformity: the same rules and routines were imposed over small and large local governments alike, and whether administered well or poorly. It should also be noted that some of its technical features (like the use of the criterion of commitment for current expenditures and cash-based competence for capital expenditures, or some arbitrariness in estimating the revenues used to cover outlays) enabled some circumventing of its prescriptions, albeit overall it was effective in terms of control of aggregate spending. In 2015 the need for flexibility led to the abolition of the Domestic Stability Pact. In its place, Law 208/2015 now applies the structural balanced budget rule to multilevel governance.

Spending Reviews

Another area of innovation has been opened by the launch of the spending reviews (Nispen van 2015), explicitly patterned on foreign experiences (notably the UK), though the overall thrust seems to be one of identifying opportunities to deliver the same service levels at a lower cost ('do the same with less'), rather than prioritising expenses. Spending reviews have been carried out as an experimental activity since the early 1980s, before being progressively institutionalised by the establishment of technical committees composed of public finance experts. However, spending reviews have been always carried out on an *ad hoc* basis by external experts operating at a distance from the budgetary mechanics, even under the centre-left government (1996–2001; 2006–08) which generally conceived of spending review exercises as part and parcel of the broader administrative reform drive. They have rarely lived up to the expectations raised. One reason for the failure of spending reviews in Italy may be attributed to their having been disconnected from the functioning of the RGS, whose centrality in the budgetary process has even further increased over the observation period of the fiscal crisis.

With the centre-right Berlusconi government in 2008 there was a shift in the approach to the spending review: technical committees led by external experts were suppressed while a network of expenditure evaluation units was established in each ministry under the leadership of the RGS. This measure was meant to internalise the capacity for expenditure analysis within public bodies. Yet, it did not yield efficiency savings as the Berlusconi government opted for the institutionalised across-the-board approach to face the first stage of the crisis (see chapter 5 on cutback management).

The Berlusconi government also launched a Program for Public Spending Revision similar to the previous ones introduced by center-left governments. An indicator of similarity is the appointment of external experts whose task was to come up with expenditure saving proposals.

However, the abrupt end of the Berlusconi government prevented the spending review to identify savings.

Late in 2011 the Monti government ushered in—once again—the external experts who used to conduct spending review under center-left governments in order to identify where cuts could be achieved with least impact on service provision (Goretti and Rizzuto 2014). Efficiency savings were the only shared policy objective of the spending review, given the discord within the grand coalition supporting the executive, which prevented priority-setting. To counteract the fragmentation of the grand coalition, an inter-ministerial committee was introduced to steer the process.

In spring 2012 the new spending review exercise ensured the transparency of public expenditure by publishing a report on its dimension and distribution. It also held an online consultation in the attempt to identify cuts supported by the broader public. In July 2012 the so-called Spending Review Law Decree 95/2012 was adopted, providing for a round of cuts which failed to abide by the efficiency gains principle, as cuts were distributed across public bodies on the basis of indicators like the spending/inhabitant or spending/employee ratio without taking into account the quality of supply and the social/economic context.

Under the Letta and Renzi government new experts were appointed to lead spending reviews. In particular, Carlo Cottarelli, former director of the Public Finance Department at the International Monetary Fund, was appointed for a three-year term by the Letta government, enjoying more powers than his predecessors and a larger scope for his mission. The latter was articulated around a work program carried out by 25 working groups composed of both experts and public managers so as to strengthen its integration with the budget process. This exercise focused on the identification of proposals for efficiency savings in specific sectors such as public procurement, state-owned enterprises, defence, retirement benefits, tax expenditures and salaries. However, when these proposals were submitted to the Renzi government in spring 2014 they were disregarded by the prime minister, who reasserted the rhetoric of the primacy of politics over technocrats. This clash led Cottarelli to resign and to publicly blame bureaucracies for the lack of collaboration and information sharing (Agasisti et al. 2015).

The politicisation of the efforts to identify efficiency savings led to the appointment as the new commissioner for the Spending Review of Yoram Gutgeld, an MP belonging to the same party of the prime minister, who was supposed to work with Roberto Perotti, an external economist. The latter resigned, however, after only a few months into his mandate, claiming that his efforts were 'useless' in a context marked by the primacy of political leadership in resource allocation.

Concluding Remarks

This chapter reviews budgetary reforms in Italy which occurred under conditions of severe fiscal crisis and political turmoil, within the historical-political context of the Eurozone crisis, which stemmed from the financial and economic crises triggered by the 2008–09 bank bankruptcies. The reform trajectory of the budget process is twofold: on the one hand, there has been a pattern of successive waves of reform, including successive spending reviews, aimed at establishing a coherent decision-making framework as well as increasing efficiency; on the other hand, there has been the progressive centralisation of the budget execution around the executive, by limiting the amendment powers of the parliament and by securing the RGS a pivotal role. In terms of outcomes, the control of overall fiscal aggregates has been achieved, leaving unaltered the input-oriented and non-transparent structural dynamics of expenditure.

Based on our analysis we argue that the intertwining of the political crisis with the fiscal crisis prevented the response to the latter from unfolding into different phases. In particular, we find no evidence of 'priority-setting' taking place in the later stages of fiscal stress, and the explanation behind this pattern of budgetary reform lies in the interaction between political crisis and the institutional legacy. In a context marked by political turmoil, coalition governments lacked the cohesion needed to implement priority-setting strategies, deemed too demanding for political leaders, also considering their demanding information and knowledge requirements. Given the lack of performance information generated by systems which have remained decoupled from the budget process throughout the reform trajectory, political executives were not in the condition—even assuming they would have otherwise been willing—to redefine performance management as a tool for strategic prioritisation of resources in the context of the economic crisis.

Political leaders of coalitions government of the 2008–16 period have rather relied on the repertoire of across-the-board cuts which had been institutionalised by the reform trajectory preceding the crisis. The uniformity of across-the-board cuts suited well the focus of political leaders on the control of fiscal aggregates in the short-term under the pressure imposed by the emergency of the Eurozone crisis, as it avoided the issue of setting priorities which could have been fraught with undesirable (for policymakers) political consequences in a context marked by political turmoil.

However, the response to the crisis through across-the-board cuts has reduced the visibility of political leadership in the budget process. To address this de-responsibilisation of political leadership, a spate of spending reviews has been launched with a focus on efficiency gains (rather than priority-setting). As it already happened throughout the reform trajectory preceding the crisis, spending reviews have been carried on an *ad hoc* basis by commissions composed of external experts operating at a distance from the budget process.

As in the past, the latter has been dominated by the RGS Department at the Ministry of Finance, which has exploited the need for more spending control imposed by the crisis to further entrench its legalistic conception of the budget in a context still marked by the lack of budgeting capacity in line ministries. Lacking policy capacity in the administration, and relying on formal adherence to the law, budgetary decision-making, including the spending reviews, has emphasised across-the-board cuts that do not require difficult choices on resource allocation and a meaningful discussion of how to connect the government program to actual policies and how these should be funded.

The dominance of the RGS resulted in effective control of spending aggregates but also a lack of integration between the budget process and the spending reviews, eventually leading external experts to give up on pursuing efficiency, as shown by the frequent turnover of spending review commissioners: spending review 'czars' lasted on average one year in the post. It is worth noting that the impact of the spending reviews has not been entirely negligible: while experts have struggled to achieve efficiency gains, they have identified large savings and a wealth of methods for pursuing efficiency, raising the public's awareness of the need to reorganise the public sector given the prospect of a tight budget situation for many years to come.

Given the lack of priority-setting and the implementation gap of spending reviews, the crisis has been effectively tackled by fiscal discipline. The latter has been ensured by more stringent rules and a more centralised budget process, further reinforcing a pattern which has emerged since Italy qualified for EMU membership. This observation raises the question of the relationship between the domestic reform trajectory and the influence of EU fiscal governance.

Until the early 2000s the impact of European pressures on the reform of Italy's budget institutions was rather limited (Stolfi 2008). Even in the run-up to the EMU, major reforms like the merging of the Treasury and Finance Ministries owed more to changed electoral incentives (the bipolarisation of electoral competition, which favours forms of delegated fiscal governance; see Hallerberg 2004; Hallerberg, Strauch and Hagen 2009) than to the influence of the EU level.

From the early 2000s on, however, domestic and European factors have more clearly interacted. The move to cash budgeting was mandated in 2009, before the 2010 crisis, and in fact cash budgeting has long been discussed in Italy; at the same time, the current push to finalise the new cash-based approach responds to the forecasting and monitoring requirements stemming from EU fiscal governance (Directive 2011/85/EU). Similarly, the reduction in the use of off-budget funds, which was already part of the 2009 law reforming the budget structure (law 196/2009), also became part of law 243/2012 implementing the changes mandated by the 2012 Treaty on Stability, Coordination and Governance (Fiscal Compact). Likewise, finally, a medium-term budget framework, another key element of top-down budgeting (Kim and Park 2006) has been central to the Italian budget process since the early 1990s, but it was reformed in 2011 to integrate it into the European Semester.

Further reform elements have an entirely supranational origin, reflecting the efforts of the EU to improve national fiscal governance in the wake of the European fiscal crisis, such as in particular the creation of the Parliamentary Budget Office and the introduction of the balanced budget requirement. However, so far transparency has actually been severely undermined by the centralisation of the control of fiscal aggregates around the Ministry of Finance through the adoption of emergency decrees which have limited the involvement of both the parliament and subnational levels in the budget process. Conversely, recent budgetary reforms could set the stage for better parliamentary scrutiny and shared responsibility between levels of government in meeting EU requirements.

Finally, it should be noted that in the last observed stage of the crisis, the prime minister (at the time this book goes to press) challenged the dominant role played by the Ministry of Finance in budget formulation as well as the role of external experts conducting spending reviews. This finding indicates the increasing politicisation of the budgetary process driven by public dissatisfaction towards a painful budgetary consolidation (read: squeeze) which is not only the consequence of past domestic fiscal profligacy but it is also deemed to be due to inappropriate EU-driven impositions ('austerity'). In particular, fiscal sustainability has been weakened by the effects of the strict fiscal discipline imposed by the EU on a country like Italy facing the exogenous constraint of a high interest burden. Fiscal improvements have been hidden by the large cyclical downturn prolonged by the lack of commitment at both the EU and domestic level to growth-friendly interventions.

Acknowledgements

The chapter is the result of a common undertaking. However, sections 'Introduction' and 'Budgetary institutions and reform trajectories preceding the crisis (1992–2008)' can be directly attributed to Fabrizio Di Mascio; section 'Concluding remarks' to Alessandro Natalini; section 'Budgetary Reforms in Times of Austerity (2009–15) was co-authored by Edoardo Ongaro and Francesco Stolfi.

References

Agasisti, Tommaso, Marika Arena, Giuseppe Catalano and Angelo Erbacci. 2015. "Defining Spending Reviews: A Proposal for a Taxonomy With Applications to Italy and the UK." *Public Money & Management* 35(6):423–30.

Blöndal, Jón, Lisa von Trapp and Erik Hammer. 2016. "Budgeting in Italy." *OECD Journal on Budgeting* 15(3):37–64.

Camera dei Deputati. 2015. *Indagine conoscitiva sulle prospettive di Riforma degli strumenti e delle procedure di bilancio.* Rome: Italian Chamber of Deputies.

De Giorgi, Elisabetta and Luca Verzichelli. 2008. "Still a Difficult Budgetary Process?" *South European Society & Politics* 13(1):88–110.

De Ioanna, Paolo and Chiara Goretti. 2008. *La decisione di bilancio in Italia.* Bologna: Il Mulino.

Di Mascio, Fabrizio, Alessandro Natalini and Francesco Stolfi. 2013. "The Ghost of Crises Past: Analyzing Reform Sequences to Understand Italy's Response to the Global Crisis." *Public Administration* 91(1):17–31.

Goretti, Chiara and Luca Rizzuto. 2014. "The Spending Review: Use and Abuse of a Term." In *Italian Politics: Technocrats in Office*, edited by Aldo Di Virgilio and Claudio Radaelli, 188–206. New York: Berghahn Books.

Gualmini, Elisabetta. 2008. "Restructuring Weberian Bureaucracy." *Public Administration* 86(1):54–76.

Hallerberg, Mark. 2004. *Domestic Budgets in a United Europe.* Ithaca, NY: Cornell University Press.

Hallerberg, Mark, Rolf Strauch and Jürgen von Hagen. 2009. *Forms of Fiscal Governance: Evidence From Europe.* Cambridge: Cambridge University Press.

Kim, John and Chung-Keun Park. 2006. "Top-Down Budgeting as a Tool for Central Resource Management." *OECD Journal on Budgeting* 6(1):87–125.

Ljungman, Gösta. 2009. "Top-Down Budgeting: An Instrument to Strengthen Budget Management." IMF Working Paper 09/243.

Ministero dell'Economia e delle Finanze. 2015. *Rapporto sullo stato di attuazione della riforma della contabilità e finanza pubblica.* Rome: Italian Ministry of Finance.

Nispen van, Frans. 2015. "Policy Analysis in Times of Austerity: A Cross-National Comparison of Spending Review." *Journal of Comparative Policy Analysis* 18(5): 479–501.

Ongaro, Edoardo. 2009. *Public Management Reform and Modernization: Trajectories of Administrative Change in Italy, France, Greece, Portugal, Spain.* Cheltenham: Edward Elgar.

Ongaro, Edoardo. 2011. "The Role of Politics and Institutions in the Italian Administrative Reform Trajectory." *Public Administration* 89(3):738–55.

Ongaro, Edoardo and Giovanni Valotti. 2008. "Public Management Reform in Italy: Explaining the Implementation Gap." *The International Journal of Public Sector Management* 21(2):174–204.

Pierson, Paul. 2004. *Politics in Time: History, Institutions, and Social Analysis.* Princeton: Princeton University Press.

Pisauro, Giuseppe and Vincenzo Visco. 2008. "Note Sulle Procedure Di Bilancio." *Politica Economica* 24(2):141–58.

Raudla, Ringa, Riin Savi and Tina Randma-Liiv. 2015. "Cutback Management Literature in the 1970s and 1980s: Taking Stock." *International Review of Administrative Sciences* 81(3):433–56.

Stolfi, Francesco. 2008. "The Europeanization of Italy's Budget Institutions in the 1990s." *Journal of European Public Policy* 15(4):550–66.

Stolfi, Francesco. 2010. "Testing Structuralist and Interpretative Explanations of Policy Change: The Case of Italy's Budget Reform." *Governance* 23(1):109–32.

Stolfi, Francesco, Chiara Goretti and Luca Rizzuto. 2010. "Budget Reform in Italy: Importing Enlightened Ideas in a Difficult Context." In *The Reality of Budgetary Reform in OECD Nations: Trajectories and Consequences*, edited by John Wanna, Lotte Jensen and Jouke de Vries, 260–80. Cheltenham: Edward Elgar.

11 Budgetary Reform in Denmark in Times of Austerity

Eva Moll Ghin

Introduction

This chapter presents an analysis of the background, content and consequences of the organic 'Budget Law' that was passed by the *Folketing*,
the Danish parliament, in 2012, taking effect in 2013. The Budget Law
was justified by the financial crisis and it implements the European Fiscal Compact, but it also contains elements that are motivated by long-
standing domestic concerns with weak expenditure control, particularly
at the level of local government, where most of the public consumption
takes place in the Danish context.

In this chapter, it is argued that the crisis was used as a 'window of
opportunity' by actors representing the government's administrative
budget guardian, the Ministry of Finance, to find support for legal instruments that had been under consideration for decades but hitherto not
found political support. The Budget Law adds to the existing trajectory
of budgetary reform by reinforcing the top-down approach to budgeting,
but it also represents path-breaking change, as it departs from the principles of informalism, local autonomy and negotiated governance that
are central to the Danish administrative tradition. Furthermore, the new
regulations pertaining to budgetary implementation have been contra-
dictory with those aspects of the NPM-inspired trajectory of financial
management reforms that have been meant to improve operational efficiency by increasing local discretion. Overall, the Budget Law represents
a centralisation of budgetary decision-making and has led to more intensive coordination of budgetary spending at the expense of managerial
flexibility.

The chapter addresses the background of the Budget Law and its consequences for both financial management in central government and the
institutional arrangements for controlling aggregate expenditure in the
98 municipalities that have independent taxing rights and are responsible for a broad portfolio of welfare services, environmental services,
infrastructure etc.[1] It thus adds to the existing analyses of recent budgetary reform in Denmark, which focus on the economic and political

circumstances that led to the adoption of the Budget Law (Jensen and Davidsen 2015; Suenson, Nedergaard and Christiansen 2016), the consequences of the Budget Law for accountability in central government (Hansen and Kristiansen 2014) or on the arrangements for steering local finances (Sørensen 2014). The analysis in this chapter is based on a combination of primary data sources and methods, including documentary analysis and qualitative interviews. Interviews have been carried out with officials from the Ministry of Finance, the Danish Association of Local Governments (LGDK) and budget officers in two line ministries at both the departmental and agency levels.

The chapter first describes the budgetary institutions and reform trajectories preceding the crisis and then presents an analysis of the budgetary reforms that were adopted in the years 2010–13. Last but not least, it discusses how the reform has changed public management.

Budgetary Institutions and Reform Trajectories Preceding the Crisis

Until recently, there were few legal stipulations of the national budgetary process. The Danish Constitution contains few rules about budgeting, including the rules that all expenditures must be decided through budgetary procedures, that no taxes can be levied without a legal mandate, and that the budget proposal must be presented to parliament no later than four months before the budget year. Further regulations of the budget process took the form of circulars issued by the Ministry of Finance or its Economic Agency (Jensen and Fjord 2010, 199). The informal approach was no less accentuated in the government's steering of local finances, which relied on an informal institutional arrangement known as the 'budgetary cooperation', which involves negotiations about the preconditions for each year's local budgeting between central government, mainly represented by its economic ministries, and the national associations of regions and municipalities (Sørensen et al. 2007).

In the next section, an account is given of the development of budgetary and financial management institutions in central government and the development of institutions for controlling local finances. The focus in each section is first on the reform motivated by concern with fiscal discipline and then reform motivated by concerns related to allocative and operational performance.

Budgeting and Financial Management in Central Government

The only major budget reform that has taken place at the national level in Denmark occurred in 1984–85. In the following, we shall consider this reform and some of the amendments that have been made since.

Reforms Motivated by Fiscal Discipline

The budget reform in the 1980s was designed to improve fiscal discipline through the introduction of a top-down budgeting process that represented a contract approach to centralisation (Hagen 2007). It meant that annual aggregate targets for government expenditures were set by the government early in the annual budget preparation process and announced to the finance committee of parliament (Jensen and Fjord 2010, 204). The target was then broken down into total ceilings for each ministry, and the ministries were expected to budget within these ceilings. However, given the political character of the targets and the need to reach agreement—first within the government coalition and then in the Folketing—about the proposed budget, there was also ample room for bottom-up negotiations about the size and distribution of public expenditure (Jensen 2008).

In the 1990s, the top-down budget process was reinforced by the adoption of a *medium-term fiscal framework* in the form of fiscal projections and plans elaborated in the Ministry of Finance. In these medium-term plans, growth targets for public expenditure were deduced from future macro-economic requirements, primarily debt reduction. The targets were not encoded in legislation, however, and they had to make their way into budgets through negotiations within government, in parliament and with the local government associations (Jensen and Fjord 2010).

Reforms Motivated by Reallocation and Operational Performance

The main mechanisms for reallocation are the *'harvester'*, an annual 2% across-the-board cut on current expenditure, which has existed since the 1980s, and *special budgetary analyses* initiated by the Ministry of Finance, which have existed since the mid-1980s but gained a more prominent position in the 1990s (Jensen and Fjord 2010, 207). The harvester is used to free up funds for political priorities in the budgeting process and for reallocation through the exemption of prioritised expenditure areas. Special budgetary studies are used to identify efficiency gains in (or across) line ministries that can be reaped and used for political priorities. The special studies are also used as input for multiyear agreements concerning the development in specific policy areas. Areas that are covered by multiyear agreements are guaranteed against further cuts in that period.

The objective of improving operational performance has motivated a series of reforms that have been based on the idea of increasing the budgetary flexibility enjoyed by public managers while keeping them accountable for results. Budgetary flexibility was a main theme of the 1980s budgetary reform in addition to top-down budgeting. For example, agencies were allowed to transfer funds between appropriations and financial years. In 1991, the budgetary flexibility theme was further pursued when the Ministry of Finance appointed 10 'free agencies' which were given extra managerial flexibility in return for commitments to improved efficiency. These free agencies became 'contract agencies' in the 1990s, and a more elaborate contract management regime was developed in which they were held accountable to their parent ministerial departments (Kristiansen 2011). The instrument was diffused to most of the agencies in central government.

In the 2000s, the theme of improving performance was pursued through the introduction of accrual accounting and budgeting in central government. In Denmark, the conversion to accruals was motivated by improving the performance in agencies rather than budget transparency, and large exemptions were made in order to avoid jeopardising short-term expenditure control; hence, appropriations for large capital spending (e.g. infrastructure, military assets) and for grants and transfers, such as pensions, remained on a cash or commitment basis (Jensen and Fjord 2010, 214).

Central Government Control of Local Finances

Since the 1970s, Denmark has delegated more of the implementation of its welfare policies to local governments. This course has been grounded in cultural and political preferences for local autonomy but has also been justified by the idea that the joint decentralisation of tasks and financial responsibility would generate good economic incentives at the local level (Pallesen 2003; Blom-Hansen et al. 2012).

Reforms Motivated by Fiscal Discipline

Over the decades, the accountability to local taxpayers has not been enough to keep local spending in line with the government's macro-economic targets. With local consumption levels exceeding 20% of GDP (Blom-Hansen et al. 2012, 26), it has been necessary for the government to steer local spending levels. Rather than regulate local expenditure through legal means, however, the governments of the 1970s and 1980s established a corporatist arrangement as the main steering mechanism: the 'budgetary cooperation' (Blom-Hansen 1998). It is centred on annual collective agreements between the central government and the two associations of local governments (one for the municipalities, the other for the counties—now regions) about the premises for local budgeting for the next financial year. The agreements contain targets for the aggregate level of operational and capital expenditure and/or the aggregate development of local taxation. They also specify the aggregate level of block grants to be paid by central government to local governments. The targets do not apply to the municipalities or regions individually, and it is up to their national associations to induce their members to respect the targets collectively (Sørensen et al. 2007).

In the 1980s and early 1990s, the budgetary cooperation was relatively successful (Blom-Hansen 1999). In the 1990s, however, municipal expenditure grew in excess of the targets in the government's medium-term plans, and this began to be perceived in the Ministry of Finance as a problem awaiting a solution (Lotz 2007). After the Conservative and Liberal parties came to power in 2001, the problem of controlling local spending climbed higher on the political agenda. A collective 'tax stop' was introduced and enforced through ad hoc reductions of block grants for regional governments that raised taxes without permission. In the prosperous climate of the 2000s, however, the local governments were able to maintain high expenditure growth rates despite the tax stop.

Reforms Motivated by Reallocation and Operational Performance

In the mid-1990s, higher than planned local expenditure growth was not a major political problem when financed by local taxes, because it was part of the Social Democrat–led government agenda to increase the coverage of local welfare services, such as public childcare. Over the decades, however, local overspending led to the unplanned expansion of local welfare services at the expense of other public services and the private sector. Furthermore, from the perspective of the Ministry of Finance, the high expenditure growth rates raised suspicions that resources were not used effectively and efficiently. Beginning in the late 1990s, the ministry began to use benchmarking and other performance analyses in the annual negotiations as an argument that local governments could deliver local services at lower cost (Sørensen 2013). The government also used the annual agreements with the local government associations to communicate its policies for the development of local services and administrations, joint performance targets and so forth. However, it remained politically contentious for central government to directly address the performance of individual municipalities (Sørensen 2013).

Budgetary Reform in Times of Austerity

In the mid-2000s, Denmark experienced a strong economic boom, leading to nominal surpluses on its public finances of almost 5% in 2007 and 3.2% in 2008 (Jensen and Davidsen 2015). In this situation, the political climate was not hospitable to reforms that would improve the level of fiscal discipline. In 2009, however, GDP contracted by more than 5%, and the economic crisis led to deteriorating public finances.

In 2010, Denmark entered the EU Excessive Deficit Procedure, and the Conservative-Liberal government presented a short-term consolidation package that included a zero-growth target for local operating expenses, and economic sanctions for overspending in the municipalities (Danish Government 2010). In 2011, it presented a medium-term economic plan with a focus on the reform of retirement arrangements (Danish Government 2011a). In this plan, the government also announced its intention to propose a new budgetary regime based on legally binding expenditure ceilings for each level of government.

In the 2011 elections, the Conservative–Liberal government lost power to a coalition consisting of the Social Democrats, the Socialist People's Party and the Social Liberals. The first two parties had run on a joint platform of rolling back most of the austerity policies of the former government. In order to take power, however, they needed to include the Social Liberals in the government, a party that has 'responsible' economic policies as an important element in its programme. After lengthy negotiations, the new government issued a coalition programme in which it pledged to continue the broad economic policies of the previous government (Danish Government 2011b). In the programme, the government promised to present an organic Budget Law in the Folketing, which would introduce legally binding expenditure ceilings on each level of government (Danish Government 2011b, 11).

In the following, the main elements of the new organic Budget Law will be presented. The extent to which the law represents path-breaking change will then be analysed together with the role that the crisis and the politics of austerity have played in the changes to the main budgetary institutions.

The New Budget Law

The Budget Law (Law 547 of 18/06/2012) introduced different types of budgeting institutions that are meant to solve the 'common pool' problem of public spending (Alesina and Perroti 1996; Hagen 2007), including (1) fiscal output rules, (2) budget procedural rules and (3) rules about the transparency and comprehensiveness of the budgetary process.

Fiscal Output Rules

The first substantial regulation in the Budget Law implements the requirement of the European Fiscal Stability Treaty that overall structural finances must be in balance or surplus. In the Danish case, it entails that, with few exemptions, the annual structural deficit can at most amount to 0.5% of GDP. The balanced-budget requirement is accompanied by an automatic correction mechanism, which obligates the Ministry of

Finance to calculate the structural deficit for the following financial year and initiate corrective measures if the deficit exceeds the requirement.

The second major element of the Budget Law is the introduction of fixed aggregate expenditure ceilings for each level of government (state, regions and municipalities). The ceilings are decided by parliament based on the government's medium-term projections and the structural balancing rule. Cyclical expenses are exempt from the ceilings in order not to disable the automatic stabilisers. The ceilings cover non-cyclical transfers and net operating expenditures for public services at each level.

Budget Procedural Rules

The Budget Law also changes the budget process. The new expenditure ceilings are decided in the Folketing on a four-year, rolling basis. This reduces the likelihood that spending levels can be adjusted as a result of bottom-up contributions from line ministries or as a result of the annual negotiations with the local government associations. It also means that parliament reduces its own competence in the annual budgetary decision-making process for coupling decisions on expenditure levels to other fiscal decisions. In the imagery of the Odyssey, parliament 'ties itself to the mast' to increase the probability of medium-term fiscal discipline (Suenson, Christiansen and Nedergaard 2016). Last but not least, the Budget Law affects the implementation of the budget. In central government, each ministry is obligated to perform regular controls and projections to prevent actual spending from exceeding appropriated spending for the financial year. Furthermore, the Ministry of Finance is mandated to perform regular controls and projections to ensure that overall spending will not exceed the expenditure ceiling for the year and to subtract any overspending from next year's appropriations (Budget Law, Law 547 of 18/06/2012, §§14–15). The Budget Law does not directly regulate the implementation of budgets in local governments, but it was accompanied—and preceded—by a set of laws mandating the government to sanction local governments in the case of overspending by reducing its block grants to local governments.

Rules Regarding the Transparency and Comprehensiveness of the Budgetary Process

The structural balance rule, which is a central element in the Budget Law, is a complex target that can be criticised for its low level of transparency (Schick 2010). However, the Budget Law also contains several mechanisms that are meant to increase transparency and accountability. First, the expenditure ceilings are designed to be simple and transparent measures that can be used by the media to keep policymakers accountable. Second, alongside the Budget Law, a law was passed that gives the existing

Economic Council the role of monitoring the administration of the structural balance rule and expenditure ceilings (Law 583 of 18/6/2012). This provision implements a requirement of the Fiscal Stability Treaty and may be regarded as a mechanism to reduce the government's scope for overly optimistic (or pessimistic) projections and for creative and strategic use of what is kept in and outside the budget (Alesina and Perotti 1996, 403). The Budget Law also increases the comprehensiveness of the national budget process since it explicitly addresses municipal and regional spending.

The Pattern of Change

This section discusses, first, whether the Budget Law represented path-breaking change of the existing budgetary institutions and, second, whether the changes were the result of a 'juncture' brought about by the international crisis or the result of a longer-term process of gradual change.

Path-Breaking Change?

The Budget Law represented path-breaking change because it provided the legal institutionalisation of public expenditure control that had been discussed on previous occasions but not found compatible with the pragmatic administrative traditions and the political preferences for an informal system (Jensen and Fjord 2010, 206–7; cp. Administrativ Debat 2013, 3). The Budget Law also departs from the previous philosophy that local tax-financing provides built-in incentives for expenditure restraint and that local fiscal policies need merely be *coordinated* with the government's policies. In the new regime, the government dictates the level of local spending.

At the same time as it departed from the principles of pragmatism and local autonomy, the Budget Law added to a long-term gradual transformation from decentralised towards centralised resource management. In central government, the Budget Law reinforced the status of the government's medium-term plans and targets and the existing top-down budgeting process. It also added a layer of new rules that makes short-term expenditure control a central element in financial management. The implementation of the law has led to new regulations that require agencies to present core periodised budgets and to follow standard cadences of spending control focusing on deviations from the periodised budget (Hansen and Kristiansen 2014, 278). These regulations are part of a broader project that is meant to lead to 'Good Financial Management', but only the requirements regarding short-term expenditure control are founded in law.

With regard to performance management, the Budget Law may be argued to reverse some of the previous reform elements that were intended to provide flexibility and incentives for long-term cost-effectiveness at the agency level. While the law does not take back the right of agencies to save funds for later spending, agencies can no longer freely spend their savings. At the end of 2012, a new rule was presented in which it was stated that in order to spend savings, an agency must have approval from its parent ministry and that the net spending of savings must be neutral or negative in total for the minister's range of portfolio in the financial year (Ministry of Finance 2012). Exemptions can be made, but only after a centralised assessment of the effects on aggregate adherence to expenditure ceiling. At the same time, the government has sought to provide new directions for performance management through its project on 'Good Financial Management'. For example, ministries and agencies have been encouraged to redirect their Management by Objectives and Results in a more strategic, effect-focused direction. The project has also provided new tools for comparative performance analysis, including cross-ministerial benchmarking data on administrative costs, absenteeism etc. However, it remains up to the ministries and agencies how they will use these tools.

The budgetary reform also adds a new, radical step to a gradual, long-term process of integrating local finances in the government's overall, top-down budgetary regime. The government still negotiates annually with the local government associations about the level and financing of expenditure for next year. However, the Budget Law has changed the reference point of the negotiations from the 'bottom-up' questions of how much local governments spent last year and how much (extra) they need next year to deliver known standards of service, to the 'top-down' question of how much expenditure society can afford based on the government's projections and policies. This is not an entirely new phenomenon, as the government's medium-term projections and economic targets have also previously constituted the reference point for the negotiations. However, since the introduction of expenditure ceilings and automatic economic sanctions, the municipalities no longer exceed the government's economic targets in their aggregate budgets or accounts. This has changed the reference point of each year's negotiations from the higher-than-planned level of last year's spending to a lower-than-planned level of spending or to the level of spending decided in the Folketing.

The Budget Law has also potentially allowed the government to extend the use of existing mechanisms for reallocation to central–local relations. In principle, the expenditure ceilings are fixed for each level of government, but the calculation of the ceilings leave a buffer for annual allocation between levels of government. In order to increase the scope for reallocation, the Liberal minority government that came to power in 2015 imposed a 'reallocation contribution' in the form of an annual 1% across-the-board reduction of the expenditure ceiling for the municipalities. The proceeds from this cut were meant to enter into the buffer that could be allocated each year. The 'reallocation contribution' is conceptualised as an extension of the existing 'harvester' in central government, but the 'reallocation contribution' proved immensely unpopular in local governments. Unlike the Budget Law itself, it failed to find support on both sides of parliament. In June 2016, the government decided to replace the 1% cut with a smaller 'modernisation and efficiency programme' to be administered by the government in cooperation with the local government association (Danish Government and Local Government Association 2016).

What Role Did the Crisis Play?

The organic Budget Law seems to confirm the idea that path-breaking changes often occur suddenly in times of economic and political crisis. In the Danish case, some of the changes were clearly motivated by the international financial crisis and the European regulations that had been designed in response to it. However, the crisis also opened a window of opportunity for internal actors to consolidate changes to the expenditure policy regime that were already in progress.

Denmark is not a member of the Eurozone due to voluntary opt-outs, but Danish governments have pursued fixed exchange-rate policies since the early 1980s. With the crisis and the turbulence in the financial markets, the credibility of the fixed exchange-rate policy came under pressure, which motivated the government to adopt and implement the Fiscal Stability Treaty rather swiftly in 2012. Hence, some elements of the Budget Law—such as the structural balance rule, the automatic correction mechanism and the new role of the Economic Council as a fiscal watchdog, represented the Danish implementation of external requirements.

However, the legally binding expenditure ceilings that are also an important element of the Budget Law are rather the result of domestic politics and of how the crisis was used as a policy window by the government's budget guardians in the Ministry of Finance to find political support for a permanent coupling of the problem of expenditure control and the solution of legal expenditure ceilings. According to the informants of this study, the main background of the Budget Law should be found in the history of local overspending. The Conservative–Liberal government that was in power from 2001 to 2011 had gradually added a number of mechanisms intended to incentivise the municipalities and regions to respect its 'tax-stop' policy and the expenditure guidelines in the annual agreements. In 2009, the local governments respected the guidelines in their budgeting but they overspent their budgets, leading to a marked increase in local spending levels. Hence, in 2010, the government asked for a permanent mandate to impose economic sanctions on the municipalities collectively and individually if their overall expenditure was not within the agreed limits in their budgets *and* their accounts (Sørensen 2014). Judging from local financial data, this legislation—which preceded the

Budget Law—solved the local overspending problem (Foged 2015). In other words, substantial changes had already been made to the expenditure policy regime in a gradual process of trial and error.

However, the mandate for economic sanctions for overspending did not relieve the government and its Ministry of Finance of the need to continually negotiate the implementation of its fiscal policies—with line ministries, with the local government associations and with the parliamentary parties. The Budget Law changed this state of affairs by making legal expenditure ceilings the fixed reference for negotiations. If we use Kingdon's Multiple Streams Model of policymaking (Kingdon 2003), the window for this change was opened in the political stream because voter preferences in the 2011 elections were significantly less in favour of expenditure growth than before the crisis (Suenson, Nedergaard and Christiansen 2016) and because the main contenders for government power on both sides of parliament were in favour of credible expenditure control. The open window enabled the Ministry of Finance to create a permanent coupling of the problem of expenditure control with the solution of expenditure ceilings; a solution modelled primarily on Swedish experiences and already in circulation at the beginning of the fiscal crisis (Ministry of Finance 2010).

Budgetary Results and Consequences for Public Management

As argued in the previous section, the crisis opened a window for changes to the rules of the game of public expenditure control. Apparently, the changes have had the wished-for consequences in terms of fiscal discipline. Since 2010, when Denmark came under the EU Excessive Deficit Procedure, projected deficits have improved markedly. This mainly reflects reforms made to retirement arrangements, but the new structural deficit target and expenditure ceilings have most likely also contributed to improving public finances (Economic Council 2015, 129). Whereas public consumption rose markedly as a percentage of structural BNP during the 2000s, it has been declining from 2009 to 2016 (Ministry of Finance 2016, 143). The main factor behind this development has been the reversal of the growth curve of current local welfare spending and the end of the tendency for local governments (particularly municipalities) to exceed their budgets.

The changes are the result of a new financial management regime that prioritises short-term expenditure control higher than the previous rules. However, we know little about how the focus on short-term expenditure control affects the pursuit of effectiveness and efficiency. This question will underlie the following analysis of financial management in central government and the steering of local finances.

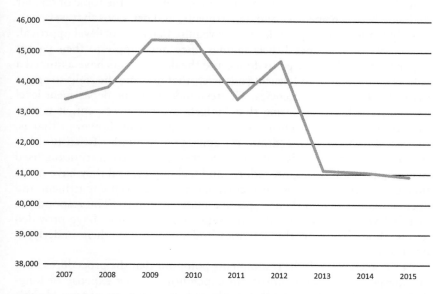

Figure 11.1 Net Operating Expenditure on Municipal Welfare Services, DKK/ Resident*

Source: Ministry of Economics and Interior Affairs 2016.

* Fixed prices 2015. National average.

Financial Management in Central Government

In central government, budgets were generally not overrun before the Budget Law; on the contrary, there was actually a tendency for *under*-spending and the accumulation of savings, which were to be spent at a later date. Nonetheless, the Budget Law and the new monitoring procedures have necessitated a higher level of managerial attention to financial management and new procedures for coordinating the use of resources so as to avoid the overspending—and underspending—of appropriated budgets.

The Ministry of Finance has assumed the role of monitoring the finances of line ministries and allocating the right to spend savings between them. The main concern of this ministry is to make sure that total spending does not exceed the expenditure ceiling, but it is also important to counter the criticism that the new regime creates incentives to hold back funds in the first months of the year not to risk overspending and to spend unused funds—to 'burn off petrol'—in the last quarter of the year. For this reason, in the perception of a respondent from this ministry, it has pursued a liberal line of making exemptions from annual ceilings and budgets.

In the line ministries, financial matters have become the topic of regular dialogue between agencies and departments, and decisions that were previously made at the agency level now require department-level approval. If agencies plan to spend their savings, they must apply to their parent departments to be allowed to do so, and the departments have assumed a role as coordinators or 'clearing agencies' that allocate the right to spend savings between their agencies. The respondents at the department level are concerned with ensuring that budgets are not overspent. It is also important for them to ensure that budgets are spent, however; that is, to ensure that there is a 'drain' on appropriated funds. To ensure that budgets are neither overspent nor underspent, they have institutionalised new regular monitoring procedures and techniques, and they have made financial matters the topic of regular meetings between department and agency managers and their respective budgetary units. The respondents at this level generally find that the reporting procedures have provided greater knowledge on the activities and resources of their underlying agencies.

At the agency level, the respondents point out that the procedures have encouraged a focus on short-term expenditure at the expense of long-term costs. As one respondent explained, the rules encourage 'double bookkeeping', where it is not money so much as the 'space under the expenditure ceiling' that counts. This respondent perceives this state of affairs as being in contradiction to the intentions of the budgetary reforms of previous decades, not least the accruals of the 2000s. The agency-level respondents also point out that useless time is spent explaining why bills are paid on the 1st of one month rather than the 31st of the previous month.

The respondents at all levels agree that the new reporting requirements generate more transparency regarding how activities drive resources and why resources are (not) spent on various projects. This knowledge can potentially be used to optimise the allocation of resources. Particularly from the perspective of the Ministry of Finance, it is useful to know where there are accounts with poor 'drainage', which may present a source of funds for reallocation to other purposes. This is also useful at the department level, but the respondents are careful to point out how they always maintain close dialogue with the agencies before suggesting the reallocation of unspent appropriations. At the agency level, one of the respondents points out that resources are often appropriated for specific programmes by parliament, and it is therefore often not possible to reallocate unspent savings.

The Budget Law is designed to keep short-term expenditure in line with budgets—not to increase the productivity or effectiveness of public spending. It is therefore not surprising that the respondents either see the law as relatively separate from those concerns or they point out how it contradicts them. In the project 'Good Financial Management', the new procedures for fiscal control are portrayed by the Modernisation Agency under the Ministry of Finance as mutually supportive with tools that are meant to improve allocative and operational performance. The respondents in departments and agencies acknowledge that the fiscal control procedures generate knowledge that can potentially be used to improve cost-effectiveness, but they generally view the reporting procedures as separate from performance concerns.

Summing up, the Budget Law has pushed the priorities in financial management in central government in the direction of closer, real-time coordination of the use of resources and away from the principle of managerial flexibility that has been central to previous financial management reforms. Conversely, it may lead to higher allocative effectiveness as it becomes more transparent to managers at higher levels how activities drive expenditure and how resources are potentially reallocated towards core activities. However, the respondents generally view the new financial monitoring procedures as bureaucratisation and a distraction from the objective of long-term resource management.

The Coordination of Local Finances

Overspending in the municipalities was the main background of the budgetary reforms that have been carried out in the recent period of austerity. It is therefore not surprising that the reforms have been accompanied by changes to the institutional arrangements for controlling municipal expenditure.

The legal expenditure ceilings have changed the point of reference of the annual negotiations between the government and association of municipalities, leaving less space for the negotiation of next year's expenditure targets. Furthermore, the introduction of economic sanctions for overspending changed the status of the targets from *guidelines* for local fiscal policies to *ceilings* that must be respected. However, the law did not abolish the collective and corporatist principle; that is, that the legal expenditure ceiling applies collectively to all municipalities and it is implemented by means of an agreement between the government and the association of municipalities about the preconditions for next year's budgeting. With the passing of the Budget Law, in principle, the Minister of the Interior received a mandate to distribute spending rights between the municipalities. In practice, however, it would be technically and politically difficult for central government to do so.

Instead, it remains up to the municipalities and their association to distribute spending rights between them, and each municipality is only affected by sanctions for overspending if the municipalities do not collectively respect the expenditure target in their budgets and in their accounts (this has yet to occur). This arrangement allows the government to stay out of the firing line of protests against local cutbacks to some degree. It also gives the Association of Municipalities a central role as the coordinator of the municipalities' fiscal policies. In 2008, the association established a collective 'phased budgetary procedure', which entails, inter alia, that the 98 mayors meet regularly to coordinate their budgeting within the limits set by the economic agreements. In the period of austerity, the phased budgeting procedure has been intensified and extended to the implementation phase of local budgets. In its new role as financial coordinator, the association also communicates more intensely with each municipality, distributes more financial figures and is more likely to have an opinion on how individual municipalities could contribute to collective expenditure restraint. From the point of view of a respondent from the Ministry of Finance, one of the most important effects of the new regime is how it has moved the association 'into centre court' in the coordination of local budgeting.

In parallel with the more intensive coordination of local expenditure levels, the issues of allocative and operational performance have become central to the budgetary coordination between the government (chaired by Ministry of Finance) and the Association of Municipalities. The parties regularly carry out joint productivity analyses of different tasks, and these analyses are often used to inform the reform of the legislative framework for local welfare services. It is also worth mentioning how the across-the-board 'reallocation contribution' introduced by the government in 2015 has been replaced with a 'modernisation and efficiency' programme to be administered jointly (see earlier discussion).

Conclusion

In the recent times of austerity, Danish budgetary institutions have undergone major changes in the direction of centralisation, formalism and coordination at the expense of local autonomy, informalism and managerial flexibility. These path-breaking changes have been motivated by the international financial crisis and the common European rules that have been devised to signal credible fiscal discipline, but they are also the result of how domestic budget guardians have used the crisis as a window of opportunity to consolidate an ongoing process of centralisation.

The most path-breaking aspect of the recent Budget Law is probably that it created a formal, legal system of expenditure control which is different in principle from the previous traditions of informalism, pragmatism and managerial flexibility. For example, the informal budgetary cooperation, which has been the main mechanism of central steering of local finances for four decades, has become embedded in a framework of legislated fiscal targets, expenditure ceilings and economic sanctions for overspending, and the budgeting process in central government has also become embedded in formal rules and targets. The new legal framework has proved effective in controlling public spending, but it has also reversed the effects of some of the previous reforms that have generated local autonomy and managerial flexibility. The priorities in financial management have thus shifted in the direction of coordination and away from flexibility.

The Budget Law also added a new layer in a long-term gradual process of centralisation. It reinforces the status of a number of existing instruments, such as the government's medium-term projections, fiscal targets and the top-down budgeting process in central government. In central government, powers have been moved from line ministries to the Ministry of Finance, and in line ministries powers have been moved from the agency level to the department level. In relation to local governments, powers have been transferred from the local government associations to the Ministry of Finance, which is now less likely to be overruled by parliamentary majorities in its firm stance on local expenditure growth. The new framework has not, however, detracted from the importance of the Association of Municipalities, which has assumed a strong role as the coordinator of local budget processes.

The new rules reduce the information asymmetries between central and decentralised budgetary units, and they potentially make it possible to reallocate unspent resources towards more productive and effective uses; however, they are also perceived as bureaucratisation at the agency level and as an impediment to a long-term perspective in public spending. Judging from the data at hand, the reform only potentially sets the course for new versions of performance management based on the closer coupling of objectives, activities and resources. It thus seems as though the times of austerity are times of strengthened fiscal discipline—but only potentially of higher performance.

Note

1 When considering the reform trajectories, it should be mentioned that the present local government structure is the result of a reform implemented in 2007, in which the 271 municipalities were amalgamated into 98 new municipalities, and the 14 second-tier 'counties' were transformed into five regions with a small portfolio in healthcare and no taxing rights. However, the analysis does not consider the effects of the local government reform, focusing mainly on the municipalities rather than the regions.

References

Agency of Modernisation. 2013. *Cirkulære om budgettering og budget-og regnskabsopfølgning*. Copenhagen: Agency of Modernisation (Ministry of Finance).

Alesina, Alberto and Roberto Perotti. 1996. "Fiscal Discipline and the Budget Process." *The American Economic Review* 86(2):401–7.

Andersen, Vibeke Normann. 2010. "Denmark." In *Changing Government Relations in Europe: From Localism to Intergovernmentalism*, edited by Michael Goldsmith and Edward Page, 47–67. London: Routledge.

Blom-Hansen, Jens. 1998. "Macroeconomic Control of Local Government in Scandinavia: The Formative Years." *Scandinavian Political Studies* 21(2): 129–53.

Blom-Hansen, Jens. 1999. "Policy-Making in Central–Local Government Relations: Balancing Local Autonomy, Macroeconomic Control and Sectoral Policy Goals." *Journal of Public Policy* 19(3):237–64.

Blom-Hansen, Jens, Marius Ibsen, Thorkil Juul and Poul Erik Mouritzen. 2012. *Fra sogn til velfærdsproducent: Kommunestyret gennem fire årtier.* Odense: University Press of Southern Denmark.

Christensen, Jørgen Grønnegård. 2013. "Budgetloven er et paradigmeskifte! Interview With David Hellemann, Permanent Secretary, Ministry of Finance." *Administrativ Debat* 2013(1): 3–9

Curristine, Teresa. 2007. *Performance Budgeting in OECD Countries.* Paris: OECD.

DanishGovernment. 2010. "Genopretningspakken:Danmarkudafkrisen—regningen betalt." Copenhagen. www.stm.dk/publikationer/genopret_10/index.htm. Accessed on 6th of October 2016.

Danish Government. 2011a. "Reformpakken 2020—Kontant sikring af Danmarks velfærd (kort fortalt)." Copenhagen. www.stm.dk/publikationer/ Reformpakken_2020_pjece_11/grafik/Reformpakken_2020_pjece_web.pdf. Accessed on 6th of October 2016.

Danish Government 2011b. "Et Danmark der står sammen. Regeringsgrundlag." Copenhagen. www.stm.dk/publikationer/Et_Danmark_der_staar_sammen_11/ Regeringsgrundlag_okt_2011.pdf. Accessed on 6th of October 2016.

Danish Government and the Association of Local Governments. 2016. *Aftale om kommunernes økonomi for 2017.* Copenhagen. www.fm.dk/nyheder/presse meddelelser/2016/06/aftale-om-kommunernes-oekonomi-for-2017. Accessed on 6th of October 2016.

Economic Council (Økonomisk Råd). 2015. *Dansk Økonomi, efterår 2015.* Copenhagen: Economic Council. www.dors.dk/files/media/rapporter/2015/ E15/e15.pdf. Accessed on 14th of December 2016.

Esping-Andersen, Gösta. 1990. *The Three Worlds of Welfare Capitalism.* Princeton: Princeton University Press.

Foged, Søren, K. 2015. "En effektevaluering på danske kommuners regnskaber, 2010–2013." *Økonomi & Politik* 88(1):57–75.

Hagen von, Jürgen. 2007. "Budgeting Institutions for Better Fiscal Performance." In *Budgeting and Budgetary Institutions*, edited by Anwar Shah, 27–52. Washington, DC: World Bank.

Hall, Peter. 1993. "Policy Paradigms, Social Learning and the State." *Comparative Politics* 25(3):275–96.

Hansen, Hanne Foss and Torben B. Jørgensen. 2009. "Den danske forvaltningsmodel og globaliseringens udfordringer." In *Globaliseringens udfordringer: Politiske og administrative modeller under pres*, edited by Martin Marcussen and Karsten Ronit, 36–65. Copenhagen: Hans Reitzels.

Hansen, Hanne Foss and Mads Bøge Kristiansen. 2014. "Ansvarlighed i en krisetid: konsekvenser af budgetloven og nye krav til økonomistyring." In *Offentlig Styring, forandringer i krisetider*, edited by Caroline Howard Grøn, Hanne Foss Hansen and Mads Bøge Kristiansen, 257–90. Copenhagen: Hans Reitzels.

Jensen, Lotte. 2008. *Væk fra Afgrunden: Finansministeriet som økonomisk styringsaktør.* Odense: University Press of Southern Denmark.

Jensen, Lotte and Sysser Davidsen. 2015. "The Global Financial Crisis in Denmark and Sweden: A Case of Crisis Management 'Lite.'" In *The Global Financial Crisis and Its Budget Impacts in OECD Nations: Fiscal Responses and Future Challenges*, edited by Evert Lindquist, Jouke de Vries and John Wanna, 174–200. Cheltenham: Edward Elgar.

Jensen, Lotte and David Fjord. 2010. "Budget Reforms in Denmark: Unheralded But Nonetheless Effective." In *The Reality of Budgetary Reform in OECD Nations, Trajectories and Consequences*, edited by John Wanna, Lotte Jensen and Jouke de Vries, 193–220. Cheltenham: Edward Elgar.

Kingdon, John W. 2003. *Agendas, Alternatives, and Public Policies*. New York: Longman.

Kristiansen, Mads. 2011. *Mål-og resultatstyring i praksis: En komparativ analyse af mål-og resultatstyring i Danmark, Sverige og Norge*. Ph.D. Dissertation, University of Copenhagen: Department of Political Science.

Lotz, Jørgen. 2007. "Spillet om kommunernes økonomi." In *Rigtigt Kommunalt*, edited by Svend Lundtorp and Max Rasmussen, 34–71. Copenhagen: Handelshøjskolens Forlag.

Ministry of Economic and Interior Affairs (Økonomi-og Indenrigsministeriet). 2016. "Net Operating Expenditure on Municipal Welfare Services (Serviceudgifter pr. indbygger)." *The Municipal Key Figures (De Kommunale Nøgletal)*. www.noegletal.dk/noegletal/servlet/nctrlman.aReqManager. Accessed 20th of December 2016.

Ministry of Finance (Finansministeriet). 2010. *Budgetredegørelse 2010*. Copenhagen: Ministry of Finance.

Ministry of Finance (Finansministeriet). 2012. "Cirkulære om afprøvning af budgetlovens bestemmelser i staten i 2013." CIR 85 af 29/11/2012. www.ret sinformation.dk/Forms/R0710.aspx?id=144280. Accessed on 14th of December 2016.

Ministry of Finance (Finansministeriet). 2016. "Økonomisk Redegørelse, maj 2016." www. fm.dk/publikationer/2016/oekonomisk-redegoerelse-maj-16. Accessed on 14th of December 2016.

Pallesen, Thomas. 2003. *Den vellykkede kommunalreform og decentraliseringen af den politiske magt i Danmark*. Aarhus: Aarhus University Press.

Pollitt, Christopher and Geert Bouckaert. 2009. *Continuity and Change in Public Policy and Management*. Cheltenham: Edward Elgar.

Schick, Allen. 2010. "Post-Crisis Fiscal Rules: Stabilising Public Finance While Responding to Economic Aftershocks." *OECD Journal on Budgeting* 2:1–18.

Sørensen, Eva Moll. 2013. *A Window for Centralisation? The Danish 'Structural Reform' and the Measurement and Steering of Municipal Service Performance*. Ph.D. Dissertation, University of Copenhagen: Department of Political Science.

Sørensen, Eva Moll. 2014. "Økonomisk Styring af Kommunerne i en Krisetid." In *Offentlig Styring, forandringer i krisetider*, edited by Caroline Howard Grøn, Hanne Foss Hansen and Mads Bøge Kristiansen, 291–317. Copenhagen: Hans Reitzels.

Sørensen, Eva Moll, Sissel Hovik, Erik Neergaard and Olaf Rieper. 2007. *Konsultationer og aftaler mellem stat og kommuner i Danmark og Norge*. Copenhagen: AKF Forlaget.

Streeck, Wolfgang and Kathleen Thelen. 2005. *Beyond Continuity, Institutional Change in Advanced Political Economies*. Oxford: Oxford University Press.

Suenson, Emil Lobe, Peter Nedergaard and Peter Munk Christiansen. 2016. "Why Do You Want to Lash Yourself to the Mast? The Case of the Danish 'Budget Law.'" *Public Budgeting & Finance* 36(1):3–21.

Thelen, Kathleen and Sven Steinmo. 1992. "Historical Institutionalism in Comparative Politics." In *Structuring Politics: Historical Institutionalism in Comparative Analysis*, edited by Sven Steinmo, Kathleen Thelen and Frank Longstreth, 1–32. Cambridge: Cambridge University Press.

12 Budgetary and Financial Management Reform in Ireland

Muiris MacCarthaigh and Niamh Hardiman

Introduction

The series of crises outlined in Chapter 1 resulted in considerable external and domestic pressures for the Irish state's budgetary and financial management processes to be reformed. A common aim of these reforms was to introduce more fiscal discipline on a political system that had hitherto paid lip-service to self-imposed controls. Given the conservative approach to such reforms for decades preceding the crisis, it can be seen as a critical juncture marking a break in the Irish state's management of public funds. During the period of crisis-inspired retrenchment, new financial and budgetary rules were agreed with the IMF–EC–ECB 'Troika' in 2010, which were further strengthened by the formalisation of the Fiscal Compact and related EU rules governing budgetary policy. Of particular importance was the requirement arising from the Fiscal Compact to achieve a structurally balanced budget by 2015.

This chapter explores the extent to which institutional reforms can inform future political behaviour and counter the adverse effects of pro-cyclical budgetary policy. It begins by outlining the rather fragmented Irish budgetary process and institutions of financial management prior to 2008, and profiles the budgetary trends leading up to the crisis. The reforms introduced after 2008 are then presented with reference to their principal drivers, that is, those that were principally EU-related, those that were Troika-related, and those that emerged from domestic pressures. Finally, the consequences of the reforms are considered, looking at their effects on the budgetary process, their implications for institutional change, and changes to the extent of public accountability for performance. We find that the centralisation of budgetary and financial controls within a new government department was an essential ingredient for the introduction of new budgetary reforms during the period of retrenchment, but that such controls become more difficult to enforce as the budgetary situation improved. The chapter is informed by official documents as well as academic sources, and is supported by a set of 61 semi-structured interviews undertaken by MacCarthaigh with senior civil servants over the 2013–15 period for a fellowship project on the work of the Department of Public Expenditure and Reform (DPER) (see also MacCarthaigh 2017).

Budgetary Institutions and Reform Trajectories Preceding the Crisis

Prior to the crisis, the general framework for Ireland's budgetary and financial oversight arrangements were specified by the constitution, relevant legislation, parliamentary rules and rules laid down by the powerful Department of Finance known as 'public financial procedures' (Hamell 2010). In a nod to democratic oversight of the state's finances, the constitution stipulates that the government should provide the Lower House—Dáil Eireann or simply 'the Dáil'—with estimates of the State's receipts and expenditure each year. This was manifested in Budget Day, when the government would reveal to the Lower House its spending plans for the year ahead and begin the process of securing legislative approval for the Finance Act.

The constitution facilitates a limited role for parliament in the budgetary process. It gives the government the exclusive right to initiate taxation and expenditure proposals (although it gives the Dáil the final say on them), to regulate the manner in which money is spent, and subsequently to present detailed accounts of government receipts and expenditure. In the context of an adversarial Westminster parliamentary system, Irish governments were incentivised to retain control over the budgetary process and to limit external input and scrutiny. The Upper House—Seanad Éireann—had virtually no veto powers over government decisions on financial allocations.

A constitutional officer, the Comptroller and Auditor-General, is charged with ensuring all public spending is accounted for, and presents its audited accounts to the Dáil's committee on public accounts. As inherited from the Westminster system, budgetary allocations to departments (and some key state institutions, such as the parliament) are known as 'votes', with each vote being managed by a minister and her/his secretary-general (the most senior level of the civil service) and smaller vote 'subheads' and 'sub-subheads' then delegated downwards. Discretion to move money between votes was possible, but not common, as departments were accountable solely for their own financial allocation within which they had discretion to move money between subheads. These subheads were traditionally allocated according to administrative budgets (e.g. salaries, office expenses, telecommunications), policy programmes according to the department's functions, and grants for those agencies under the respective department's remit. Taxation is gathered by the Revenue Commissioners, and a 'National Treasury Management Agency' with specialist responsibility for managing the national debt and for borrowing on behalf of the state was created in 1990.

An OECD review of Irish parliamentary budget oversight, published in 2015, noted that in Ireland the government 'has primacy, to the point of dominance, in budgetary matters' (OECD 2015, 11) with expenditure proposals not subject to any adjustment in parliament. Furthermore, the report criticised the fact that the formal parliamentary vote on proposed expenditure did not take place until after the start of the budgetary year has begun.

Prior to the 1990s, Irish fiscal reports confined themselves to central government budgets and covered only cash transactions and debt. Their focus did not go beyond the year ahead. They presented virtually no data on the achievement of policy outcomes. They did not follow an internationally recognised classification system; neither was there any examination of fiscal risks. Furthermore, Irish budgetary and fiscal policy had not been the subject of any major domestically inspired reform initiatives. Indeed, a survey by the IMF published in 2013 suggested that prior to (EU-required) alterations in the 1990s, the Irish system of government budgeting and accounting was largely unchanged from that which it had inherited from the UK at independence in 1922 (IMF 2013, 7). Some of the financial oversight procedures were even premised on the Exchequer and Audit Departments Act of 1866, and were performed in a secretive manner, reflecting a view that key national policy decisions were not to be subjected to meaningful public scrutiny.

Successive governments had resisted 'performance budgeting' reforms that had spread globally during the 1980s. National budgets were generally planned, spent and accounted for on an annual basis, with all stages managed by the Department of Finance. That department was widely regarded as the most powerful institution in the Irish politico-administrative system, possessing considerable powers of policy veto in virtue of its role as the sole authority with responsibility for the state's finances (Considine and Reidy 2012, 88). As a result, it was often thought of as a bastion of procedural as well as fiscal conservatism with an aversion to organisational and procedural reform. The economic and financial crisis severely damaged its reputation for prudent management and regulation. Deficits in its capacity for macroeconomic analysis and financial regulation were identified as key contributory factors to the severity of the effects of the financial crisis (Independent Review Panel 2011; Houses of the Oireachtas 2016).

Such reforms as had been made to the Irish budgetary system had arisen as a result of EU membership. In particular, the Maastricht Treaty introduced reporting requirements that obliged Irish governments to produce fiscal statistics that followed a common system (the European System of Accounts from 1995). The 1997 Stability and Growth Pact was also important in initiating multiyear planning, as were the requirements for ex ante and ex post evaluations necessary for securing EU Structural and Cohesion funding. Also driven by EU compliance requirements, multiannual planning for capital expenditure was introduced in 2004. Multiyear planning for current expenditure did not take root until after 2008.

The content of budgets was traditionally closely guarded and subject to state secrecy provisions, and only released on Budget Day. Prior to the crisis, there had been no state-funded budgetary or fiscal institutions. The partially state-funded Economic and Social Research Institute (ESRI) was virtually the only body capable of providing an independent institutional voice on financial, fiscal and macro-economic policy. Budget formation was largely driven by bilateral meetings between the Department of Finance and individual spending ministries, with the former holding significant veto powers.

Until 2002, the Irish financial year had begun in the first week of April with the presentation of the budget. From 2002 onwards, the financial year was aligned with the calendar year. But the presentation of the budget in early December remained a major 'set-piece' event, and was generally interpreted as a test of the incumbent government's authority in parliament. The process leading up to Budget Day followed a well-practiced series of events. Preparation of expenditure estimates began early in the financial year with an open call for interest groups and others to make submissions to be considered in the forthcoming budget. In parallel, government departments collected expenditure estimates from their subdivisions, as well as agencies funded by them, for the year ahead. The Department of Finance published a Budget Strategy Memorandum in July, setting out the general expenditure parameters within which government departments would be expected to make their spending plans (even though the final expenditure level was not usually confirmed until Budget Day).

Once each department had made an aggregate estimate of its spending needs for the year ahead, also accounting for inflation, they would then each negotiate a budget with the Department of Finance. Typically, departments always overestimated their needs in anticipation of Department of Finance resistance, while that department's stance was usually characterised as one in which any increases in spending were opposed. Final budgets would be agreed by the respective ministers in each case. This informal political negotiation over final budget packages would on occasion also involve the *Taoiseach* (Prime Minister) in a mediator role. The Minister for Finance would then publish the government receipts and current and capital expenditure plans on Budget Day.

As noted previously, following Westminster tradition, the agreed budgetary allocations were distributed by departmental 'Votes'. A three-year forecast was also published with the budget in line with the EU Annual Stability Programme Update. But this was indicative only, and featured weak medium-term projections that required constant updating; forecasting usually started de novo each year. A 'White Paper on Receipts and Expenditure' was usually published the weekend before the budget, but this was purely a reference document based on the assumption that there would be no policy changes from the previous year. Its figures were also immediately displaced by those published days later in the budget (OECD 2015, 18)

Prior to the crisis, the only reform of note that had not been mandated by the EU was the introduction in 2007 of a requirement on public bodies to publish 'annual output statements' in respect of their work. These statements, which were considered ex-ante alongside annual estimates, were an attempt to address criticisms of the lack of information available to the public and parliaments about how effectively public money was being spent. The experiment was not successful, owing to the poor quality and timeliness of the information provided (OECD 2008, 145). A 2008 OECD review of the Irish public service called for more comprehensive use of performance information across the public service, including better integration of such information in the resource allocation process (OECD 2008).

The 12-month nature of the Irish budgetary financial cycle provided for an annual system of expenditure control, and was generally viewed as robust. However, they also noted some questions 'about the de jure paper policies and de facto practice of budget-making in Ireland' (Considine and Reidy 2012, 99), in which considerable discretion was given to the Minister for Finance to approve increases in expenditure or tax cuts on Budget Day. This did not allow time for informed debates or discussion over national fiscal policy and expenditure trends. Moreover, the budget was largely a cash-based process and did not involve full consideration

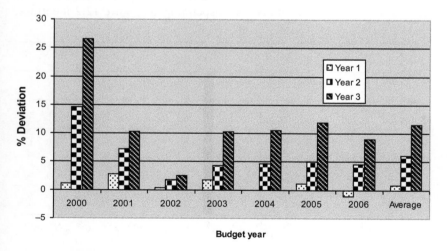

Figure 12.1 Deviation of Actual and Gross Current Expenditure from Budget Projections 2001–06

Source: Department of Finance 2011, 3.

of state assets or liabilities. And with few institutional constraints on the exercise of executive discretion in the Irish parliamentary system, these practices facilitated egregious pro-cyclical expenditure policy (Hallerberg, Strauch and Hagen 2007). The unfettered ability of Irish governments to spend surpluses facilitated large increases in expenditure, including spending deviations of over 10% in the years preceding the crisis, as Figure 12.1 shows. The causes of these budgetary trends require some further analysis.

Budgetary Trends Prior to the Crisis

The Irish economy had been growing rapidly after 1994 in the wake of the completion of the European Single Market, as a fresh round of mostly US investments kick-started the 'Celtic Tiger'. Macroeconomic performance in the run-up to European Monetary Union in 1999 was very good: budgetary processes were disciplined by the external constraints of the Maastricht Treaty. However, in the context of a political system in which the two largest parties frequently contested power on the basis not only of competence in office but also on promises about spending and other commitments, public spending tended to increase rapidly and rising tax revenues made this possible without visible deficits emerging. Thus, since the 1970s, Irish fiscal policy had tended to follow a pattern of strong pro-cyclical measures, in which elections in the good times featured competitive 'auction politics', while downturns saw the sudden adoption of recession-amplifying fiscal retrenchment (Hardiman 2014).

Between 2000 and 2008, net expenditure by Irish governments doubled as buoyant revenues facilitated extra spending, as Figure 12.2 identifies.

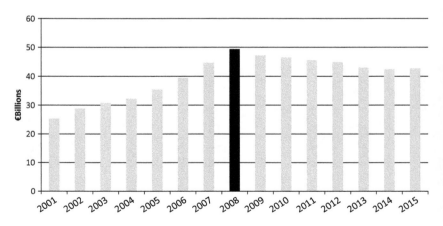

Figure 12.2 Net Expenditure by Irish Governments, 2001–15 (Not Adjusted for Inflation)

Source: Department of Public Expenditure and Reform Databank, http://databank.per.gov.ie/

Ireland, like Spain, did not run a fiscal deficit at all during the 2000s, and indeed in some years actually recorded a fiscal surplus. But the fiscal basis of this dual strategy was weak, as much of the increased revenue came from construction-related taxes and from additional income tax from extra employment in construction. Meanwhile, the base of the income tax system was steadily eroded, as governments engaged in steady tax cuts to support both job creation and to stabilise employee wage demands. Therefore, although Ireland was ostensibly running a small fiscal surplus during some of this period, the underlying fiscal sustainability of the public finances was becoming increasingly compromised.

A report into the Irish financial crisis (Independent Review Panel 2010) noted that public spending had accelerated in line with the growing economy from the early 2000s, but critically noted that the Department of Finance had not been able to assert control over this growth in expenditure (13.8% in one year alone). With one exception (2003), between 1999 and 2007 inclusive, governments had committed on Budget Day to more public expenditure than previously indicated. With a rapid decline in activity in the property sector, government revenues contracted at an alarming rate from 2007, leading to a large gap opening up in government finances.

The combined banking, financial and economic crises in Ireland resulted in a fourfold increase in government debt over the 2007–12 period, and the Irish debt-to-GDP ratio moved from being one of the lowest to the fourth largest in the Eurozone (Barnes and Smyth 2012). As well as the growing structural problem in the state's annual budget, this rapid increase in public debt arose from the government decision to recapitalise huge losses in Irish banks. In September 2008, the government extended a blanket guarantee to all banking liabilities, apparently without full knowledge of their scale at the time. By the spring of 2009, it was clear that Irish bank losses arising from the property crash were very much larger than realised (Whelan 2014). In December 2010, the government was forced to enter a 'bailout' loan programme from the Troika of the IMF, ECB and EU. As part of this programme, the state was required to use public funds not only to recapitalise the guaranteed banks, but to do so without requiring any corresponding 'bail-in' of owners of distressed assets—a source of deep discontent in Irish politics and a recurring grievance between the Irish government and the ECB (Whelan 2014). This resulted in an enormous increase in public debt. It is from this period that substantial reform of the Irish budgetary and financial management systems began to manifest itself.

Budgetary Reforms in Times of Austerity

The Irish post-crisis budgetary reforms involved institutional innovation at the national level. But in effect, very little changed in the process until after the election of a new government in early 2011, which came to power with a large majority and a mandate for reform (see also Chapter 7). Evidence from interviewees indicates that the crisis undoubtedly provided a 'window of opportunity' for implementing reforms to the fiscal process that had been mooted for several years, hitherto without success. Reform of the Irish budgetary process was already a prominent feature of political and media discourse by 2010. In particular, there was much criticism of the tendency of Irish governments since the 1970s (see preceding) to engage in pro-cyclical fiscal policy and the limitations of the 'big bang' approach to Budget Day, which inhibited ongoing analysis of budgetary policy.

The *National Recovery Plan 2011–14*, published by the government immediately after the Troika loan programme agreement was signed, stated that:

> . . . the budget system will be comprehensively reformed and updated to bring greater sustainability to the management of public finances; to achieve maximum value for money in public expenditure; and guard against the emergence of structural budgetary imbalances
> (Government of Ireland 2010, 59).

Boyle and Mulreany (2015, 299–300) note that the budgetary reforms in the plan reflected the conclusions of a parliamentary report on fiscal and economic governance published earlier in 2010. It had been strongly critical of the traditional budgetary process of votes and subheads, and had also questioned the efficacy of the system of organisational Annual Output Statements introduced as recently as 2007 (see preceding). That report had called for a new system to more clearly link expenditure to all projects 'so that all activity including costs, current, capital, administrative etc. are fully captured and recorded against a project' (Houses of the Oireachtas Joint Committee on Finance and the Public Service 2010, 8).

Many of the reforms were the result of external pressures, namely those arising from reforms initiated at EU level, and those that arose from the loan programme signed with the Troika in December 2010. However, it is important to note that many of the Troika demands on budgetary and financial management reform were in fact proposed by the Irish negotiators from the Department of Finance, who had drawn up plans for a more regulated budgetary process following the onset of the crisis and who saw the loan program memorandum as the chance to have these formalised. The sections that follow will outline what these reforms involved respectively. Finally, a series of domestically inspired reforms are identified, with a particular emphasis on the institutional decoupling of the Irish revenue-raising and expenditure functions.

EU-Related Reforms

Irish budgetary reforms were deeply influenced by changes initiated at the European level. The EU Council's Task Force on 'Strengthening

Economic Governance in the EU' resulted in amendments of the Stability and Growth Pact in 2011 and stronger 'preventive' and 'corrective' dimensions of budgetary policy for member-states. The former dimension involved a new European budgetary 'semester' as well as better analysis of economic risks, while the latter involved setting targets for deficit and debt reductions, as well as associated financial penalties for breaches of the targets (see also the description of the 'Six Pack' in Chapter 3).

In line with other EU states, from 2013 the annual budget day was moved forward from December to mid-October. As well as giving the European Commission an opportunity to comment upon national budgetary plans, this also presented national parliaments with a larger window to comment on government budgetary plans. The Irish government was also obliged to produce a Stability Programme Update (SPU), identifying aggregate fiscal plans and related macroeconomic projections for the forthcoming budget year and into the medium term. Prior to 2011, the SPU was published as part of the December Budget day documentation, but was moved to April that year in line with EU-wide reforms.

The government passed key legislation—the Fiscal Responsibility Act 2012—to further provide for its EU obligations under the Fiscal Compact, which was adopted in 2012. But this legislation was controversial. It could not be enacted by government initiative alone: because it entailed a transfer of sovereign powers from the state, the Irish Constitution required that it be put to referendum. The Thirtieth Amendment to the Constitution was carried in June 2012—but without any great popular or indeed political enthusiasm. Many economists warned that it was ill-advised. But Ireland was at that time deeply entangled in loan obligations—dependent, in effect, on the kindness of strangers, as it was put by some at the time; and the government's position was that it would be unwise if not ruinous to appear to resist this initiative.

The centrepiece of the Fiscal Responsibility Act was to provide a legal anchoring for the work of a new body, the Irish Fiscal Advisory Council (IFAC), which had been created on a provisional basis in July 2011. The legislation assigned to IFAC the task of assessing and monitoring the forecasts of the Department of Finance, compliance with European budgetary rules and the general appropriateness of the government's fiscal stance. It is also mandated to comment publicly on whether the government is meeting its budgetary targets and objectives, allowing it a policy role not common to national fiscal oversight bodies elsewhere.

The legislation also created a new 'budgetary rule' which determined that the public finances be in structural balance or in surplus, save for exceptional circumstances, or that annual structural balance shall be converging towards the medium-term objective in line with the determined time frame (the 'adjustment path'). The law also contains a debt rule, and it sets a lower limit of the medium-term budgetary objective at an annual structural balance of minus 0.5% of GDP (Fiscal Responsibility Act 2012). The act also specified a correction mechanism in case of failure to comply to the budgetary rule. Furthermore, it provided for the 'expenditure benchmark' whereby in the absence of additional tax policy measures, expenditure growth should not exceed medium-term economic growth. A final reform of note attributable to the EU level, though not provided for in the Fiscal Responsibility Act, was to remove responsibility for reporting on General Government Deficit and General Government Debt from the Department of Finance. It was transferred to the Irish Central Statistics Office in 2013, in line with Eurostat's recommended best practice.

The Irish budgetary retrenchment over the 2009–14 period followed an 'orthodox' line. In other words, it was more heavily based on spending cuts than on tax increases in a 2:1 ratio. It successfully brought the annual general budget deficit within 3% of GDP as required by the Maastricht Treaty and the Stability and Growth Act.[1]

Troika-Related Reforms

In March 2011, the Department of Finance published 'Reforming Ireland's Budgetary Framework: A Discussion Document' (Department of Finance 2011). It was framed around the commitments the Irish state had undertaken in its loan programme agreement with the EU–ECB–IMF Troika.

The proposed new budgetary architecture involved considerable institutional reforms to the Irish annual budgetary process with a view to restoring Ireland's international credibility as well as better domestic fiscal governance and budgetary outcomes. There were two major reforms to the new budgetary regime, as follows:

1.   Introduction of multiannual expenditure ceilings

The newly elected administration agreed a Programme for Government in March which included a commitment to a 'Comprehensive Spending Review to examine all areas of public spending. . . and to develop multi-annual budget plans with a three-year time horizon', and that performance information would be 'published in a new, audited annual Public Service Delivery Reports'. The two key reforms arising were legislated for in the Ministers and Secretaries (Amendment) Act 2013. The first was new aggregated multiannual ceilings on current expenditure—known as 'Ministerial Expenditure Ceilings'—announced by government in an attempt to switch from short-term (annual) to medium-term (three-year) considerations of spending at budget time. Once published, the idea was that subsequent annual expenditure plans were expected to respect these pre-defined ceilings for that year. This idea was not copper-fastened in law however, but set out in an administrative circular, a shortcoming noted by the European Commission in its country peer-review of fiscal governance when it noted that 'consequences for non-compliance with minsterial and government ceilings are thus far not well defined' (European Commission 2013, 43).

2. New performance reporting regime

Allied to the 'three-year ceilings' was the second reform in the Ministers and Secretaries (Amendment) Act 2013. It was a requirement placed on all government departments to produce performance statements, with a view to better alignment of decisions on spending with policy outcomes. Building on recommendations in the 2008 OECD review of the Irish public service, as well as Troika requirements, a 'Public Service Reform Plan' published by the government in November 2011 stated that

> Performance Budgeting will be implemented across all Government Departments by January 2013, ensuring that the allocation of resources is more closely aligned to the outcomes and outputs to be achieved with those resources
> (Department of Public Expenditure and Reform 2011a, 9).

A pilot 'performance budgeting' experiment was carried out in a number of departments for the 2011 Estimates. The aim was to provide parliamentarians and the public with a clearer indication of funding and staffing investments, as well as subsequent policy results and performance indicators, which would be presented alongside expenditure estimates for the years ahead. This was designed to improve the quality of public debate over future resource commitments. Separate documents summarising output targets and results for public bodies were integrated, aligning financial allocations and performance information. The Estimates information was also presented in a 'programme' format (rather than by departmental vote), which aligned them with the format used in the Statements of Strategy prepared by public bodies. Each programme was restricted to a single page and also contained output indicators (for the budget year and the previous year), as well as 'context and impact indicators' with three-year historical trends.

A final element of the move to a more evidence-based budgetary and estimates process was the initiation of a new public web-based database called IrelandStat (www.irelandstat.gov.ie). The purpose of the website was to provide information about government progress in achieving policy goals, as well as trends over time, in a user-friendly format. It sat alongside new databank websites that provided information on public expenditure and personal numbers that were previously only available to those working within the public service.

Domestic Reforms: Institutional Decoupling

The most tangible reform to the Irish budgetary process involved the institutional decoupling of the state's revenue-raising and expenditure functions following the election of the new government in 2011. As described in Chapter 7, the grand coalition of centre-right Fine Gael with the centre-left Labour Party resulted in a political agreement to split the Department of Finance in two. A new Department of Public Expenditure and Reform (DPER) brought together two key Divisions of the Department of Finance (which had public servicewide oversight of government spending) with the small Public Service Modernisation Division of the Department of the Taoiseach. The Department of Finance was left with responsibility for overall budgetary policy, taxation and spending parameters.

DPER was granted the entirety of functions relating to the public service, including public service reform matters which, for the first time, were placed on a statutory footing. As such, it was a new and very important veto player in the architecture of Irish government. It was also presented with responsibility for managing public expenditure, with the Minister for Finance retaining responsibility for overall budgetary parameters. Significantly, new secretaries-general, both with private sector career experience, were appointed to manage both departments. And politically, the two departments were led by very senior figures from the coalition parties.

The new department brought together public spending, industrial relations and public-sector reform for the first time, providing the necessary levers to ensure administrative reforms would be linked to expenditure allocations (and pay) across the public sector. In terms of budget-making, the decoupling may be considered a centralisation and concentration, rather than a diffusion of authority. The new department was given full authority over public expenditure matters including medium-term expenditure ceilings, annual budgetary parameters, budgetary allocations ('votes') for each department (following negotiations), public service remuneration, budgetary implementation and expenditure reviews. The transfer of controls over spending to DPER from the Department of Finance led to greater concentrations of responsibility amongst fewer officials in that department, and thus a centralisation of budgetary management. Interviews also suggest the institutional split between revenue-raising and expenditure functions also had a 'buffering' effect. Prior to DPER's creation, any new expenditure proposal from a 'line' department was assessed by the relevant section in the Department of Finance, and the merits of raising taxation or other forms of revenue to support the measure were considered. With the decoupling, the new ministry could point out to spending departments that it had no power to raise extra revenue and thus departments had to live within their means rather than appeal to them for revenue-raising measures.

Although DPER's creation led to a centralisation of control over budgetary expenditure and the reform agenda, in practice there was decentralisation of the implementation of the cuts. Departments were given targets to achieve not just in terms of personnel, but also in terms of their financial envelope for the year ahead. This meant officials, and political advisers, working together within departments to decide on what to cut and by how much in order to meet their target as set by DPER. Ministers would have to defend any inability to meet a budgetary target, with the Economic Management Council having the final say on where further cuts would need to occur.

The Economic Management Council was an inner cabinet committee where key budget decisions were now concentrated. It comprised the Taoiseach, Tánaiste (deputy-PM) and Ministers for Finance and Public Service and Reform, as well as their top civil servants and a number of economic advisers. Popularly referred to as a 'war cabinet', its original remit was to oversee and manage implementation of the Troika loan programme but its policy focus expanded over time. Questions persisted about its democratic legitimacy throughout the 2011–16 period, however, given that other Ministers were effectively excluded from its workings and its decisions presented to them as a fait accompli. The government subsequently elected in early 2016 decided not to continue with its use, given that economic growth and the public finances were now back under control.

An important development in the government's financial and budget management reform was the creation of a new economic service to address criticisms of weak economic skills leading up to the crisis. The 'Irish Government Economic and Evaluation Service' (IGEES), housed in the Department of Public Expenditure and Reform, had a large number of graduate economists recruited into it at a time when recruitment elsewhere in the public service was embargoed. In early 2014, IGEES began to publish its economic evaluations, exposing policy to external opinion at the formulation stage in a manner that was previously unusual for central departments in Irish government.

In early 2013, the Departments of Finance and Public Expenditure and Reform invited the IMF to conduct a pilot Fiscal Transparency Assessment for Ireland. In its report, the FTA proposed that fiscal disclosure in Ireland 'remains somewhat fragmented and diffuse', and made a series of recommendations for reform:

- The government should expand the institutional coverage of budgets, statistics and accounts;
- Fiscal reports should recognise all assets, liabilities and associated fiscal flows;
- The government should modernise and harmonise accounting standards across the public sector;

- The timetable for submission and approval of the annual budget and financial statements should be accelerated; and
- Analysis of forecast changes, long-term trends and fiscal risks should be improved.

Comprehensive Expenditure Reviews

In parallel with these changes, DPER undertook two 'root-and-branch' Comprehensive Reviews of Expenditure in 2011 and 2014. The first of these resulted in the publication of the 'Comprehensive Expenditure Report 2012–14' in December 2011 alongside the Coalition's first Budget, for the calendar year 2012. It was the culmination of a process initiated almost immediately by the new government involving a detailed analysis and assessment of all programmes of expenditure, with all government departments required to identify options for savings. Within the CER was a plan for reform of the annual estimates and budgetary process, with the key features being:

- Confirmation of the move from annual to three-year current expenditure allocations
- Greater alignment between spending and outcomes
- Better use of evaluation analysis in the allocation of funds
- Improved engagement of the parliament in the estimates process

The Comprehensive Expenditure Report 2012–14 also called for an 'opening up the budgetary process to the full glare of public and parliamentary scrutiny' (Department of Public Expenditure and Reform 2011b, 92). In this context, a 'whole-of-year' approach to budget development was proposed, which would more closely align with information about reforms in how public services were being implemented. The 2nd Comprehensive Expenditure Report and an associated plan for capital investment were published in October 2014 as part of Budget 2015. In line with the reformed public spending code, the Comprehensive Expenditure Report set out multiannual expenditure ceilings for all 'Votes' for each of the years 2015, 2016 and 2017. These new practices have continued but as the next sections identifies, have come under pressure as economic fortunes have improved.

Budgetary Results and Effects on Public Management Emerge

The EU-related, Troika-related and domestically inspired budgetary and financial management reforms identified in the previous section had a number of effects on public management. In the first instance they substantially recast the Irish annual budgetary process, and aligned it with the EU semester system. This has provided for a less opaque budgetary process and more scheduled in-year parliamentary discussion concerning the government's proposed fiscal and budgetary policy stances in advance of the October budget. The potential for EU sanctions also plays a role in guarding against excessive spending. Troika conditionality has also been important in this respect not just as a driver of reform, but also for providing the window of opportunity for implementing domestically initiated ideas around protecting the budgetary process from politically short-term thinking.

Second, the crisis has resulted in considerable institutional reform in respect of the character of the state's financial management and budgetary processes. The ensuing reforms create a more complex and decentralised institutional environment for governments to develop and defend its annual estimated process, with more 'voices' now to be heard and more robust justifications needed for spending decisions. The creation of the new Department of Public Expenditure and Reform alongside the old Department of Finance, and the transfer of key expenditure roles to it, created an important new veto player at the heart of Irish government. Between 2011 and 2016, coordination of budgetary policy was successfully managed in large part due to the harmonious personal relationships and agreement on national objectives between the respective ministers holding departmental office. This coordination was also facilitated by the work of the powerful Economic Management Council, which provided for strong coordination of fiscal strategy during the period of the bailout.

Another new institution, the independent Irish Fiscal Advisory Council, has been quite publicly vocal in its critiques of government policy vis-à-vis adherence to EU rules. For example, as the Irish economy began to improve into 2015, and government revenues increased as the state met the 3% deficit target (Figure 12.3), pressure came on the Department of Public Expenditure and Reform to breach these ceilings. A decision to increase public spending in the budget for 2016 led to criticism of the government's fiscal stance by the council, which stated in its review of the budget that 'the decision to loosen the fiscal stance in 2015 was a deviation from prudent economic and budgetary management' (IFAC 2015, 1). The Department of Finance contested this view, insisting that it had been operating within agreed parameters. The Council's criticisms are made in the context of the Fiscal Compact and 'preventive arm' rules, which limit the instincts to spend amongst Irish political elites after years of austerity measures.

The Fiscal Advisory Council also voiced a note of concern in 2015 about pressures that were undermining the multiyear expenditure framework which formed part of the post-crisis fiscal reforms. They noted:

> The system of multi-year expenditure ceilings—a core component of the Government's budgetary framework—is not being implemented effectively owing to continuous upward revisions to spending. The failure to respect expenditure ceilings raises the risk of funding increases in expenditure from windfall revenue sources. The domestic Medium-Term Expenditure Framework should be strengthened

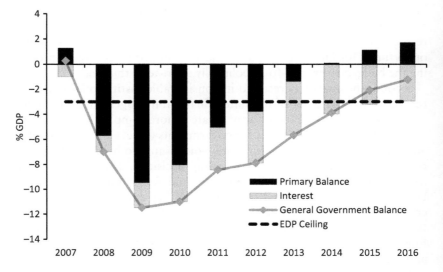

Figure 12.3 General Government Balance (% GDP), 2007–16

Source: Irish Fiscal Advisory Council, www.fiscalcouncil.ie

to ensure that multi-annual planning becomes a central element of the budget process.

(Irish Fiscal Advisory Council 2015, 2)

It would appear from this that, as an advisory body relying on powers of suasion alone, the IFAC could not easily overturn older political temptations to yield to the electoral pressure for an upward trend in public spending commitments. In the context of rising expectations, after years of curtailment of spending on essential services, and with many grievances emerging over restoration of public-sector pay, this clash of perspectives between government and its advisory council is hardly surprising.

Third, and finally, the reforms played a role in advancing accountability for public-sector performance by creating a larger volume of publicly available knowledge concerning the allocation of funds over the medium term, and the performance of individual policy programmes. The Irish budgetary framework certainly now involves a greater range of performance data, including trend analyses, emerging from ministries. However, the use and analysis of this information by the parliament has been poor and an OECD review published in 2015 found room for much greater political engagement in budgetary priority-setting and oversight using this information (OECD 2015, 54). The OECD report also indicated an ongoing lack of accountability in respect of meeting performance targets and greater room for consistency in the quality of performance measures being used (OECD 2015, 53).

Conclusions

The enormous scale of the Irish financial, banking and economic crises resulted in considerable pressure for reform of the state's budgetary and financial management processes. A critical juncture was reached with the arrival of the Troika in 2010, and the signing of the three-year loan programme memorandum which committed the state to a number of initiatives in this area. These developments were quickly followed by reforms mandated by changing rules governing European Monetary Union, including the introduction of the European Semester. As noted in Chapter Seven, the mantra that one should 'never waste a crisis' was also invoked by domestic reformers seeking to introduce regulation of pro-cyclical budgetary behaviour.

It remains to be seen if the reforms collectively and completely arrested the problematic 'boom and bust' approach to public spending, and political pressures to spend over budget limits remain strong. Despite a large underlying debt arising from the Irish state guarantee of bank liabilities, improved economic statistics in 2015 resulted in calls for greater government spending arising from a desire to end 'austerity' measures. Pressure also emerged from public-sector trade unions for an accelerated unwinding of the salary and pension reductions introduced over the 2009–13 period, which had amounted to reductions of up to 25% of salary in some cases. Thus the pre-crisis pattern of focusing on short-term spending has not completely dissipated due to the crisis.

The weight of the influence that new bodies such as the Irish Fiscal Advisory Council and the Irish Government Economic and Evaluation Service can exert also remains uncertain. In the context of a wavering economic recovery, older trends toward pro-cyclical relaxation of budget disciplines, driven by the government electoral cycle, seemed all too likely to re-emerge—notwithstanding the ongoing constraints of EMU and the emergent external disciplines of the Fiscal Compact. The reforms moderated but did not fundamentally alter a tendency toward pro-cyclicality in budget formation. Time will tell what the ultimate consequences may be of the institutional and procedural reforms to the Irish budgetary and financial processes that emerged over the 2008–15 period.

Note

1   As part of the requirement of the Stability and Growth Pact in the Eurozone, the Irish General Government deficit was required to be at or below 3% of GDP. In response to the worsening economic situation, however, the European Council recommended in 2009 that this deficit target be achieved by 2013, extending it to 2014 later that year. Arising from the 2010 Troika loan programme memorandum of understanding, the deadline was further extended to 2015; a target which was achieved (see Figure 12.3). An assessment of the Stability Programme for Ireland published in 2016 subsequently established a new target of 0.5% by 2018.

References

Barnes, Sebastian and Diarmuid Smyth. 2012. *The Government's Balance Sheet After the Crisis: A Comprehensive Perspective.* Dublin: Irish Fiscal Advisory Council.

Boyle, Richard and Michael Mulreany. 2015. "Managing Ireland's Budgets During the Rise and Fall of the 'Celtic Tiger.'" In *The Global Financial Crisis and Its Budget Impacts in OECD Nations: Fiscal Responses and Future Challenges,* edited by John Wanna, Evert Lindquist and Jouke de Vries, 284–308. Cheltenham: Edward Elgar.

Considine, John and Theresa Reidy. 2012. "The Department of Finance." In *Governing Ireland: From Cabinet Government to Delegated Governance,* edited by Eoin O'Malley and Muiris MacCarthaigh 88–105. Dublin: Institute of Public Administration.

Dellepiane-Avellaneda, Sebastian, Niamh Hardiman and Jon Las Heras. 2013. "Building on Easy Money: The Political Economy of Housing Bubbles in Ireland and Spain, UCD." Geary WP2013/18. www.ucd.ie/geary/static/publica tions/workingpapers/gearywp201318.pdf.

Department of Finance. 2011. *Reforming Ireland's Budgetary Framework: A Discussion Document.* Dublin: Department of Finance.

Department of Public Expenditure and Reform. 2011a. *Reforming Ireland's Fiscal Framework: Expenditure Aspects.* Presentation at 'Seminar on Reform of Ireland's Budgetary Framework', Dublin, May 30, 2011.

Department of Public Expenditure and Reform. 2011b. *Comprehensive Expenditure Report 2012–14.* Dublin: Department of Public Expenditure and Reform.

European Commission. 2013. *Fiscal Frameworks in the European Union: Commission Services Country Factsheets for the Autumn 2013 Peer Review, European Commission Occasional Papers 168.* Brussels: European Commission, Directorate-General for Economic and Financial Affairs.

European Council. 2010. *Strengthening Economic Governance in the EU: Report of the Task Force to the European Council.* Brussels. www.consilium.europa. eu/en/press/press-releases/2010/10/pdf/strengthening-economic-governance-in-the-eu-report-of-the-task-force-to-the-european-council/.

Fiscal Responsibility Act. 2012. www.irishstatutebook.ie/eli/2012/act/39/enacted/en/ print#sec6.

Government of Ireland. 2010. *The National Recovery Plan 2011–2014.* Dublin: Stationery Office.

Hagen von, Jürgen. 1992. "Budgeting and Fiscal Performance in the EC." In *Economic Papers* Vol. 96. Brussels: European Commission: 1–85.

Hallerberg, Mark, Rolf Strauch and Jürgen von Hagen. 2007. "The Design of Fiscal Rules and Forms of Governance in European Union Countries." *European Journal of Political Economy* 23(2):338–59.

Hamell, Philip. 2010. "Financial Oversight." In *The Houses of the Oireachtas: Parliament in Ireland,* edited by Muiris MacCarthaigh and Maurice Manning, 340–57. Dublin: Institute of Public Administration.

Hardiman, Niamh. 2012. *Irish Governance in Crisis.* Manchester: Manchester University Press.

Hardiman, Niamh. 2014. "Repeating History: Fiscal Squeeze in Two Recessions in Ireland." In *When the Party's Over: The Politics of Fiscal Squeeze in*

Perspective, edited by Christopher Hood, David Heald and Rozana Himaz, 139–60. London: The British Academy.

Houses of the Oireachtas. 2016. *Report of the Joint Committee of Inquiry Into the Banking Crisis*. Dublin: Houses of the Oireachtas.

Houses of the Oireachtas Joint Committee on Finance and the Public Service. 2010. *Report on Macroeconomic Policy and Effective Fiscal and Economic Governance*. Dublin: Houses of the Oireachtas.

Independent Review Panel. 2010. *Strengthening the Capacity of the Department of Finance*. Dublin: Department of Finance.

Independent Review Panel. 2011. "Strengthening the Capacity of the Department of Finance (Wright Report)." www.finance.gov.ie/documents/publications/reports/2011/deptreview.pdf.

International Monetary Fund. 2013. *Ireland: Fiscal Transparency Assessment*. Washington, DC: International Monetary Fund.

Irish Fiscal Advisory Council. 2015. *Fiscal Assessment Report*. Dublin. www.fiscalcouncil.ie/wp-content/uploads/2015/11/FAR_Draft_30.11.15-Website-Final.pdf.

MacCarthaigh, Muiris. 2017. *Public Sector Reform in Ireland: Countering Crisis*. Basingstoke: Palgrave Macmillan.

OECD. 2008. *Ireland: Towards an Intgrated Public Service*. Paris: OECD.

OECD. 2015. *Review of Budget Oversight by Parliament: Ireland*. Paris: OECD.

Whelan, Karl. 2014. "Ireland's Economic Crisis: The Good, the Bad, and the Ugly." *Journal of Macroeconomics* 39(B):424–40.

13 Budgeting and Financial Management Reforms in Estonia During the Crisis of 2008–10 and Beyond

Ringa Raudla, Tiina Randma-Liiv and Riin Savi

Introduction

Since regaining of independence 1991, the Estonian public administration has aspired to move away from the inherited Soviet system and work towards European integration (OECD 2011, 99). The governments have usually been coalition governments consisting of two to three different parties. The government is composed of a prime minister and twelve ministers.

In budgetary policy, Estonia is often viewed as a poster child of fiscal discipline: a champion of balanced budgets and low public debt (Raudla and Kattel 2011). In other fields of public management, the government of Estonia has also aspired to be 'modern' and 'progressive'. In light of these two tendencies, one would expect that the experience of the crisis in 2008–10, when the Estonian government undertook major cutbacks in order to consolidate the budget, would trigger reforms in the area of budgeting and financial management. On the other hand, the competing prediction would be that as Estonia's commitment to conservative fiscal policies since the early 1990s has been more strongly influenced by unwritten political norms than any explicit fiscal rules, the crisis might not necessarily generate pressures to undertake major budgeting reforms. This chapter gives an overview of the reform trajectories in Estonia in the field of budgeting and financial management and explores whether the experience of the crisis in 2008–10—whereby the GDP fell by more than 18 percentage points—led to any major reforms.

This chapter shows that the crisis period (2008–10) did coincide with some reforms—the consolidation of accounting in the public sector and the imposition of additional borrowing restrictions on local governments—but in general, the crisis reinforced existing reform trajectories in Estonia. After the acute phase of the crisis was over, more extensive reforms in the field of budgeting and financial management have been undertaken, but these, for the most part, have been influenced by other factors—especially the external pressures from the EU and the spillovers from the Eurozone crisis—rather than Estonia's own experience of the fiscal crisis in 2008–10.

The sources of data for the analysis included: existing academic studies on budgeting and fiscal policy in Estonia, laws and policy documents as well as semi-structured interviews with officials in the Ministry of Finance. The interviews were conducted between 2010 and 2015 within the framework of various research projects undertaken by the authors. Altogether, 15 Ministry of Finance officials were interviewed, with each interview lasting between one and three hours.

Budgetary Institutions and Reform Trajectories Preceding the Crisis

Fiscal Rules

Although Estonia has become widely regarded as a poster child of fiscal discipline and low public debt, its commitment to conservative fiscal policies since the early 1990s has been more strongly influenced by unwritten political norms than any explicit fiscal rules (Raudla 2010a; Raudla and Kattel 2011). The 1991 constitution, for example, does not prescribe any numerical fiscal rules or balanced budget requirements.[1] Also, until 2014, the organic budget law (the State Budget Act), which is the main framework law governing the budget process in Estonia, did not contain any *deficit* limits.[2] The analysis of political debates during the 1990s, however, indicates that the politicians often claimed that the 'fiscal constitution' of Estonia requires a balanced budget (see Raudla 2010a; Raudla and Kattel 2011 for a more detailed discussion). There were some provisions in the organic budget laws that stipulated constraints on *debt* between 1995 and 2004, but because the government never even came close to these limits, they cannot be viewed as having been de facto constraining.[3] Between 2004 and 2014, there were no fiscal rules in the organic budget laws of Estonia. Instead, after Estonia joined the European Union (the EU), the Maastricht criteria for deficit and debt limits have been regarded as the fiscal rules that the government has to conform to, though it has usually adopted a stricter fiscal stance than the Maastricht criteria prescribes (Raudla and Kattel 2011).

With regard to the centrally imposed fiscal rules for *local governments*, the acts governing local-government budgeting and finances between 1998 and 2011 stipulated that the total debt of a local government should not be allowed to exceed 60% of current revenues. In addition, the local governments had to inform the Ministry of Finance in the central government of the taking of loans. If a loan was taken without informing the Ministry of Finance, then it had the right to suspend transfers from the equalisation fund.

Budget Procedures

Comparatively speaking, Estonia has been viewed as having rather centralised *budgetary institutions* governing the preparation, adoption and implementation of the budget since regaining its independence in 1991 (Raudla 2010a; 2010b; 2013b). The organic budget law adopted in 1994—after regaining independence—foresaw a top-down approach to budget *preparation* and granted the Ministry of Finance extensive powers in the budget process. These included the authority to establish expenditure ceilings for the line ministries at the beginning of the annual budget cycle (from which the ministries had to proceed when compiling their annual budget bids) and to delete or change the line items in the ministerial budget proposals after their submission to the finance ministry (Raudla 2010a; 2010b).[4]

Thus, despite the fact that Estonia has only had *coalition governments* since 1992, the fiscal-governance arrangements resembled the 'delegation' mode (with a strong minister of finance enforcing fiscal discipline) rather than the 'contracts' (or commitment) mode more characteristic to coalition governments (Hallerberg, Strauch and Hagen 2009). The centralised approach to fiscal governance was partially influenced by historical legacies (the 1938 organic budget law was used as a blueprint for the 1994 law) but also environmental factors. In 1992–94, the first government of the newly independent country faced severe fiscal constraints and had to implement extensive austerity measures. Thus, having a strong finance minister was viewed as helpful (Raudla 2010a; 2010b). Although the revised organic budget law, adopted in 1999, somewhat increased the budgetary decision-making powers of the *cabinet* as a whole (at the expense of the *finance minister*), the overall orientation of the budget process still remained top-down, with the overall expenditure target and ministerial ceilings established early in the budget-preparation process.

During the *boom years* of 2004–07, however, the tax revenues repeatedly overshot the projections, and positive supplementary budgets—adopted in the middle of the fiscal year—became the rule (Kraan, Wehner and Richter 2008). As a result, the line ministries came to perceive the stipulated expenditure ceilings as 'negotiable' in view of higher than expected tax revenues. Although the cabinet still retained final decision authority over how these windfalls would be spent, the line ministries started to submit higher and higher budget requests, instead of proceeding from the expenditure targets stipulated for them at the beginning of the budget cycle. In other words, patterns of *bottom-up budgeting* emerged in negotiations between the Ministry of Finance and the line ministries (Raudla 2013b).

With regard to the *adoption* phase of the budget process (i.e. the adoption of the budget law by the legislature), the developments since the early 1990s can be characterised by an increasing domination of the *executive* over the legislature. Although in the early 1990s the legislators played a more active role in discussing and amending the budget, their de facto role has decreased over the years (see Raudla 2010a; 2010b). While the legislature can amend the draft budget proposed by the cabinet, the amendments have to be offsetting. It is mostly the members of the opposition who propose amendments, and they are usually not approved. Since 1994, several procedural restrictions have been added to the legislative budget process (e.g. pertaining to when and by whom the amendment proposals can be submitted) via changes to the organic budget law and the acts regulating the working procedures of the parliament.

Since the early 1990s, the *implementation* phase of the budget in Estonia has also become increasingly centralised, and the treasury (in the Ministry of Finance) has assumed an important role in controlling the expenditure flows, aided by the use of ICT solutions. At the same time, the breakdown of the input-based expenditure categories has become less detailed since the 1990s: instead of more detailed classification of operational expenditures, the budget law started to provide lump-sum appropriations, leaving it up to the cabinet to decide on the more detailed line items. Thus, the general practice since the early 2000s has been for the cabinet to decide on the items dividing the operational expenditures between personnel and other administrative expenses (after the budget law has been adopted by the parliament), leaving the ministries some leeway in shifting funds within those categories. During the fiscal year, the ministries also have a possibility to ask for the cabinet's permission to reallocate spending between the different line items.

Performance Budgeting

While the reform efforts in the 1990s were focused on creating the basic frameworks for budgeting, in the 2000s the government attempted to 'modernise' budgeting and financial management in Estonia. The reform efforts included the establishment of a medium-term fiscal framework and taking steps towards performance budgeting (in the form of creating links between strategic planning, performance management and budgeting) (Kraan, Wehner and Richter 2008; Raudla 2012; 2013a).

The *performance-budgeting* system in Estonia was created in 2002–05 via amendments to the organic budget law (the State Budget Act) and the adoption of a regulation on strategic planning.[5] The resulting system can be categorised as *presentational performance budgeting*, whereby performance information is added to the main budget documents (i.e. the state budget strategy spanning four years and the annual budget) but without any direct linkages between performance information and budgetary allocations. Although the system created in the early 2000s required the ministries to produce a lot of performance information (to be included in the four-year development plans of the ministries, the one-year action plans and the strategic plans for different policy sectors), the increasing concern of the reform actors was that the performance information was not taken into account in actual budgetary decision-making (Kraan, Wehner and Richter 2008; Raudla 2012). Thus, in the mid-2000s the Ministry of

Finance started working on reform blueprints for moving Estonia closer to a performance-*informed* budgeting system (Raudla 2013a).

The State Budget Strategy (SBS) is also the instrument for medium-term fiscal planning: in addition to performance information, it covers macro-economic projections for the next four years and targets for expenditure, deficit and debt (Kraan, Wehner and Richter 2008). The provisions governing the compilation of the SBS did not foresee the establishment of sectoral or ministerial expenditure ceilings (as is the case in several countries). Before the crisis, however, some of the SBS documents did outline expenditure projections for the different ministries (Raudla 2015).

While several other countries in Europe (and elsewhere) have attempted to use instruments for consciously reallocating spending between different policy areas (e.g. spending reviews), no such instruments have been used in Estonia. Instead, the reallocation between areas of government has been ad hoc and ideologically motivated, rather than resulting from any specific analytical instruments.

Public-Sector Accounting

In the area of accounting, the major reform has been the switch from cash-based to *accrual accounting* (mandatory for all public-sector organisations) in 2004 (Tikk 2010)—ahead of many other European countries. Overall, however, since the early 1990s public-sector financial accounting in Estonia has been decentralised and fragmented, with each public-sector organisation having its own accountants (and also its own financial accounting software). Such a decentralised and fragmented system of public-sector accounting led to an uneven quality of the financial reports (especially after the introduction of the accrual principles) and made it difficult for the government to have a real-time overview of the state finances. Although the Ministry of Finance in Estonia tried to encourage the consolidation of financial accounting throughout the 2000s, it did not have a sufficient legal mandate for it; and because of the resistance of the public-sector organisations, the progress in consolidating public-sector financial accounting was limited (Raudla and Tammel 2015).

Budgetary Reforms in Times of Austerity

Between 2000 and 2007, the Estonian economy witnessed an unprecedented boom: the average annual GDP growth during that period was around 8%. These high growth rates were, however, accompanied by signs of overheating, like double-digit inflation, a housing boom, accelerating wage growth, a fast accumulation of net foreign liabilities and soaring current-account deficits (Raudla and Kattel 2011; 2013; Kattel and Raudla 2013). Although the government was running nominal budget surpluses, it also undertook several tax reductions and repeatedly adopted positive supplementary budgets in the middle of the fiscal year—which added fuel to the boom (Kattel and Raudla 2013; Raudla and Kattel 2013).

The economy started slowing down in 2007, after the two main banks in Estonia began tightening the lending conditions. The global financial crisis—as was the case with many other countries in Central and Eastern Europe—exacerbated the negative effects of the burst of Estonia's domestic property bubble. The GDP plummeted dramatically, falling by 5.4% in 2008 and by 14.7% in 2009 (Eurostat). As a result, the tax revenues undershot the projected levels and the forecasted budget deficit rose significantly.

Although many other countries in Europe sought to tackle the recession with economic stimulus measures, the Estonian government responded to the economic crisis with extensive austerity measures (amounting to about 17% of GDP for 2008–10). What was essentially an 'economic crisis' was viewed as a 'fiscal crisis' by the Estonian government (Raudla and Kattel 2011; 2013; Kattel and Raudla 2013). The coalition parties in power in 2009 hoped that joining the Eurozone would help Estonia to exit the crisis (Raudla and Kattel 2011). Thus, despite the fact that the government had accumulated significant reserves (circa 10% of GDP), it implemented austerity measures—combining both expenditure cuts and tax increases—in the midst of a major recession (Raudla and Kattel 2011; 2013; Kattel and Raudla 2013).

Budgetary Reforms During the Acute Phase of the Crisis in 2008–10

During the 'acute' phase of the crisis, the following changes to budgeting and financial management took place in Estonia: the reinforcement of top-down budgeting, closer monitoring of expenditures in the implementation phase of the budget process and the adoption of restrictions on municipal borrowing.

Reinforcement of Top-Down Budgeting

Although the boom period had led to the emergence of bottom-up elements in the budget process, after the onset of the crisis in 2008 we can observe a clear return to *more centralised* and *top-down* decision-making in the budget process (Raudla 2013b). The cabinet resumed the role as a central forum for negotiations between the coalition partners, and the minister of finance reinforced the ministry's role as the central mediator between the cabinet and the line ministries in setting the budgetary ceilings. The existing budgetary institutions (including provisions in the organic budget law, according to which the cabinet and the Ministry of Finance have extensive budgetary powers) enabled the government to reinforce the top-down mode of decision-making in the budget preparation phase (Raudla 2013b).

Closer Monitoring of Budgetary Expenditures in the Implementation Phase of the Budget Process

In addition to reinforcing the centralised decision-making in the budget *preparation* phase, the Ministry of Finance increased its control over the *implementation* phase by engaging in closer real-time monitoring of expenditures. This was, in particular, driven by the need to provide more accurate and timely estimates of the fiscal indicators considered necessary to ensure compliance with the Maastricht criteria. If, in real time, the deficit projections worsened, the government was able to implement additional austerity measures in order to achieve the fiscal targets.

Restrictions on Local-Government Borrowing

Another expression of more 'centralised' fiscal policymaking was the adoption of a legal provision (in 2009) that allowed *local governments* to incur loans only after receiving consent from the minister of finance. Such a restriction was considered to be necessary for ensuring that Estonia meets the Maastricht deficit criterion for joining the Eurozone (the deficit requirement applies to the *general* government budget position, which also includes the local governments).

Decreased Focus on Performance Information in the Budget Process But Continued Plans to Reform the Performance Budgeting System

The role of performance information (PI) in budgetary decision-making actually declined during the acute phase of the crisis (Raudla and Savi 2015). During 2008–10, the amount of performance information submitted by the line ministries (to the Ministry of Finance) decreased, as witnessed by shorter performance documents (i.e. the organisational development plans and annual action plans) and also less focus on performance indicators in the State Budget Strategy (Raudla 2015). In making the cutback decisions, the Ministry of Finance officials made almost no use of the performance information provided by the line ministries, and in the cutback decisions at the ministry level only a limited utilisation of PI was reported (see Jõgiste, Peda and Grossi 2012; Raudla and Savi 2015). During the acute phase of the budget, the focus of the Ministry of Finance and the line ministries was on ensuring that the aggregate cutback targets were met rather than on improving allocational efficiency or enhancing organisational performance. The interviewed officials pointed to the following reasons for why PI was not used in cutback decisions: the sense of urgency in achieving cutbacks and the lack of time for analysing PI, limited analytical capacities, insufficient linkages between performance information and funding, and political considerations of equity (Raudla and Savi 2015).

With regard to *reforming* the existing performance budgeting system *as a whole*, the Ministry of Finance *continued* with reform preparations that had commenced in 2006 by procuring studies and analyses from various think tanks and consultants (Raudla 2013a) and conducting some pilot projects in selected ministries. As mentioned earlier, the overall goal of the reform preparations has been to move beyond presentational performance budgeting and closer to performance-informed budgeting, in order to facilitate greater use of performance information in resource allocation and create closer linkages between strategic planning and budgeting (Raudla 2013a). During the crisis, preparing the strategic planning and performance budgeting reform, however, was not a priority for the Ministry of Finance as a whole (as its focus was on maintaining fiscal discipline and achieving cutbacks). Rather, it continued because of the initiative of some individual civil servants and because funding was available from the EU structural funds for procuring studies and analyses.

Consolidation of Support Services (Including Accounting)

In 2009, during the peak of the financial crisis, the Estonian government launched a project aimed at consolidating support services. The aim of the reform was to standardise fragmented central-government support services (such as financial accounting, payroll accounting and personnel records), to consolidate these functions to the ministerial level (i.e. remove accounting functions from the agencies to the ministries) and to impose the adoption of common software SAP on all central-government organisations. As mentioned above, the Ministry of Finance had attempted to consolidate public-sector accounting already in the pre-crisis years but had not succeeded. Thus, the crisis provided a window of opportunity for the Ministry of Finance—with the support from the cabinet—to impose consolidation of financial accounting in the Estonian central government. The crisis pointed to the importance of obtaining real-time overviews of the finances of the state in order to allow the government to evaluate the effects of fiscal consolidation efforts. In addition, given its goal to cut expenditures, the cabinet was looking for opportunities to reduce operational costs of the public sector, and consolidating financial accounting (and other support services) appeared to be one possible option for achieving significant cost-savings (Raudla and Tammel 2015).

Budgeting and Financial Management Reforms After the Acute Phase of the Crisis (Since 2011)

Although during the acute phase of the crisis in 2008–10, no major budgetary or financial management reforms were undertaken in Estonia (instead, the existing institutional arrangements were reinforced), a significant package of reforms was adopted in 2014 when the parliament passed the new organic budget law (the State Budget Act). The enactment of the new law was primarily motivated by the need to implement the requirements of the Fiscal Compact (or the Treaty on Stability, Coordination and Governance), obligatory for all Eurozone members. The Ministry of Finance, however, used the need to adopt a new organic budget law to advance other reform initiatives, as well. The new organic budget law foresaw the following major reforms: (1) the provisions allowing the adoption of programme-based performance budgeting by the line ministries; (2) the establishment of a new fiscal rule requiring the state budget to be in structural balance (or surplus); and (3) the creation of an independent Fiscal Council. In the field of accounting, the Ministry of Finance went ahead with the consolidation of support services and created a shared service centre. Also, starting in 2017, the government plans to move from cash-based budgeting to accrual budgeting.

The Provisions for Programme-Based Performance Budgeting

As mentioned above, the Ministry of Finance started planning a reform of performance budgeting in 2006. It continued with the reform preparations throughout the crisis and in its aftermath. The focus of the reform, however, changed over time. Overall, the general goal of the reform efforts of the Ministry of Finance over the past decade has been to move towards performance-informed budgeting, but more recently, there has been a growing emphasis on *programme* budgeting (called 'activity-based budgeting' in Estonia).

Despite the reform preparations between 2007 and 2013, no clear blueprint for reform had emerged (Raudla 2013a), and in 2013 the main members of the reform team left the Ministry of Finance. Because of the time limit imposed by the Fiscal Compact for implementing its requirements, the Ministry of Finance drafted the new organic budget law in a considerable hurry. Thus, there was not sufficient time to thoroughly discuss different options and, as a result, the provisions of the new organic budget concerning performance budgeting reflect pragmatic compromises and flexibilities. For example, the new law provides a *possibility* for the government to adopt a programme-based budget format but does not *mandate* it. Thus, the law includes provisions that *allow* ministries to move from an input-based categorisation of their budgetary expenditures to a programme-based budget format in which the expenditures would be categorised according to performance areas, programmes and subprogrammes. As of 2016, only the Ministry of Education and Science has switched from an input-based format to a programme format in their budget.

The adoption of such a gradual, ministry-by-ministry approach reflects the understanding that ministries are at different stages of preparedness in developing their systems for performance measurement and activity-based costing. The increased flexibility in using budgetary resources is expected, by the Ministry of Finance, to make the adoption of a programme format attractive to the line ministries. Ministries can petition the Ministry of Finance to adopt the programme-based format. The Ministry of Finance would then verify if the ministry's systems for strategic planning, activity-based costing and accrual budgeting would be sufficient to justify the switch. The Ministry of Finance is in the process of drafting the regulation for programme-based approach budgeting. The first draft of that regulation was sent out to the line ministries for comments in 2015, but in light of the critical feedback received, the Ministry of Finance is reconsidering its approach.

In sum, the experience of the crisis appears to have slowed down the performance budgeting reform. Given that only limited (if any) use was made of performance information during the crisis, the Ministry of Finance and line ministries started to reconsider the trajectory of the reform. While the Estonian government generally has preferred radical, big-bang, comprehensive reforms when it came to performance management and budgeting, the realisation emerged that a radical approach may not be feasible.

The Adoption of New Fiscal Rules: The Structural Balance Rule and the Expenditure Ceilings

Before the enactment of the Fiscal Compact, Estonia did not have a fiscal rule stipulating budget balance or a deficit target in their domestic legislation; instead, the budgetary process was governed by the informal norm of a balanced budget. The Fiscal Compact (enacted in 2013) required the members of the Eurozone to introduce a structural deficit ceiling (of 0.5% of GDP) in their domestic legislation. The structural position of the budget is calculated on the basis of a cyclically adjusted position, which is adjusted for one-off and temporary transactions. The cyclically adjusted budget position, in turn, is found by subtracting the cyclical component (or the output gap) from the nominal budget position. The new State Budget Act of Estonia, adopted in early 2014, however, establishes a stricter rule than prescribed by the Fiscal Compact and requires that the structural budget position be 'in balance or in surplus'. As the interviewed Ministry of Finance officials from Estonia explained, the drafters of the law hoped that the structural *balance*—rather than deficit—requirement would provide a 'buffer', in case calculations of the output gap by the Ministry of Finance deviated from those of the European Commission (Raudla et al. 2016).

According to the interviewed Ministry of Finance officials, the introduction of a structural balance/deficit rule can be considered to be one of the biggest reforms in the fiscal policy arena during recent years. At the same time, they noted that *without* the Fiscal Compact, the structural balance target would *not* have been written into domestic legislation. It was felt that there was actually no need for such a rule, given the political culture of fiscal conservatism in Estonia. They also pointed out that if a fiscal rule had to be established at all, the local preference would have been for one with a *nominal*—rather than structural—target (Raudla et al. 2016).

When the drafts of the new organic budget law were debated in the Estonian parliament in 2013–14, the discussions over the structural balance rule focused on the technical complexities involved in calculating it and how the real-time estimations might differ from the ex post assessments. There was also some discussion over whether a structural balance requirement should be preferred over a nominal balance rule and how it is also important to pay attention to the nominal balance. Generally, however, there was very little discussion about it; the elected officials simply accepted that since the Fiscal Compact required such a rule, it had to be incorporated into the domestic legislation (Raudla et al. 2016).

After the enactment of the new organic budget law, the structural balance rule triggered shifts in fiscal policymaking discussions. Most of the interviewed Estonian officials noted that *after* the adoption of the structural budget balance rule, the *main focus* of fiscal policymaking has switched from the nominal balance (which has been the traditional focus in Estonia so far) to the *structural* position (Raudla et al. 2016).

In sum, the enactment of the structural balance rule in Estonia was only indirectly influenced by the fiscal crisis of 2008–10. The Fiscal Compact itself was indeed adopted in response to the Eurozone crisis, but its provisions were mostly aimed at countries that have problems with fiscal discipline—which is not the case with Estonia. Curiously, in Estonia, the adoption of the structural balance rule has in fact allowed the government to take a somewhat more relaxed stance towards deficits. While it previously tried to maintain a nominal balance (or surplus) irrespective of the position of the economic cycle, the stabilisation function written into the structural balance rule has made nominal deficits more acceptable for the government in the context of economic downturns (Raudla et al. 2016).

Another important change that came into force with the new State Budget Act in 2014 is the binding nature of the multiyear expenditure ceilings for the areas of government. Although previous SBSs had also outlined multiyear financial plans for the governing areas before, these were not mandatory according to the previous framework law (Raudla 2015). The provisions in the new State Budget Act now state that once the SBS is approved by the cabinet (the SBS is still approved by the cabinet and not the parliament), the multiyear expenditure ceilings contained in it are 'binding', in the sense that they should become the starting point in compiling the subsequent SBSs in the following years.[6] Again, the adoption of the expenditure ceilings was primarily motivated by the EU requirements rather than by the crisis experience.

The Creation of an Independent Fiscal Council

The Fiscal Compact requires the members of the Eurozone to establish independent fiscal councils. The function of such a council is to monitor the government's fiscal policy, provide independent evaluations and assess whether the budget complies with fiscal rules. When the fiscal compact was discussed in the EU, the Estonian government was in fact against the provision *requiring* all member countries to establish such an institution: it was felt that Estonia does not in fact need a new institution like that, considering its political commitment to fiscal discipline. Given that the creation of such a council became mandatory for all Eurozone members, the government did go ahead with its institutional design. In 2014, a fiscal council was established in the form of an independent advisory board, aided in its work by the Central Bank of Estonia.

Further Consolidation of Public-Sector Accounting: The Creation of a Shared Service Centre

The ambition of the Ministry of Finance in consolidating support functions has been to move from the establishment of the accounting centres in the line ministries to the provision of support services by an inter-ministerial shared service centre. This process was kick-started at the beginning of 2011, when the Ministry of Finance and the Ministry of Justice agreed to establish a 'State Service Centre' (SSC) on the basis of the already functioning courts' shared service centre. The Ministry of Justice, in whose governing area the centre had been created in 2005, became the first client of the 'new' centre and handed over all its accounting functions to the SSC on 1 January 2012. As a result, the Ministry of Justice itself did not have accountants working within the ministry anymore. In addition to the Ministry of Justice, other ministries were invited to become customers (and hand over their accounting) to the new SSC. By 2015, the Ministry of Finance, the Ministry of Economic Affairs and Communications and the Ministry of Social Affairs also handed their accounting functions over to the horizontal SSC. In 2015, the government announced that it sought to transfer the accounting function from all remaining ministries to the SSC, as well. Crisis-related arguments—including ensuring the transparency of accounting and cutting administrative costs—were often used by policy actors in advocating this reform (Raudla and Tammel 2015; Tammel 2015).

Preparations for Accrual Budgeting

As mentioned above, Estonia adopted an accrual *accounting* system in 2004. Since then, the Ministry of Finance has been considering the reform of accrual *budgeting* as well. The argument often made by the reform actors in the Ministry of Finance is that if the annual budget system is also accrual-based (rather than cash-based), the two systems—accounting and budgeting—fit better together. In addition, it has been argued that accrual-based budgeting is 'more transparent' and 'reliable' (Õepa 2016). According to current plans, the annual budget for 2017 will be accrual-based. In justifying the reform, the reform actors have so far not made use of any arguments referring to the crisis experience.

Budgetary Results and Broader Consequences of Budgetary Reform to Public Management

Generally speaking, the centralised budgetary institutions of Estonia have been considered to be conducive to the maintenance of fiscal discipline. Indeed, the possibility to revert to a very centralised mode of budget preparation and adoption (including procedural provisions allowing the cabinet to bypass parliamentary discussions over negative supplementary budgets) at the onset of the crisis facilitated the swift adoption of the austerity measures and allowed the government to curb budget deficits and the public debt (Raudla 2013b). At the same time, we can observe that after the introduction of the structural balance rule in 2014, the government has started to adopt a somewhat more relaxed position with regard to the nominal deficit (reflected in the adoption of budgets with projected nominal deficits for 2015 and 2016).[7]

While the previous rounds of changes to the organic budget law (in 1999 and 2002–04) had witnessed the introduction of additional constraints on the parliament in the budget process, the 2014 law did not add any additional constraints. Still, the introduction of programme budgeting (and the more detailed provisions regulating it) have been left to the cabinet, which can be seen as potentially weakening the role of the parliament (as it may reduce the level of detail in the annual budget and loss of legislative control over the format of the budget law). On the other hand, the new Fiscal Council may somewhat enhance the power of the legislature vis-à-vis the executive by providing the members of parliament with an additional source of independent evaluation of fiscal policy.

The crisis only indirectly affected the other ongoing public-management reforms, such as the mergers of government agencies (nine mergers took place at the peak of the crisis in 2008–10), attempts to further centralise strategic planning and the central government policy to amalgamate local-government units. All these reforms—like the public financial management and budget reforms described earlier—reflect the more general reform direction in the Estonian public administration: steps towards greater centralisation. The fiscal crisis did not have an effect on reforming coordination practices in the Estonian government.

In addition to the trajectory of increased centralisation, the Estonian public-management reforms have been driven by cost-efficiency motives since the early 2000s, and cost-efficiency continued to be one of the main aims of reform even during the years of economic boom. This has to do with prevailing anti-state attitudes among the citizens, fuelled by legacies of the past as well as consecutive neo-liberal governments. In this regard, the goal of 'more cost-efficiency' during the years of fiscal crisis was nothing new in the government rhetoric. Thus, alongside greater centralisation, there have also been attempts to increase cost-efficiency by providing the managers with more flexibility in their more detailed decisions. For example, the efforts at (re-)asserting macro control over the fiscal policy have been accompanied by plans to introduce more flexibility for the line ministries and agencies via programme budgeting.

All in all, the evidence from Estonia shows a weak and indirect link between the crisis and public-management reform. The Estonian government did not initiate any public-management reforms due to fiscal crisis, but the crisis environment gave a boost to a few ongoing reforms. One could even say that the fiscal crisis served to *justify* politically motivated reforms more than actually *necessitating* them. The Estonian government's response to crisis predominantly followed a combination of straightforward cutbacks and incremental change in public administration. The crisis intensified the pressure to reform public management to some extent, but these pressures did not translate into large-scale structural reforms and/or specific reform trajectories in Estonia. The response to the crisis displayed many elements of continuity rather than change vis-à-vis the reform trends and tools that had already been evolving before the crisis. The evidence from Estonia thus shows that fiscal crisis provided neither a 'change event' nor a 'critical juncture' in the ongoing process of public-management reforms. This finding is in line with Pandey's (2010) argument that decision makers tend to draw a clear distinction between restoring the fiscal balance and modernising public administration by carrying out structural reforms.

Conclusion

In the Estonian case, the experience of an acute crisis in 2008–10 appears to have reinforced existing budget practices, instead of triggering path-breaking changes and major reforms. The need to achieve ambitious cutback targets led to *a path-dependent return* to a very top-down approach in the budget-preparation process—with clear ceilings set by the cabinet (together with the Ministry of Finance) at the beginning of the budget-preparation cycle. The crisis also reinforced ongoing reforms in the direction of centralisation and organisational mergers. The preparations for performance management and budgeting reform were not completely abandoned during the acute phase of the crisis but they certainly lost some momentum, and the limited use of PI in budgetary decision-making during cutbacks forced the Ministry of Finance to reconsider the reform trajectory. Thus, it slowed down but did not permanently halt ongoing changes in the direction of performance-budgeting practices that potentially centralise allocative decisions but also provide public managers with more flexibility in the management of funds.

There were, however, some reforms that were more directly motivated by the crisis experience: the adoption of additional borrowing restrictions for local governments and the consolidation of public-sector accounting. While the restrictions on local governments were *directly* motivated by the need to secure fiscal discipline (in order to fulfil the Maastricht criteria), the crisis provided a *window of opportunity* for the Ministry of Finance to proceed with its already *existing* plans to reduce the fragmentation of public-sector accounting.

After the acute phase of the crisis was over, preparations for reforming budgeting and financial management continued, but the Ministry of Finance opted for a more *incremental* approach, especially in the field of performance budgeting. What can be considered to be more *path-breaking* changes for Estonia, however, have been the reforms triggered by the spillovers from the Eurozone crisis and the requirements of the Fiscal Compact: the adoption of the structural balance rule, the stipulation of expenditure ceilings and the creation of the Fiscal Council. These changes to the framework law for budgeting, enacted in 2014, entailed major changes for the Estonian budgetary system, where fiscal discipline had hitherto been primarily driven by the *informal* rule of a balanced budget. Had it been up to the Estonian government itself, it would not have adopted such rules.

Acknowledgements

The research leading to these results has received funding from the Estonian Research Council Grant PUT-1142.

Notes

1   The constitution does, however, entail some procedural restrictions. For example, the legislative amendments to the draft budget have to be offsetting, and the executive needs the approval of the legislature in order to incur debt (Raudla 2010b).
2   The organic budget law that was adopted in 1994 did state that 'the budget has to be balanced' but, at a closer look, this requirement was purely formal, since 'loans' were listed as 'revenues'. Thus, according to these provisions, the budget would be 'balanced' even if loans were used to cover expenditures (Raudla 2010a).
3   In 1999, with changes made to the organic budget law, a golden rule was established, stipulating that the maximum amount of loans taken should not be larger than the amount foreseen for investment and that the loans should not exceed 10% of the budget revenues for that year. With changes made to the organic budget law in 2002 and 2004, these provisions were abolished,

however. The Foreign Borrowing by the Republic of Estonia and State Guarantees for Foreign Loan Agreements Act, which came into force in 1995, stipulated that 'the total amount of foreign loans taken by the Republic of Estonia in a current budget year cannot exceed 15 per cent of the state budget revenue approved by the *Riigikogu* and that the total amount of all foreign loans cannot exceed 75 per cent of the budget revenue for the current budget year'. In 2003, this act was abolished.

4   Most of the provisions in the organic budget law of 1993 were copied from the organic budget law of 1938 (which had governed the budget process in a regime strongly dominated by the executive branch). Such provisions were also seen as beneficial in light of the financial constraints facing the first government of the newly independent Estonia (Raudla 2010a, b).

5   An important motive for the reform was to modernise the budgeting system in order to show that Estonia is a developed country with advanced management practices. The reform actors argued that adding performance information to budget documents would increase efficiency and transparency. The reform was influenced by the doctrine of New Public Management and also recommended by external actors (i.e. the IMF and the EU) (Raudla 2012; 2013a).

6   The organic budget law does, however, allow for adjustments to take place, in case the main directions of the state fiscal policy, the macroeconomic forecast, financial forecast or legislation have materially changed.

7   Ex post, these deficits did not actually materialise, however.

References

Hallerberg, Mark, Rolf R. Strauch and Jürgen von Hagen. 2009. *Fiscal Governance in Europe.* Cambridge: Cambridge University Press.

Jõgiste, Kadri, Peeter Peda and Giuseppe Grossi. 2012. "Budgeting in a Time of Austerity: The Case of the Estonian Central Government." *Public Administration and Development* 32(2):181–95.

Kattel, Rainer and Ringa Raudla. 2013. "The Baltic States and the Crisis of 2008–2011." *Europe-Asia Studies* 65(3):426–49.

Kraan, Dirk-Jan, Joachim Wehner and Kirsten Richter. 2008. "Budgeting in Estonia." *OECD Journal on Budgeting* 8(2):87–126.

OECD. 2011. *Public Governance Reviews. Estonia: Towards a Single Government Approach.* Assessment and Recommendations. Paris: OECD.

Õepa, Aivar. 2016. "Riik läheb üle tekkepõhisele eelarvele" [The government will adopt accrual-based budgeting]. *Postimees*, January 22. http://majandus 24.postimees.ee/3478115/riik-laheb-ule-tekkepohisele-eelarvele.

Pandey, Sanjey K. 2010. "Cutback Management and the Paradox of Publicness." *Public Administration Review* 70(4):564–71.

Raudla, Ringa. 2010a. *Constitution, Public Finance, and Transition: Theoretical Developments in Constitutional Public Finance and the Case of Estonia.* Frankfurt am Main: Peter Lang, Europäischer Verlag der Wissenschaften.

Raudla, Ringa. 2010b. "The Evolution of Budgetary Institutions in Estonia: A Path Full of Puzzles?" *Governance: An International Journal of Policy, Administration, and Institutions* 23(3):463–84.

Raudla, Ringa. 2012. "The Use of Performance Information in Budgetary Decision-Making by Legislators: Is Estonia Any Different?" *Public Administration* 90(4): 1000–15.

Raudla, Ringa. 2013a. "Pitfalls of Contracting for Policy Advice: Preparing Performance Budgeting Reform in Estonia." *Governance* 26(4):605–29.

Raudla, Ringa. 2013b. "Fiscal Retrenchment in Estonia During the Crisis: The Role of Institutional Factors." *Public Administration* 91(1):32–50.

Raudla, Ringa. 2015. "The Role of State Budget Strategy in the Execution of Fiscal Policies." In *Estonian Human Development Report 2014/2015*, edited by Raivo Vetik, 255–9. Tallinn: SA Eesti Koostöö Kogu.

Raudla, Ringa, Aleksandrs Cepilovs, Rainer Kattel and Linda Sutt. 2016. "Pulling the Discursive Trigger? The Impact of Structural Deficit Rule on Fiscal Policy-Making in Estonia and Latvia." Paper presented at the WINIR Annual Conference in Boston, September 2016.

Raudla, Ringa and Rainer Kattel. 2011. "Why Did Estonia Choose Fiscal Retrenchment After the 2008 Crisis?" *Journal of Public Policy* 31(2):163–86.

Raudla, Ringa and Rainer Kattel. 2013. "Fiscal Stress Management During the Financial and Economic Crisis: The Case of the Baltic Countries." *International Journal of Public Administration* 36(10):732–42.

Raudla, Ringa and Riin Savi. 2015. "The Use of Performance Information in Cutback Budgeting." *Public Money & Management* 35(6):409–16.

Raudla, Ringa and Kaide Tammel. 2015. "Creating Shared Service Centres for Public Sector Accounting." *Accounting, Auditing & Accountability Journal* 28(2):158–79.

Tammel, Kaide. 2015. "Collective Institutional Entrepreneurship in Initiating Public-Sector Shared Service Centers." *Administrative Culture* 16(2):161–79.

Tikk, Juta. 2010. "The Internationalization of the Estonian Accounting System." *Annals of the University of Petrosani, Economics* 10(2):341–52.

Part IV

Comparative Analysis and Conclusion

14 Comparative Analysis and Conclusion

Eva Moll Ghin, Hanne Foss Hansen and Mads Bøge Kristiansen

Introduction

The aim of this book is to provide insight into austerity and its effects on public management. We understand austerity as policies, adopted in response to the crisis, that represent a tough stance on public spending, and we have chosen to focus on the policies of cutting back spending in central government and reforming budgetary institutions in ways that are meant to strengthen budget guardians vis-à-vis the spending pressures from various social groups and administrative units. We are guided by the idea that the policies of austerity could possibly become a catalyst for new ways of managing and reforming the public sector but also by the realisation that it is perhaps just as likely to be used to reinforce existing reform trajectories or that it may even slow down the pace of existing reforms. In the present context of public management reform, it is not least relevant to know how austerity relates to the ongoing transformation towards 'post-NPM' reform priorities, such as the strengthening of central steering, coordination, and organisational reintegration in a 'whole-of-government' perspective. This led us to formulate three research questions in Chapter 1:

1. What is the character of the changes that are taking place under present-day austerity?
2. Does austerity lead to path-breaking and/or path-dependent change?
3. Why are different and/or similar patterns of change found in different countries?

We have approached the task through case studies of cutback management and budgetary reform in five European countries that vary with respect to economic factors, such as the severity and duration of the crisis and their fiscal records, and with respect to their political systems and administrative structures, traditions and reform trajectories. The case selection is based on a 'most different' strategy according to which the idea is to extract common findings from widely different experiences of crisis and austerity, but we also use the variations to look for patterns of correspondence between economic factors, political and administrative institutional factors and the respective countries' approaches to austerity and reforms. The main methodological approach, however, is in-depth analysis of each individual case in its particular context.

The case studies show that the current austerity appears to reinforce the existing 'post-NPM' tendencies in the direction of centralisation, larger-scale organisations and coordination. Beneath these broad patterns, however, we find many nuances and variations. For example, we find that the centralisation of aggregate budgetary control is both accompanied by decentralisation to the public managers of detailed decisions on budgetary allocations and by intensified central monitoring of budgetary implementation and that personnel policies simultaneously move in the directions of deregulation, standardisation and a return to the privileging of civil service 'insiders' over 'outsiders'. We also find that austerity has mostly reinforced existing public management reform trajectories but that it was more of a critical juncture for public management modernisation and innovation in a country like Ireland, which was hit hard by the crisis and where the political system also favours a boom–bust reform pattern.

In the following sections, we will present a more detailed comparative analysis and conclusion. In the second section, we describe and compare the crisis and the turn to austerity in the five countries, and in the third and fourth sections we compare their cutback strategies and measures and their budgetary reforms. We then consider the consequences of austerity for four components of public management reform: financial management, organisational issues, personnel management and the use of performance measurements. Last but not least, we draw the overall conclusions and discuss the implications and limitations of the case studies and findings presented in this book.

From Crisis to Austerity

The five case countries in this volume represent very different crisis experiences and responses. Estonia was hit by a deep, albeit short, recession and responded with substantial cutbacks from 2008 to 2010. Ireland was hit by a deep recession and major fiscal crisis, to which it responded with very substantial cutbacks from 2008 until 2013. Italy and Denmark were hit by more moderate crises and first initiated major cutbacks in 2010, but since then they have both reduced their (relatively high) levels of public spending. Germany was affected relatively little by the crisis and has been able to avoid implementing most of its planned cutbacks. In the following, we elaborate on the characteristics of the crisis and responses in the countries and present some comparative figures.

The Crisis and Responses

For each case country, Table 14.1. summarises the economic and fiscal situation prior to the crisis, the crisis characteristics, the main elements in the overall responses and the role of international actors.

Among the case countries, Germany was relatively mildly affected by the crisis. Its GDP only fell in one year, 2009, and although it experienced

Table 14.1 Country Situations Prior to the Crisis, Crisis Characteristics, Crisis Responses and the Role of International Actors

Germany
- Relatively high growth prior to the crisis (after a prolonged period of low growth and reforms at the beginning of the century). Modest deficits, moderate public debt.
- Banking crisis. Moderate, short recession. Deficits exceeding Maastricht criteria in 2009 and 2010.
- Immediate focus on solving banking crisis, later growth stimulation. Extensive fiscal consolidation launched but not implemented due to economic recovery.
- In the EU excessive deficit procedure 2009–13.

Italy
- Relatively low growth prior to the crisis. High budget deficits, very high public debt.
- Moderate recession in 2009 followed by long-term stagnation and decline. Deficits exceeding Maastricht criteria despite primary surpluses.
- Emergency fiscal packages with wage freezes, cutbacks and revenue increases. Some growth stimulation more recently.
- In the EU excessive deficit procedure 2009–12. Contagion from other high-debt countries threatened by sovereign default. Pressure from EU and other international bodies to carry out fiscal consolidation.

Denmark
- Relatively high growth prior to the crisis. Housing bubble. Large budget surpluses and little public debt.
- Banking crisis, moderate recession followed by a longer period of economic stagnation. Increasing deficits and debts but generally below Maastricht criteria.
- Immediate focus on solving banking crisis, later initiatives to stimulate growth hand in hand with fiscal consolidation including cutbacks.
- In the EU excessive deficit procedure 2010–13.

Ireland
- Very high growth prior to the crisis. Bubble economy in construction. Budget surpluses and little public debt.
- Banking crisis. Deep but not very long recession. Large increases in deficits and debts due to bank guarantees and gap between revenue and expenditure.
- Bailout of national banks. Emergency fiscal packages followed by more targeted cutbacks.
- In the EU excessive deficit procedure 2009–15. Troika conditionality 2010–13.

(Continued)

Table 14.1 (Continued)

Estonia
- Very high growth prior to the crisis. Housing bubble. Budget surpluses and very little public debt.
- Deep but short recession. Deficits remained below Maastricht criteria throughout the crisis.
- Immediate fiscal consolidation through budget cuts, tax increases and reduced transfers to local government and social security.
- The interest in joining the Eurozone was an important motivating factor for fiscal consolidation.

Source: Our own elaboration based on the case analyses of the volume.

deteriorating deficits and debts and entered the excessive deficit procedure, economic growth promptly resumed, allowing it to avoid implementing much of the fiscal consolidation it initiated at the beginning of the crisis.

Ireland and Estonia experienced deep recessions that had already begun in 2008 after the bursting of the economic bubbles that prevailed in both countries prior to the crisis. Estonia already returned to positive growth rates in 2010, however, and Ireland again posted relatively high growth in 2013. Nevertheless, these two countries have experienced very different degrees of fiscal crisis; Estonia already responded to the economic crisis with substantial fiscal consolidation in 2009. It was also aided in this regard by the fact that its banking sector was foreign-owned, and it did not have to spend public money bailing out banks. Not so in Ireland, where the losses in the construction industry spilled over to the substantial domestic banking sector. The government issued a blanket guarantee to cover banking liabilities, which led to very large losses of public money. A gap also opened between government revenues and expenditure, which, combined with the bailout costs, led to very large deficits and an explosion in public debt levels. In 2010, the government had to apply for emergency assistance from international financial institutions, and the country carried out much of its fiscal consolidation under Troika conditionality from 2010 to 2013.

The two remaining countries, Italy and Denmark, are different on many accounts, but they both experienced relatively moderate recessions in 2008–09, and their deficits remained below the EU average, although near or above the 3% limit. They have also both found it difficult to return to sustained economic growth. The situation has been particularly dire in Italy, where the historic record of high deficits and high public debt contributed to pulling it deeper into recession when the sovereign debt crisis in other high-debt countries made financial investors demand larger premiums for investing in Italy. Denmark, on the other hand, has a better fiscal record and has benefited from the role of 'safe haven' in financial markets. Both countries have carried out substantial fiscal consolidation, and they have both been in the EU excessive deficit procedure, but in Italy the external pressure for consolidation has been much harder and more sustained due to its central and precarious role in the Eurozone.

All in all, the varying character of the crisis in the respective countries led to different responses, and the different political and administrative cultures and histories also influenced how each country responded. In Germany, reform and cutback efforts had been considerable before the crisis, which became a factor contributing to the rapid recovery after the crisis. The Italian response proved inadequate to restore market confidence. Several crises regarding political legitimacy and shifts in government resulted, probably prolonging problems further. In Denmark, prior experiences with banking crises made rather prompt responses possible in relation to this crisis element. In Ireland, the response to the fiscal crisis was initially modest, but after a restructuring of what was considered weak state capacity, more rigorous responses became possible. In Estonia, a strong culture of fiscal discipline rendered it possible for the government to implement major consolidation measures in a short time span. Finally, the role of international actors and EU policy differed. Germany was an important actor in setting the EU agenda. In Estonia and Denmark, the EU agenda primarily played a role because it was convenient for domestic policy. In Italy and Ireland, the EU and other international actors put extensive pressure on domestic agendas.

Fiscal Consolidation and Austerity

Expenditure reductions have been a main instrument of consolidation in all of the case countries. Measuring and comparing the 'size' of public expenditure reduction is no simple matter, and the validity of detailed comparisons is limited by the difficulty of harmonising the expenditure registrations that feed into international statistics. However, we have chosen to attempt to provide the reader with an impression of the size of the cutbacks as illustrated in some aggregated figures.

First, Figure 14.1 presents the size of total public expenditure as a percentage of GDP.

This figure shows us, first, how the percentage of the national product spent by the different governments varies greatly. Denmark has the highest level of government expenditure followed by Italy, EU28, Germany, Ireland and Estonia (although the Irish state has spent a lower percentage of GDP than Estonia since 2014, which primarily reflects the high Irish GDP growth rates in recent years). It also shows us how the level of government expenditure as the proportion of the economy increased in the early years beginning of the crisis. This reflects both the declining size of the economies and the increasing levels of public expenditure resulting from rising unemployment, social expenses, and stimulus measures. Ireland in particular experienced a peak after the crisis, which was, however, largely driven by its considerable bailout costs. The graphs also show us how the rising proportion of public expenditure was marked but relatively short-lived in Estonia (and mostly caused by a denominator effect), whereas the increased share of public spending seems more permanent

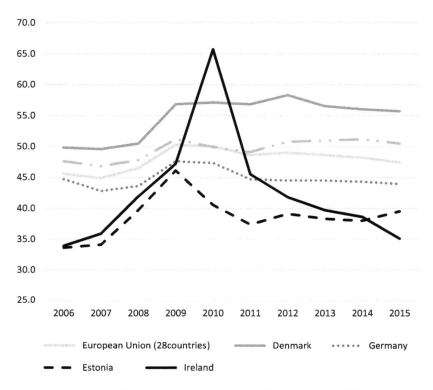

Figure 14.1 General Government Expenditure as Percentage of GDP
Source: Eurostat (2016).

in Denmark and Italy. As already argued, however, these numbers partly reflect the very different levels of economic growth after the crisis, so we also include a figure for the level of public expenditure calculated as index figures, with 2010 as the base year.

The reductions of public expenditure have affected both capital and operational expenditure, subsidies, pensions and other social transfers. In this volume, we are mainly interested in cutbacks on the operating costs of running the public sector, and we have chosen to include one figure (Figure 14.2.) as a proxy for this; that is, government final consumption expenditure.

Figure 14.2. confirms the impression that Estonia carried out substantial cutbacks from 2008 to 2010, and Ireland carried out very substantial cutbacks from 2008 until 2013. Italy and Denmark did not reduce consumption expenditure until 2010, but since then the level has been slightly falling in Denmark and more so in Italy. Germany has not cut back its level of consumption expenditure.

In the following, we examine the process of implementing cutbacks at the state level of government, including the German Länder but excluding the regions and municipalities in all of the countries.

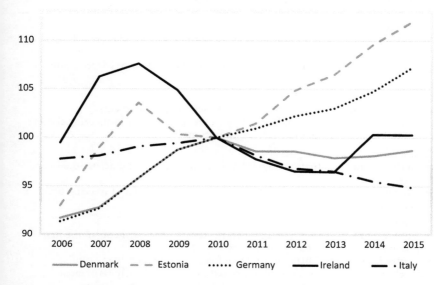

Figure 14.2 Government Final Consumption Expenditure*
Source: OECD (2016).
* Calculated as index 2010.

Cutback Management

We introduced the main distinction in the cutback management literature between across-the-board and targeted cutback strategies as well as the intermediate 'managerialist' strategy in Chapter 2, and we argued that each strategy may lead to cost reductions through different measures, including staff layoffs, hiring freezes, wage reductions or savings on office space, acquisitions and so forth. They may also be differently associated with reforms, such as reorganizations. When we consider the case studies in this volume, a mix of cutback strategies and measures appears, as summarised in Table 14.2.

When the crisis hit, all of the countries chose to initiate across-the-board cuts. The decision is hardly surprising, as this is a quick and easy approach to cutbacks that reduces decision-making costs, minimises conflict and is perceived as being equitable—at least for the overall decision makers who delegate the unpleasant cutback decisions to ministries and agencies. Germany, Ireland and Denmark also made use of targeted cuts, whereas Estonia and Italy seem to have relied primarily on across-the-board cuts, at least at the national government level. Across-the-board cuts are well suited in a political context marked by fragmentation and instability, as in Italy, whereas the short duration of the consolidation period in Estonia may contribute to explaining the reliance on across-the-board strategies.

Table 14.2 Cutback Management Strategies and Measures

Germany
- Cutback strategies (national govt level): Both targeted and across-the-board cuts.
- Cutback measures: Hiring freeze and to a limited extent pay freeze. Some reorganisations.

Italy
- Cutback strategies (national govt level): Across-the-board cuts.
- Cutback measures: Hiring freeze, pay freeze, pay cuts and squeezing the size of staff by replacement rates. Reorganisations.

Denmark
- Cutback strategies (national govt level): Both targeted and across-the-board cuts.
- Cutback measures: Hiring freeze, voluntary resignation and freezing unfilled vacancies, dismissals. Reorganisations.

Ireland
- Cutback strategies (national govt level): Across-the-board cuts in the first phase of the crisis, later targeted cuts.
- Cutback measures: Hiring freeze, pay freeze, comprehensive pay cuts, incentivised career breaks, voluntary redundancy and early retirement schemes, mobility of staff (reshuffling). Significant reorganisations.

Estonia
- Cutback strategies (national govt level): Considerable, across-the-board cuts.
- Cutback measures: Hiring freeze, pay and salary cuts, dismissals and reduced work time and unpaid leave. Some reorganisations.

Source: Our own elaboration based on the case chapters of this volume.

In the literature, it is expected that when the crisis grows longer and deeper, decision makers will move from decremental towards strategic approaches (Jørgensen 1981). If we consider the national government level, we do not find clear support for the so-called stages model (maybe with Ireland as an exception), and the patterns appear blurred, with much overlap in approach. When across-the-board cuts were sent down in the hierarchy of delegation, however, the cuts were transformed to and implemented as targeted cuts in several cases. Following a 'cascading' logic of centralisation (Raudla et al. 2015), target-setting was centralised, but power over implementation was decentralised. Thus, although our cases support expectations concerning the centralisation of decision-making during the fiscal crisis, as through an increase of the relative power of the Ministry of Finance (and the Irish Department of Public Expenditure and Reform), they also show decentralisation of power over implementation.

In practice, departments were given cutback targets, which were delegated down the line. When cutbacks were delegated to a subordinate level, they were often implemented through both managerial and strategic savings (Pollitt 2010), achieved by, among other things, reorganisations. At the organisational level, in ministries and agencies, some of our case studies find support for the stages model, as it was found that cutback decisions were influenced by previously adopted cutbacks (e.g. in Estonia, Denmark), and that more selective approaches were implemented in later stages of the crisis as further rounds of fiscal packages made cuts increasingly painful (Italy).

Demands for cutbacks were met with a broad range of cutback measures. Hiring freezes were commonly used across countries as a convenient measure to buy time and preserve options in the short run. Hiring freezes were insufficient to fulfil the cutback ambitions, however, and they were combined with other—more radical and/or long-term—measures. In Germany, hiring freezes were combined with pay freezes; in Italy with pay freezes, pay cuts and replacement rates; and in Ireland with pay freezes, pay cuts, incentivised career breaks, voluntary redundancy, early retirement schemes and mobility of staff. In Denmark, hiring freezes were combined with dismissals as well as voluntary resignation, including early retirement and by freezing unfilled vacancies, while in Estonia they were combined with pay and salary cuts, dismissals, unpaid leave and reduced work time.

The applied measures were largely influenced by country-specific administrative traditions related to civil service systems and labour market structures. In Estonia the use of both wage cuts and dismissals was feasible because there is no civil service tenure and the legislation allows for dismissing personnel and cutting pay. Moreover, Estonia has low levels of unionisation and had widespread acceptance of the necessity of cutbacks among civil servants, which may have allowed more room for radical measures. Conversely, dismissals are not an option in Germany, as public-sector staff are rigorously protected against dismissal and pay cuts. Between Estonia and Germany, we find Italy, Ireland and Denmark. Italy would generally appear to apply hiring freezes and replacement caps, as the unions were in a position to avoid outright dismissals. In Ireland, a broad range of cutback measures, including considerable pay cuts, were applied; when isolated strikes took place, however, the government negotiated a new pay deal with public service unions that did not involve dismissals and further pay cuts. In Denmark the limited number of staff with a tenured career as civil servants and the 'flexicurity' labour market model made the use of dismissals possible while the decentralised labour market negotiation system stood in the way of pay cuts.

Although in principle the right to decide how to achieve the set level of cuts was delegated to the organisational level, our cases show how the room for decision-making was influenced by a number of factors, including administrative traditions, the regulation of civil services and labour market structures. In some countries public employees had strongly entrenched unions and fought to avoid erosions of their basic conditions of service (Italy and Ireland), in one case the constitutions limited the measures available (Germany), and in another the decentralised labour market negotiation system made it impossible to consider pay cuts (Denmark). In the final case (Estonia), resistance was less organised and less embedded in legal rights, and it was easier to adopt a broader scope of more radical measures.

Furthermore, a tight timeline, a limited number of flexible budget lines and the share of savings before the crisis period influenced decision-making. Besides these constraints on decision-making, our cases revealed how ministerial-level decisions on cutbacks seemed to be influenced by the pool of popular management ideas, as across-the-board cuts were often transformed to managerial and targeted cutbacks through reorganisation in the form of mergers, shared service centres and the centralisation of functions.

Budgetary Reform

All of the case countries have carried out major budgetary reform motivated by the goal of improving fiscal discipline, whereas the goal of more performance-oriented budgeting seems to have been crowded out for a time in most countries. In the following, we will (1) account for the major budgetary reform in the case countries; (2) analyse how they are meant to contribute to fiscal discipline; and (3) reflect on the fate of performance-oriented budgeting under austerity.

The major budgetary reform in each country is represented in Table 14.3. Among other things, the table illustrates how the main innovations of the

Table 14.3 Major Budgetary Reforms

Germany
2010. Constitutional Amendment. *Introduction of a debt brake, including the rule of structurally balanced budgets (max. deficits of 0.35% of structurally adjusted GDP) and the establishment a Fiscal Stability Council.*
2010–. Federal and Länder Budgetary laws. *Binding deficit and debt reduction targets, such as corrective mechanisms and sanctions.*

Italy
2009. Law on Fiscal Federalism, Budget Reform.
2011. Law. *Alignment of budget planning with European Semester.*
2012. Constitutional Law and Reinforced Law: *legal structural balance rule, establishment of fiscal council in the shape of Parliamentary Budget Office, increased scope of Budget Law.*
2014. Legislative decree. *Implementation of EU Six Pack.*
2015. Law. *Shift from Internal Stability Pact to balanced budget.*

Denmark
2008+2010+2011. Amendment Laws on local government grants: *Economic sanctions in case of elicited tax raises and overspending in local governments.*
2012. Budget Law + Amendment Law on the Economic Council. *Legal structural balance rule, legal multi-year expenditure ceilings, automatic correction mechanism. Existing Economic council given role as Fiscal watchdog.*

Ireland
2012. Fiscal Responsibility Act. *Established the Irish Fiscal Advisory Council as a statutory body and legislated for the implementation of national and EU fiscal rules, including structural balance rules and deficit reduction targets.*
2013. Ministers and Secretaries (Amendment) Act. *Provided for all government expenditure to be budgeted for on the basis of three-year ceilings.*

Estonia

2009–11. Government decisions, Ministry of Finance decisions. *Reinforcement of top-down budgeting. Closer monitoring of budgetary expenditure in the implementation phase. Restrictions on local government borrowing. Consolidation of central government accounting.*

2014. State Budget Act. *Provisions for programme-based performance budgeting. Structural balance rule. Automatic correction and compensation mechanism. Binding multi-year expenditure ceilings. The creation of an independent fiscal council (supported by the Bank of Estonia). Accrual budgeting.*

Source: Information from the contributors to this volume.

Note: Text in normal type refers to the name of the relevant legislation. Text in italics refers to its main contents.

German 'debt brake' (i.e. structural balance rules and fiscal stability councils) were made part of European legislation (in the Fiscal Compact) and subsequently adopted by the other case countries. It also illustrates how, particularly in Italy, adaption to EU substantial and procedural requirements were an important driver of budgetary reform.

Budgetary Reform From the Perspective of Fiscal Discipline

The aim to improve fiscal discipline has motivated several reforms that represent more centralised budgeting based on at least three types of budgetary institutions: (1) rules concerning the transparency and comprehensiveness of budgeting (2) fiscal targets or rules, (3) budgetary procedures (cp. Chapter 2 and Alesina and Perotti 1996; Hagen 2007).

All of the countries have carried out reforms to improve the transparency and comprehensiveness of budgeting. The best example is probably the establishment of independent *fiscal councils* as required by the European Fiscal Compact. These councils are meant to generate transparency by holding governments accountable for their calculations of structurally adjusted budget deficits. Budgeting has also been rendered more comprehensive in several cases by legislation aimed at curbing the use of off-budget funds (e.g. Law 243/2012 in Italy or Fiscal Responsibility Act 2012 in Ireland). Last but not least, most case countries have increased the comprehensiveness of the national budget process by imposing restrictions on the borrowing and spending autonomy of local governments.

All of the countries have also adopted fiscal rules. The best example is the structural balance rule, as required by the Fiscal Compact. It is more demanding than the preexisting deficit and debt targets of the Maastricht Treaty, as it limits deficits to 0.5% of GDP under normal circumstances. It is also more flexible, as it is calculated in a manner that takes account of economic cycles. It thus represents a 'second-generation' fiscal rule (Schick 2010). In some cases, the structural balance rules were supplemented with medium-term expenditure ceilings. In Ireland and Estonia, these ceilings were adopted for the executive, whereas in Denmark the parliament strengthened the existing executive ceilings by adopting legal expenditure ceilings on a four-year running basis.

The budgeting procedures have also become more centralised. In the preparation phase, budgeting is increasingly a top-down procedure, taking its point of departure in medium-term plans and expenditure ceilings. In Germany, top-down budgeting was a new phenomenon, whereas in other cases the existing top-down character of the budget process was reinforced. In Denmark and Estonia, for example, the predetermined ceilings had become seen as negotiable by line ministries during the 'good years' preceding the crisis. After the crisis, top-down budgeting was reinforced, and expenditure ceilings were made more binding. At the adoption phase of the budget, the scope for upwards adjustments in parliament was reduced, e.g. through the Italian use of 'maxi-amendment' technique or through the Danish self-limitation of parliament through medium-term expenditure ceilings. At the implementation phase, we find increased centralisation in the shape of the closer real-time monitoring of expenditure by the ministries of finance.

The finding of centralisation is consistent with the predictions in the literature on budgetary institutions. Here, crises are expected to increase the level of popular support for strong expenditure control. As argued in Chapter 2, this is likely to open a 'window of opportunity' for 'budget guardians' (typically ministries of finance) to propose reforms that centralise budgeting. In Germany, for example, the fiscal crisis in 2009–10 helped generate political support for the idea of the debt brake, which had been developed in the federal Ministry of Finance in the previous years; however, the cases do not confirm that the severity of the crisis predicts the degree of centralisation.

The case countries have adopted some very similar rules and institutional elements. These similarities are the result of how reform ideas are circulated in the community of budgetary policymakers (e.g. the German debt brake was inspired by similar developments in Switzerland), and of how institutional innovations were made part of common European regulations. Given the prominence of legal instruments of expenditure control, the recent reforms also represent a formalisation of the budgetary process which reinforces the legalistic traditions that characterise Germany and, to some extent, Italy. However, the formalisation represents more of a departure from the informal and corporatist governing traditions in Denmark, the reliance on a conservative fiscal culture (and an informal commitment to a balanced budget) in Estonia, and the culture of executive dominance in Ireland. One might also argue that the use of legal fiscal targets and independent fiscal councils is more in line with the 'contracts' approach to budgetary centralisation and that it represents more of a path-breaking change in the Irish and Italian cases, which previously relied on a delegation approach with a strong Ministry of Finance exerting control over line ministries.

Budgetary Reform From the Perspective of Performance

There is mixed evidence concerning the fate of performance budgeting under austerity. In Ireland, the introduction of medium-term expenditure ceilings for government departments was allied to a new requirement to produce performance statements. In Denmark, Estonia and Italy, however, austerity did not increase the role of performance information in budgeting, and in Germany the debt brake did not do away with the traditional scepticism towards the use of performance information.

Spending reviews appear to have played a somewhat larger role as an instrument of rationalising budgetary allocations. Again, Ireland seems to have made the largest changes, as the new Department of Public Expenditure and Services made comprehensive spending reviews a major instrument in its negotiations with line ministries. In Italy, several different governments commissioned external spending reviews as a way of identifying more efficient and effective ways of spending public money, but politicians were reluctant to let their expenditure priorities be guided by the reviews, and they have played a more indirect role as inspiration for the implementation of cutbacks in line ministries. In Denmark, austerity has led to more intensive use of the existing 'special budget analysis' instrument, albeit not the invention of new instruments.

Summing up, austerity has involved centralising budgetary reform in all of the case countries. The countries have adopted rather similar legal fiscal rules and institutions, and in some cases these instruments have represented a departure from more informal traditions of budgetary governance and/or from the 'delegation' mode of budgetary centralisation. Austerity does not seem to have done much to advance the agenda of performance-oriented budgeting at national levels—except in Ireland, where this agenda seems to have been weakly developed previously.

Austerity and Changes to Public Management

Now we turn more directly to answering the main research questions raised in the book concerning the consequences of austerity for public management. We analyse how austerity and expenditure cutbacks affected the reform trajectories in our five case countries, focusing on the reform components that relate to financial management, personnel management, organisational restructuring and performance measurement. Table 14.4. summarises our main findings on the character of changes and the patterns of change regarding each of the four reform components.

Table 14.4 Character and Patterns of Change

	Character of change	Pattern of change
Financial management	Centralisation of overall expenditure decisions. Decentralisation of detailed budget allocations. Centralised monitoring and coordination of budgetary implementation.	Reinforcement of centralising elements in top-down budgeting. Punctuation in countries where top-down budgeting did not previously exist. Path-dependent development of decentralising elements.
Personnel management	Varying directions of change: Towards decentralisation of personnel authority and less secure public-sector careers in Estonia and Denmark. Towards standardisation, coordination and coherence in Ireland. Retaining the traditional career-based system in Germany, and back towards a more traditional career-based system in Italy.	Path-dependent changes in Germany. Path-dependent development but also elements of reversal of ongoing reforms in Italy. In Estonia and Denmark reinforcement of ongoing reforms. More radical changes in Ireland.
Organisational restructuring	Towards larger-scale organisations, centralisation and both single-purpose and multipurpose organisations.	Reinforcement of ongoing organisational restructuring in most countries. Punctuation in Ireland where the restructuring of agencies had not yet begun.
Performance measurement	Less attention to and resources for performance measurements in the short term. Some signs of increased demand for performance information in the longer term.	Path-dependent and gradual developments in most countries. Punctuation in Ireland.

Source: Our own elaboration based on the case chapters of this volume.

Financial Management

Financial management reforms have been partly driven by pressures to restrain the growth of public expenditure and partly by pressures to increase the effectiveness of public spending. As argued in Chapter 2, the 'savings' objective often speaks for centralisation. In top-down budgeting, however, the central setting of overall expenditure ceilings is often combined with the delegation of detailed resource allocation decisions and managerial freedoms in the implementation phase (Kim and Park 2006). This combination of centralisation and decentralisation is symptomatic to NPM as a paradigm that both recommends the centralisation of overall decision-making powers towards the core executive and decentralisation to line managers who can 'get things done'.

Among our cases, we find some countries that have combined centralisation and decentralisation in their previous reform trajectories. Beginning in the 1980s, for example, Denmark's financial reform trajectory combined top-down budgeting with increases in managerial discretion and accountability for performance. Italy has also aimed at a combination of centralisation and managerial discretion, but its reform trajectory has been characterised by the weak implementation of the managerialist elements. Germany, on the other hand, has maintained a more traditional bottom-up budgeting process.

The recent period of austerity has reinforced the centralising elements in the countries that already had a trajectory of top-down budgetary reform, such as Denmark, Italy and Estonia. At the same time, new top-down budgeting procedures became institutionalised in Germany and Ireland. The findings are murkier when it comes to the fate of the decentralising reform elements. We find that governments decentralise the responsibility for detailed cutbacks to line ministries, but we do not find signs of increasing managerial discretion in budgetary implementation. In Italy, austerity seems to have strengthened the tendency that the managerialist reform elements are weakly implemented, and in Denmark the intensified monitoring and regulation of budgetary implementation seems to reverse some of the managerial discretion allowed by previous reforms. Moreover, we do not find many signs indicating the reinforcement of the trajectories towards accrual accounting and budgeting: in Italy, the movement went from accruals towards cash-based principles, and in Denmark the tighter monitoring and coordination of real-time expenditure was felt by public managers to counteract the principles of accruals. In Estonia, the existing system of accrual accounting is to be extended to budgeting, but the reform actors did not make reference to the crisis experience in promoting this reform.

Personnel Management

A civil servant was traditionally assumed to be a tenured career appointment, promoted in relation to qualifications and seniority, and part of a unified civil service within a distinct national framework of terms and conditions. These features made being a civil servant different from most private sector jobs. NPM-inspired reforms generally changed personnel management towards less secure careers, linking promotion more clearly to performance and decentralising personnel authority so that managers were able to hire and fire according to local conditions (Pollitt and Bouckaert 2011, 90–5).

The reform intensity related to personnel management prior to the fiscal crisis varied, however, across our five countries, and their starting points differed significantly. Germany had retained a traditional career-based personnel system with strong protection against dismissal. In Italy, NPM-inspired reforms were introduced in the 1990s and 2000s, but successive governments had been unwilling to implement them, and the formal-legalistic tradition had largely survived. In Denmark and Estonia, on the other hand, the NPM-inspired reform of personnel management had increased managerial flexibility and made public-sector careers less secure.

In two countries (Germany and Italy), austerity led to path-dependent patterns of change (including some reversals in Italy) in the existing systems of personnel management. The traditional career-based system was retained in Germany, and new recruitments are largely related to voluntary or age- and health-related departures. In Italy, those already in post ('insiders') were secured by the replacement rate, meaning that the burden of cuts shifted to the shoulders of non-unionised temporary workers ('outsiders'). This meant the exclusion of non-unionised younger candidates from public service and privileging those with civil servant status. Thus, the non-flexibility in Germany and Italy affected the room of manoeuvre for decentralised public managers, leading to an ageing workforce.

In Estonia and Denmark, austerity seems to have reinforced existing reform trajectories, increasing managerial flexibility, making careers of public-sector employees less secure and encouraging larger inflows and outflows of staff. In Estonia, one-quarter of the civil servants lost their civil service status and became employed according to the private sector Employment Act. These changes were prepared before the crisis hit, but the crisis paved the way for its approval. In Denmark, dismissals became more normal during austerity and they seem to have been used to renew the workforce in some areas, replacing senior (expensive) staff with younger (cheaper) staff. Moreover, agreements concerning working conditions were changed in some areas, increasing managerial flexibility to organise working hours individually with staff.

In Ireland, the essential framework of tenured employment remained in place despite pressure to make dismissals easier, but a number of other reforms were adopted, including redeployment arrangements and the creation of a single public service labour market. Working conditions were standardised and the Human Resource function in the civil service was professionalised. As new recruitment began (from 2014), the profile of advertised positions was designed to attract persons with specialist legal, auditing and other skills—rather than open competition for general roles, as had previously been the case. Furthermore, arising from the crisis, all senior positions were now open to external appointment rather than internal-only approaches, as had been the case for the majority of positions prior to the crisis.

Organisational Restructuring

As argued in Chapter 2, the main thrust of NPM-inspired reforms was towards organisations that were more specialised, decentralised and smaller, whereas the main thrust during the 2000s and 2010s was towards multipurpose organisations, recentralisation and larger-scale organisations.

In four of the case countries (Germany, Italy, Estonia and Denmark) ideas about organisational mergers, shared service centres and the centralisation of procurement were launched and adopted in the years before the crisis. In Ireland, agency reform had emerged as a subject of discussion from the mid-2000s, but agency merger and terminations did not take place on a significant scale before the crisis.

In all of the countries, agency mergers and shared service centres were adopted in response to the fiscal crisis. Ireland stands out, however, as agency mergers and rationalisations appear more far-reaching, as the crisis, in combination with the recommendations of a previous OECD report, gave way to a series of agency terminations through mergers, dissolution, abolitions, centralisation of functions and shared service initiatives. Organisational changes were adopted at a smaller scale in the remaining four countries, evolving more slowly in the continuation and acceleration of previous reforms.

Performance Measurement

At the beginning of the book, we asked whether the tougher attitudes towards public spending will also be associated with higher levels of ambition for public money to be spent effectively and efficiently, for example by using performance measurements in financial management, in the allocation of cutbacks or in personnel management.

Among the case countries, performance measurement was an important element in the public management reform trajectories preceding austerity in Denmark, Estonia and also in Italy, although the latter was characterised by weak implementation. The German administrative culture was less hospitable to performance management, and Ireland was a 'reform laggard'.

Austerity seems to have primarily led to a path-dependent development of the use of performance measurement. In Estonia, austerity slowed the development of performance-informed budgeting and management. During the acute phase of the crisis, policymakers paid less attention to performance information, fewer resources were available for performance pay in personnel management, and the ongoing efforts to move towards performance-informed budgeting were slowed down and turned in the direction of programme budgeting. In Italy, austerity also dried up the resources for performance pay and reinforced the tendency for the weak implementation of performance-oriented reforms. In Germany, austerity had little impact on sceptical attitudes towards performance measurement.

Conversely, in Denmark, having to cut back expenditure generated new demand from among top managers to have more comparative economic performance indicators, which led to the creation of a new set of benchmarking data at the central level of government, which was added to the existing performance measurement systems contributing to the gradual development of performance-informed management in central government. Ireland represents the only country where austerity seems to have created something akin to punctuation in the realm of performance measurement.

Conclusions and Discussion

This section sums up and discusses our main findings related to the main research questions posed in the book: What is the character of changes to public management under austerity? Does austerity involve path-breaking and/or path-dependent change? And why are different and/or similar patterns found in different countries?

What Is the Character of the Changes Taking Place Under Austerity?

Judging from the five case countries in the book, austerity led to the centralisation and formalisation of decision-making on aggregate budget parameters, top-down budgeting processes and stronger administrative budget guardians. This centralisation was often accompanied by the decentralisation of detailed decisions on budgetary allocations and cutbacks, but at the same time the central monitoring and coordination of budgetary implementation was intensified in some countries.

In personnel management, the character of the changes was more mixed. In Estonia and Denmark, the main thrust was towards the decentralisation of personnel authority, making public-sector careers less secure and encouraging increased personnel turnover. In Ireland, the changes moved in the direction of standardisation, coordination and coherence in a unified civil service, while the changes in Germany and Italy were limited or went in the direction of the traditional career-based systems.

We also find that austerity reinforced the existing trend towards agency mergers, the reintegration of agencies into departmental structures and/or centralisation of back-office functions. The main thrust of organisational restructuring was towards larger-scale organisations and centralisation, whereas the effects on organisational specialisation were mixed, as mergers led to less specialisation and more multipurpose organisations, and shared service centres and the centralisation of procurement functions led to a higher degree of specialisation and the development of single-purpose organisations.

We do not find that austerity has generally increased the use of performance information in the public sector; in some countries, the demand for performance statements and spending reviews increased, while elsewhere austerity appears to have reversed or slowed the development of performance-informed public budgeting and management.

Overall, austerity seems to have reinforced the ongoing transformation of public management reform in the direction of a 'post-NPM' paradigm, where centralisation, coordination and larger-scale organisations are central values, whereas the findings are mixed regarding its effects on the deregulatory and decentralising elements of ongoing reforms.

Did Austerity Lead to Path-Breaking and/or Path-Dependent Patterns of Change?

In the case studies presented in this book, austerity often led to the reinforcement of existing reform trajectories, such as towards top-down budgeting and organisational mergers, whereas sudden path-breaking changes of the kind normally associated with a critical juncture mainly occurred in the Irish case, which seems to have been pushed from the position of a 'reform laggard' towards more active modernisation strategies. There are, however, also many examples of non-change or delays or reversals of existing reforms, particularly with respect to the decentralisation of budgetary implementation, deregulation of public employment and the use of performance measurements. Last but not least, it is worth noting how the same reforms may be path-breaking in some aspects and path-dependent in others. For example, the German adoption of the debt brake was path-breaking inasmuch as it led to top-down budgeting and increased the level of fiscal discipline, but it was path-dependent in the sense that it relied on the respect for legal instruments that is typical of Germany. In Denmark, the adoption of legal expenditure ceilings reinforced the existing traditions regarding top-down budgeting, but it was also path-breaking in the sense that it represented a new, legalistic approach to financial management.

How Should the Cross-Country Similarities and Differences Be Understood?

As argued in Chapter 2, a common topic of discussion in the literature is whether economic forces and ideas lead towards similarities in public management reform and possibly even convergence and/or how economic factors and political and administrative institutions intermediate the common pressures in ways that lead to continued divergence. In the following, we will briefly discuss why similarities and differences are found based on the in-case analysis presented in the case studies.

Similarities

The main similarities between the cases concern the centralisation of financial management and organisational structures. The widespread similarities in budgetary reform and their consequences for financial management are largely the result of how the countries were obligated by common European fiscal policies; in other words, economic integration and international regulation seem to be the main explanatory factors. The similarities in organisational reform are more about how public managers sought out inspiration in other countries and sectors when faced with the task of realising cutback targets. This process of drawing inspiration was sometimes facilitated by international economic organisations, as in the Irish case, where agency terminations were based on the recommendations of an OECD report. In other words, European regulations and the circulation of popular management ideas pulled in the direction of similarity in budgetary and financial and organisational reform under austerity.

Differences

The main differences between the cases concern how austerity affected the decentralising, deregulatory and performance-oriented elements of reforms and whether the pattern of change was characterised by continuity (path-dependence) or discontinuity (i.e. potentially path-breaking change). In the following, we will discuss how these differences depend on economic, political and administrative factors.

As argued, the findings are mixed with regard to the *decentralising and deregulatory elements* that would lead to increased managerial discretion at the level of line ministries and agencies. In Germany, the introduction of top-down budgeting potentially increased the scope for managerial discretion, but this discretion has yet to be used due to favourable economic developments, and the level of managerial discretion in personnel policy has not increased. In Italy, budgetary reform policies and cutbacks slowed down or reversed the managerialist stream of reform with respect to both financial and personnel management. In the Estonian case, the findings mainly point in the opposite direction; here, the decision to implement large cutbacks over a short period of time meant that line managers enjoyed greater discretion, and the crisis was used to push through reforms that made it easier to manage and dismiss public employees at the decentralised level. In the Danish and Irish cases, the findings are mixed internally. In Denmark, the more centralised monitoring and coordination of budgetary implementation was felt to reduce the level of discretion in resource management at the agency level. At the same time, some line managers received greater leeway to organise work. In Ireland, austerity had no clear effects on the level of managerial discretion in financial or personnel management. On the one hand, the terms and conditions of public service employment were changed through pay cuts, increased productivity demands and compulsory mobility; on the other, more standardised public working conditions were introduced across the entire public sector to eliminate the anomalous arrangements that had accrued.

The emerging pattern seems to be that austerity did not increase the level of managerial discretion in Germany and Italy whereas it increased some elements of discretion in Estonia, Ireland and Denmark. This pattern of variation is likely to reflect differences in both political systems and administrative structures and traditions. Germany and Italy are federal or quasi-federal states with many veto points in both decision-making and implementation, which makes it difficult to advance administrative reforms from the national level, although some Länder and regions may be active reformers in their own right. At the same time, Germany and Italy share administrative traditions with strong legalistic foundations, although Italy has attempted to modernise them. These traditions seem more reconcilable with the centralising tendencies of contemporary public management reform than with the decentralisation and deregulatory elements. In comparison, Denmark, Estonia and Ireland are all small, unitary states with fewer veto points and more flexible administrative traditions and civil service systems.

As regards the question of *continuity or discontinuity in public management reform*, Ireland is the only case of the five where austerity led to several sudden radical changes (i.e. critical junctures). This calls for separate discussion of the Irish case. On the other hand, Germany and Italy seem to have been characterised by relatively continuous patterns of change except in the area of budgeting, where Germany changed to a new kind of fiscal rule and top-down procedures for the first time. Estonia and Denmark were mainly characterised by the reinforcement of existing reforms or by path-dependent changes; except that the new legal framework for budgeting and financial management constituted a rather path-breaking change in relation to the informal Danish administrative traditions.

If we first consider the prevalence of discontinuous changes in the Irish case, the most obvious explanatory factor is an economic one. Ireland experienced a relatively deep, protracted crisis, and it was the only country subject to Troika conditionality, including requirements to reform public management. Political system factors can also contribute to our understanding of the Irish case, since the absence of clear ideological poles appears to favour a boom–bust pattern of reform where long periods of clientelist politics are interceded by periods of necessary and relatively radical reform. This explanation adds new insights to the significance of political systems to administrative reform compared to the model and explanatory factors presented in Chapters 2 and 3, as it does not relate to the type of government or state but to the ideological composition of the party system. Administrative structures can also contribute to the understanding of the Irish case, as it is a small country with centralised administrative structures and relatively few veto points in the implementation of administrative reforms. It is also worth noting that the Irish government created a centralised administrative reform actor, the Department of Public Expenditure and Reform, before proceeding to the more strategic and managerialist phase of cutbacks and reform. Last but not least, it is likely to have played a role that Ireland was a reform laggard which had not yet embarked on the reforms that had already been pursued in other countries for some years. This concerns, for example, organisational mergers and rationalisations in central government or the policy of making publicly available performance measures and plans an element in the budgetary process.

The findings of path-dependent patterns of change in Germany and Italy can be attributed to several factors. In the German case, the relative absence of economic pressure seems important to understanding the low degree of change except in matters of fiscal policy and budgeting procedures. In the Italian case, however, the economic pressure was not enough to lead to significant reform other than the budgetary reform that was imposed by EU policy; indeed, economic pressure appears to have contributed to the destabilisation of its political system and, hence, its limited capacity for other aspects of reform. In other words, we must consider the administrative structures and political systems in addition to the level of economic pressure to understand the low pace of change. Germany and Italy both have federal or quasi-federal structures and many veto points, which does not usually speak for radical reform. As regards the type of government, the German case seems to indicate that grand coalitions can carry out radical changes, even overcoming veto points when the confluence of problems, politics and ideas makes it possible to find internal agreement on a new policy such as the debt brake. However, they are probably not likely to adopt radical reform on a broad scale of administrative policies, as their views on administrative policy are likely to differ internally. In Italy, the instability of the political system and the reliance on technocratic and grand coalition government for lack of better options during the crisis is probably an important explanatory factor for the path-dependent patterns of change found in this case.

Implications and Limitations of the Analysis

Overall, the findings of the case studies point in the direction of the reinforcement of the centralising and regulatory elements of 'post-NPM' reform, and recent reforms would appear to have done more to promote and disseminate legalistic approaches to public administration in Europe than previous generations of reform, which disseminated elements from the public interest–based traditions. Furthermore, we find few indications of radical departures from accustomed ways of organising, managing—and reforming—public organisations and services. This conclusion might appear somewhat disheartening for the reader who is looking for signs of new, innovative ways of doing public management and hoping that the conditions of crisis and austerity might have provided the pressure that makes reformers look more actively for new ways of doing things. However, we do not claim to be able to conclude that austerity has not contributed to advancing the agenda of a more networking, innovative or co-producing public sector. Indeed, our findings are likely to reflect to some degree the methodological choices we made when designing this book. First, we have decided to focus on budgetary reform and cutbacks that were decided and implemented in a relatively short period of time following the financial, economic and fiscal crisis. It is hardly surprising that the cutbacks and reforms mainly had the effect of increasing the level of control exerted by the core executive and administrative budget guardians over the rest of the public sector. It is a common expectation in the literature that short-term responses to a crisis are likely to focus on controlling the level of aggregate expenditure whereas the more strategic and innovative responses to increased scarcity may first become visible in the longer term. Second, we have focused on cutbacks and reforms at the central level of government, and the lens has been 'top-down' rather than directed at the process of reforming individual public organisations or their services. The room for managerial discretion and for innovation in public administration and services likely becomes more apparent if public management reforms are studied more from the perspective of decentralised agencies or local governments.

With respect to the contribution of the comparative approach of the volume, it should be clear from the preceding analysis that it is nearly impossible to disentangle the different explanatory factors from each other and assess their relative powers given the low number of cases and interacting nature of the factors. However, it does seem possible for us to confirm the general viewpoint in the literature that economic pressure and international ideas and regulations lead towards similarity in some aspects of public management reform, particularly in times of crisis and austerity. Indeed, a general pattern of variation among the cases would appear to be that the most path-breaking changes occurred in relation to the aspects on which the countries diverged from contemporary international standards. For example, the adoption of fiscal rules led to top-down budgeting in Germany, where bottom-up procedures had still been in use until 2010. In Denmark, it led to an unprecedented formalisation of financial management, and in Ireland the position of reform laggard probably contributed to the radicalism of its reforms.

We can also confirm that other aspects of reform were so heavily intermediated by the specific economic situations of the countries and their political and administrative systems that they are likely to continue following divergent reform trajectories for example in matters of personnel management, financial management, and performance management.

Last but not least, it is interesting to note that a high level of economic pressure and international intervention can provide the necessary impetus to overcome clientelist political patterns and help pass overdue reforms in some cases, as in Ireland, whereas it can also contribute to the destabilisation of political systems and thus stand in the way of reform, as in Italy. These varying effects of economic pressure are obviously related to a country's economic and fiscal records, but the implication may also be that international economic and fiscal policies must be designed in ways that do not presume more uniformity in the political and administrative systems of European states than exists. International policymakers should consider taking more account of the consequences of austerity on both the political systems in Europe and on the progress of the more entrepreneurial aspects of public management reform.

References

Alesina, Alberto and Roberto Perotti. 1996. "Fiscal Discipline and the Budget Process." *The American Economic Review* 86(2):401–7.

Eurostat. 2016. "Total General Government Expenditure: Percentage of GDP." From the dataset *Government Revenue, Expenditure and Main Aggregates [gov_10a_main]*. http://appsso.eurostat.ec.europa.eu/nui/show.do?dataset=gov_10a_main&lang=en.

Hagen von, Jürgen. 2007. "Budgeting Institutions for Better Fiscal Performance." In *Budgeting and Budgetary Institutions*, edited by Anwar Shah, 27–52.Washington, DC: World Bank.

Jørgensen, Torben Beck. 1981. *Når staten skal spare*. Copenhagen: Nyt fra Samfundsvidenskaberne.

Kim, John and Chung-Keun Park. 2006. "Top-Down Budgeting as a Tool for Central Resource Management." *OECD Journal on Budgeting* 6(1):87–235.

OECD. 2016. "Government Final Consumption Expenditure, Volume," *OECD Economic Outlook*, No 99–June 2016. http://stats.oecd.org/index.aspx?DataSet Code=EO. Accessed 8th of December 2016.

Pollitt, Christopher. 2010. "Public Management Reform During Financial Austerity." *Statskontoret*. www.statskontoret.se/globalassets/publikationer/om-offentlig-sektor-1-11/om-offentlig-sektor-2.pdf.

Pollitt, Christopher and Geert Bouckaert. 2011. *Public Management Reform: A Comparative Analysis: New Public Management, Governance, and the Neo-Weberian State*. Oxford: Oxford University Press.

Raudla, Ringa, John W. Douglas, Tiina Randma-Liiv and Riin Saavi. 2015. "The Impact of Fiscal Crisis on Decision-Making Processes in European Governments: Dynamics of a Centralization Cascade." *Public Administration Review* 75(6):842–52.

Schick, Allen. 2010. "Post-Crisis Fiscal Rules: Stabilising Public Finance While Responding to Economic Aftershocks." *OECD Journal on Budgeting* 2:1–18.

About the Contributors

Jobst Fiedler is Professor Emeritus of Public and Financial Management and Resident Senior Fellow at the Hertie School of Governance in Berlin. From 2004 to 2008 he served as founding associate dean of the School. After his studies of law, economics and political science in Berlin, London, Göttingen and Berkeley, Jobst Fiedler worked as research fellow at the Social Science Research Center Berlin (WZB); he holds a PhD from the University of Hanover.

Beginning in 1980, Fiedler worked in executive positions within the city state of Hamburg and was member of several working groups of the OECD and the EU. He was elected Hanover Executive Mayor in 1990. In 1996, Jobst Fiedler switched to the private sector and joined Roland Berger Strategy Consultants as managing partner. During his private sector career, Fiedler continued publishing and teaching in the field of public management, e.g. at the University of Potsdam and the Bocconi School of Management in Milan. In 2009, he was visiting professor at the Columbia University of New York, USA. In addition, he has continued to teach at partner institutions of Hertie School including Ecole des Sciences Politiques in Paris and Getulio Vargas Business School in Sao Paulo. The main focus of his research activities has been directed to the effects of fiscal rules on budgeting and administrative modernisation activities.

Davide Galli is assistant professor of management at the Università Cattolica del Sacro Cuore, Piacenza, Department of Economic and Social Sciences, Italy. Previously he was at Bocconi University and the SDA Bocconi School of Management. He has also been president of the Independent Evaluation Unit at the Italian Ministry of Environment. His research interests include performance management and comparative public administration.

Eva Moll Ghin is postdoctoral researcher in public administration at the Department of Political Science, University of Copenhagen, Denmark. She holds a PhD from the University of Copenhagen and MAs from the University of Copenhagen and the University of Sussex, and she has previously worked in the Danish Institute of Local Government Research. Her main research interests are cutback management, budgetary reform, organizational change, performance management, central-local government relations and local government affairs. She has published in several journals, including *Public Organization Review*, *Politica, Public Governance Research* and *Energy Policy*.

Gerhard Hammerschmid (Dr. soc. oec., Vienna University of Economics and Business) is professor of Public and Financial Management at the Hertie School of Governance, and academic director of the Institut für den öffentlichen Sektor e.V. in Berlin. His research focuses on public management (reform), performance management, financial management, comparative public administration and institutional theory. He has been co-project leader for the EU FP 7 research project Coordinating for Cohesion in the Public Sector of the Future (COCOPS) and is involved in several international projects on public administration reform. Gerhard Hammerschmid is co-author of several books on public management reform and his research has been published in various peer-reviewed international journals.

Niamh Hardiman is professor at the School of Politics and International Relations a University College Dublin, and has interests in comparative politics, political economy and public policy. Her recent work has appeared in *Governance, European Journal of Political Research, European Political Science Review* and the *Journal of Comparative Policy Analysis*.

Hanne Foss Hansen is professor in public administration and organization at the Department of Political Science, University of Copenhagen. Her main interests are public organization and management, public-sector reform, evaluation, evidence-based policy and practice and higher education and research policy. Her recent publications include articles in *American Journal of Evaluation, European Journal of Higher Education, Science and Public Policy, Scandinavian Journal of Public Health* and *Scandinavian Journal of Public Administration* as well as contributions to edited volumes published at Sage, Springer, Edward Elgar, Palgrave and Routledge. She has also worked as a consultant for various governmental organizations including the National Audit Office, the Ministry of Science, Technology and Development, the Swedish Parliament, the Swedish Research Council, the Norwegian Ministry of Education and Research, the Norwegian Research Council and OECD.

Mads Bøge Kristiansen is associate professor at the Department of Political Science and Public Management, University of Southern Denmark. He holds a PhD from the Department of Political Science, University of Copenhagen. His research focuses on public administration and management, public management in times of austerity, budgetary reforms and financial management, cutback management, public management reforms and performance management. His recent publications concern the topics of performance contracting and performance management, and appear in *Public Performance and Management Review*, *International Journal of Public Sector Management* and the *Scandinavian Journal of Public Administration*.

Lorenz Löffler is research associate at the Hertie School of Governance, Berlin. He holds a Masters in Public Policy and Management from the University of Potsdam and is an alumnus of the The Washington Center's Political Leadership Program, Washington, D.C. His research focuses on public management reform, performance management and digitization of the public administration in Germany.

Muiris MacCarthaigh is lecturer in Politics and Public Administration at Queen's University Belfast, School of Politics, International Studies and Philosophy, Northern Ireland. His current research interests relate to the politics and practice of state retrenchment and administrative reform. His recent publications concern the topics of state agency governance, shared services, and the Irish experience of public-sector reform in a time of crisis, and have appeared in *Governance*, *Public Administration*, *Public Administration Review* and the *Journal of Comparative Policy Analysis*.

Fabrizio di Mascio is associate professor of Political Science at the Interuniversity Department of Regional and Urban Studies and Planning, University of Turin, Italy. He holds a PhD in Political Science from the University of Florence. He has been policy advisor at the Italian Ministry for Simplification and Public Administration. His research interests include fiscal retrenchment, public management reform, policy advice and open government in comparative perspective. His work has been published in journals such as *Public Administration*, *Public Management Review*, *International Review of Administrative Sciences* and *International Public Management Journal*.

Alessandro Natalini is an assistant professor of Political Science at the Parthenope University, Naples, Department of Law. He has been policy advisor of the Italian Ministry for Simplification and Public Administration. His research interests include better regulation, fiscal retrenchment, public management reform and policy advice in comparative perspective. His work has been published in journals such as *Public Administration*, *Public Management Review*, *Journal of European Public Policy* and *International Public Management Journal*.

Edoardo Ongaro is professor of International Public Services Management Department of Social Sciences and Languages at Northumbria

University, UK. Since September 2013 he is the president of the European Group for Public Administration (EGPA). He has served in various academic and expert committees and has contributed to numerous international research projects; he is visiting professor at Bocconi University. He is editor of *Public Policy and Administration*.

Professor Ongaro has published extensively on the topic of administrative reforms and comparative public management. Publications include: *Philosophy and Public Administration: An Introduction* (2017, Elgar); *The Palgrave Handbook of Public Administration and Management in Europe* (2017, Palgrave, editor, with Sandra van Thiel); *Strategic Management in Public Service Organisations: Concepts, Schools and Contemporary Issues* (2015, Routledge, co-authored with Ewan Ferlie); *Multi-Level Governance: The Missing Linkages* (editor, 2015, Emerald); and *Public Management Reform and Modernization: Trajectories of Administrative Change in Italy, France, Greece, Portugal and Spain* (2009, Edward Elgar).

Professor Ongaro is Fellow of the Academy of the Social Sciences of the United Kingdom.

Tiina Randma-Liiv is professor and chair of Public Management and Policy at Tallinn University of Technology, Ragnar Nurkse School of Innovation and Governance, Estonia, where she currently also serves as vice dean of the Faculty of Social Sciences and Member of the University Council. Randma-Liiv previously served as professor and chair of Public Management at the University of Tartu, and as visiting professor at the Catholic University of Leuven, the University of Gdansk, Vienna University of Economics and Business Administration, and Florida International University. Randma-Liiv is currently a member of the Advisory Board to the Estonian Minister of Public Administration, previously she has been a member of the Academic Council of the President of Estonia and of the Prime Minister's Advisory Board on Administrative Reform. She has served in the academic advisory board of the European Public Service Award, in the advisory board of the UNDP Regional Centre for Public Administration Reform, and in the OECD Expert Group of the Partnership for Democratic Governance. Her research interests include the impact of fiscal crisis on public administration, public-sector structure, civil service systems, public administration reforms in post-communist countries, policy transfer and small states. Her recent publications include articles in *Public Administration Review*, *Public Management Review*, the *American Review of Public Administration*, *Administration & Society*, *International Review of Administrative Sciences*, *Journal of Comparative Policy Analysis*, *Public Organization Review*, and *Public Administration and Development*. She received the Estonian National Science Award in 2016.

Ringa Raudla is professor of Public Finance and Governance, Tallinn University of Technology, Ragnar Nurkse School of Innovation and Governance, Estonia. Her main research interests are fiscal policy, public budgeting, public administration reforms, institutional economics, and fiscal sociology. She has also worked as a consultant for various governmental organizations, including the Ministry of Finance of Estonia, the National Audit Office, and the World Bank. Her recent publications include articles in *Public Administration Review, Governance, Public Administration, Policy Studies Journal,* the *American Review of Public Administration, Journal of Public Policy, Administration & Society, Public Money & Management, International Review of Administrative Sciences, Journal of Comparative Policy Analysis,* and *Europe-Asia Studies.* She is a member of editorial boards of various journals, including *Governance, Urban Affairs Review, Perspectives of Public Management and Governance, Journal of Public Budgeting, Accounting & Financial Management,* and *International Journal of Public Sector Management.*

Riin Savi is a research fellow in the Chair of Public Management and Policy at the Tallinn University of Technology, Ragnar Nurkse School of Innovation and Governance, Estonia. Her main research interests include comparative public policy with a focus on impact of fiscal crisis to public administration and public-sector reforms, policy transfer and organization theory. Savi has published numerous co-authored peer-reviewed articles in the journals of *Public Administration and Development, Journal of Comparative Public Administration, International Review of Administrative Sciences* and book chapters in Routledge Critical Studies in Public Management and Edward Elgar Publishing. Correspondence: Tallinn University of Technology, Ragnar Nurkse School of Innovation and Governance, Akadeemia tee 3, Tallinn 12618, Estonia; E-mail riin.savi@ttu.ee

Juliane Sarnes is a research associate at the Hertie School of Governance, Berlin, and a PhD candidate at the University of Potsdam, Germany. She holds a Master's in Public Administration from the London School of Economics and a Master's in Sociology from the University of Munich. Taking politico-cultural and capital market perspectives into account, the focus of her research activities lies with fiscal frameworks and fiscal performance in developed countries.

As a London-based finance professional at a global credit rating agency, Juliane Sarnes has analytical responsibility for the credit ratings of European subsovereigns, including regional and local governments and public corporations in Austria, Germany and Switzerland. She has published numerous pieces of research on the sectors she covers. In addition, she has translated several sociological books from English and French into German.

Previously, Juliane Sarnes was a visiting scholar/analyst at the European Bank for Reconstruction and Development (EBRD); the International Monetary Fund (IMF) and the UK Treasury's Office for Budget Responsibility (OBR).

Francesco Stolfi is assistant professor of Political Science at the University of Nottingham, School of Politics and International Relations, Faculty of Social Sciences, Malaysia Campus. Previously he was at the University of Exeter and University College of Dublin. He holds a PhD in Political Science from the University of Pittsburgh. His research interests include the impact of regional integration on national policymaking and the politics of economic policymaking and of administrative reform. His work has been published in journals such as *Governance, Journal of European Public Policy* and *Public Administration.*

Index

For Product Safety Concerns and Information please contact our EU
representative GPSR@taylorandfrancis.com
Taylor & Francis Verlag GmbH, Kaufingerstraße 24, 80331 München, Germany